THE BANKERS

Some of the material in this book first appeared in *Triple A, Business Review Weekly, Asian Finance* and *Money Management*. Permission to use it is gratefully acknowledged.

Also by the author:
Sandakan: The first hundred years, 1879–1979
Bank Negara Malaysia: The first twenty-five years, 1959–1984
On the Sulu Sea

THE BANKERS

Australia's leading bankers talk about banking today

Supriya Singh

Allen & Unwin

First published in 1991
Allen & Unwin Australia Pty Ltd
8 Napier Street, North Sydney, NSW 2059 Australia

National Library of Australia
Cataloguing-in-Publication entry:

Singh, Supriya (Supriya S.), 1929–
The bankers

Bibliography.
Includes index.
ISBN 0 04 442244 X.

1. Bankers—Australia—Biography. 2. Banks and banking—Australia—History. I. Title.

332.1092294

Set in 10/11 pt Times New Roman
by Graphicraft Typesetters, Hong Kong
Printed by Chong Moh Offset Printing Pte Ltd, Singapore

Contents

Illustrations

With love to
Lata Bhaini and Nandy Virji

Preface

This book attempts to make sense of the Australian banking system through a study of bankers, past and present. Coming to Australia from Malaysia in late 1986, I was struck by two facets of banking in the country. Firstly, it differed from banking elsewhere in the scope of its national branch network, the number and variety of financial institutions and the use of banking as an avenue of social mobility. Secondly, it was changing at an unprecedented pace.

To understand both these characteristics, I had to look to history. The history of the major banks has been told before in great detail, and I am indebted to these works. However, the focus in the earlier histories is on the banks, not on the bankers. This book puts the bankers first, and through them the history of their banks and the banking system is told.

The focus is on seven bankers and their banks. Stuart Fowler heads Westpac Banking Corporation, the first and largest banking group in Australia. Will Bailey leads the Australia and New Zealand Banking Group (ANZ), the most international Australian bank. Nobby Clark is the managing director of the National Australia Bank, the recognised leader in retail banking. Don Sanders is chief of the government-owned Commonwealth Bank of Australia. These four bankers lead banks representing nearly two-thirds (65.4 per cent at end-March 1990) of the assets of all banks in the country.

Bill Moyle till recently headed the State Bank Victoria, the fifth-largest bank and the largest state bank in the country. Known for its success in regional retail banking, it stumbled as it grew too fast in a deregulated environment.

Mark Johnson, the sixth banker whose story is told, occupies a pivotal position in Australian history because he was the first managing director of the Australian Bank, the first new national bank to open in

Australia in more than 50 years. Though he failed with his vision of a new bank that would take on the major banks and do everything better, the venture signalled the beginning of a new breed of banker and a new way of banking.

The Australian Bank also bred another chief executive who, in a different way, tried to do what the Australian Bank failed to do. Bill Gurry, managing director of the National Mutual Royal Bank, is one of the few new bankers who set his sights on building a national retail network. It was seen as the bank most likely to succeed. But by the end of May 1990, his bank was sold to ANZ and Gurry himself was due to leave.

As the book proceeded, many asked me, Why study bankers? The answer is that I was writing about bankers for *Triple·A*, a magazine dealing with corporate finance and banking in Australia, Asia and the Pacific. I had written of bankers before in Malaysia, so I felt that I had a worthwhile regional perspective. On the other hand, why *not* study bankers?

Researching this book has provided a valuable perspective into Australian social history. The history of bankers this century covers the Depression years in the mallee country; what it felt like to drop out of school and become an office boy because there was not enough money to go around; the Second World War; growing up Catholic in Melbourne in the 1950s. Because these bankers in the main come from families of tradesmen, farmers and teachers, their history provides a middle class view of Australia from the 1930s to the 1960s.

Some particulars stand out: how far one could come in Australia with no tertiary education, and the relative egalitarianism of Australian society. It would not be possible in Malaysia or India, for instance, for a chief executive of a large bank to live next to a plumber — or more correctly, for a plumber to afford a house next to the chief executive — but offsetting this, was the very exclusive character of the directors of a bank board.

It has been a rewarding book to write. It was possible to come as a stranger to the country and venture on such a personal project because of the accessibility of people at the top of Australian financial institutions. They were generous with their time, and in many cases their wives also shared their perceptions of a banking life. This is something not easily come by in many parts of Asia. It was possible just to pick up the phone and ask for an appointment with the chief executive of a large bank. And get it.

It has also been a hard book to write. I have written of bankers and their banks as they were at the end of May 1990. It is important to keep this cut-off point in mind, for Australian banking is changing so fast that facts become outdated nearly as soon as they are recorded. The people move on, and it is likely that in the near future their banks will not exist in the same form. However, in a fast-changing environment, it becomes even more pertinent to understand the history and the human dimensions of Australian banking. Only then can we understand the present and deal with the future.

Some important changes have already taken place since the end of May 1990. On 26 August 1990, it was announced that the State Bank Victoria would be sold to the Commonwealth Bank. To fund the purchase the Commonwealth Bank will be partially privatised. This momentous change is discussed in the Postscript to this book.

This book would not have been possible without the help of the bankers, and often their wives, who gave freely of their time. I am indebted to Nugget Coombs, Bob Johnston, Bede Callaghan, John Brady, Bill Norton, Bob White, Stuart Fowler, Will and Dorothy Bailey, Nobby and Peggy Clark, Don Argus, Trevor Bennett, Don Sanders, Vern Christie, Ian Payne, Bill and Judy Moyle, Mark Johnson, Bill and Meg Gurry, Leigh Scott-Kemmis, David Saunders and Richard Beetham.

I am indebted also to David Uren, editor of *Triple A* in the first 18 months I was there. I would like to thank Mr M. R. Hill, adviser with the Reserve Bank of Australia, for reading the chronology, the first three chapters and the ones on the Commonwealth Bank and the State Bank Victoria; Dr David Merrett for reading the first two chapters and that on the ANZ; Professor Geoffrey Blainey for looking at the chapter on the National Australia Bank; and Clive Smith for checking the historical aspects of the chapter on Westpac.

Supriya Singh
Melbourne, 1990

Note: Unless otherwise stated, all references to dollars are to Australian dollars.

Chronology 1817–1990

The chronology is drawn from published history works listed in the bibliography, but the listing of trading and savings banks particularly draws on Butlin's *The Australian Monetary System: 1851–1914* (1986).

1817 Apr.	The Bank of New South Wales, the first commercial bank of Australia, opens — forerunner of Westpac. Governor Lachlan Macquarie initiates its establishment, so that one paper currency will underpin the financial development of the colony. He goes beyond his legal powers to issue a charter to support the bank.
1819 July	The New South Wales Savings Bank, also known as Campbell's Bank, the first Australian savings bank, is established for safekeeping the money of the newly arrived convicts, small settlers, mechanics, servants and labourers. Deposits are received from 2 shillings and 6 pence 'from any poor person of his neighbourhood, male or female, married or single'. This starts two separate streams of Australian banking: trading banks and savings banks. This distinction holds till 1988.
1824 Mar.	The Bank of Van Diemen's Land is founded in Hobart, modelled on the Bank of New South Wales.
1826 Feb.	The Bank of Australia is formed by pastoralists and free settlers. This distinguishes it from the Bank of New South Wales, which has previous convicts on its board. Referred to as 'the pure merino bank', it collapses in 1843 during Australia's first recession.
1828 Jan.	The Derwent Bank starts business in Hobart. It introduces the overdraft to Australia and pioneers branch banking and the London agency to collect deposits for Australian banks. It fails in 1849.
1828 May	The Cornwall Bank is established in Launceston, Tasmania. Later it becomes the first Launceston branch of the Bank of Australasia.
1829 June	The Commercial Bank of Tasmania is founded by John Dunn. The first trading bank to be founded by a

	single individual, it becomes a partnership in 1832. In 1829 there are more banks in Tasmania than in New South Wales, with all the banks being one-branch operations. In 1921, the bank is taken over by the English, Scottish and Australian Bank.
1829	First efforts are made to colonise Western Australia as a government-sponsored company settlement.
1830–35	Wool exports quadruple, leading to the opening up of half of the Australian continent. This leads to the official opening of a settlement at Port Phillip (now Melbourne) and is behind moves to colonise South Australia. It also increases the flow of capital and immigration from Britain. Population doubles from 50 000 to 100 000.
1832 Aug.	The Savings Bank of New South Wales is established by an Act of Parliament. It takes over the business of the New South Wales Savings Bank (Campell's Bank).
1834 Aug.	South Australia becomes a province by an Act of Parliament. Settlement is in 1836.
1834 Nov.	The Commercial Banking Company of Sydney opens, spurred by early signs of the pastoral boom. Unlike the older banks, which rely on shareholders' funds and note issue for their resources, it offers interest on deposits, 3 month fixed and current; but after 3 months it withdraws its interest on current deposits.
1835 Mar.	The Launceston Bank for Savings is set up.
1835 Dec.	The Bank of Australasia, the first British bank, opens in Australia. The Anglo-banks, as they come to be called, organise themselves on a branch basis and emphasise deposits as a source of funds. They also create a bankers' market in foreign exchange, replacing the Commissariat and the merchant middlemen.
1837 April	The Bank of South Australia, the first bank in South Australia, opens in Adelaide. It is taken over by the Union Bank of Australia in April 1892.
1838 May	Union Bank of Australia starts operations in Australia.
1838 Aug.	The Bank of Australasia opens a branch in Melbourne, becoming the first bank in the new settlement.

1839 Aug.	The Union Bank agrees to open a branch in New Zealand, becoming that country's first bank.
1840 Feb.	The Treaty of Waitangi is signed between the British Crown and the indigenous Maori people. New Zealand thus becomes a British colony.
1841 Mar.	The South Australian Savings Bank is established. It closes in 1847, to be succeeded by the Savings Bank of South Australia in 1848. All the profits of the bank, after deducting expenses and the sum set apart for the Security Fund, are to be paid out in interest. It is now known as the State Bank of South Australia.
1841 June	The Western Australian Bank opens in Western Australia.
1842 Jan.	The Savings Bank of Port Phillip, opens for business — forerunner of the State Bank of Victoria.
1845 Mar.	The Hobart Savings Bank is formed.
1850 June	The Colonial Bank of Issue opens. It is set up in New Zealand to solve the colony's currency problem. It holds the monopoly of the note issue for New Zealand till the bank is wound up in 1856.
1851 Feb.	Edward Hammond Hargraves, a coachman returned from California, discovers gold near Bathurst, 200 kilometres west of Sydney. It is reported in the *Sydney Morning Herald* on 15 May 1851. This starts the gold rush. The newly established state of Victoria offers a reward for the discovery of gold in Victoria to prevent an exodus. In August, T. Hiscock discovers the rich alluvial field at Ballarat. With the gold rush, the banks set up agencies and branches at the diggings.
1851 July	Victoria becomes an independent colony, separate from New South Wales.
1851–91	In 1851, there are only eight trading banks with 25 branches; but in the next 40 years, 21 new note-issuing banks open, most of them in Melbourne. Retail banking is established by 1891, with 1553 branches. Victoria in 1891 is the most populous state in Australia and has 36 per cent of the bank branches.
1852 Oct.	The English, Scottish and Australian Bank starts.

1853 Feb.	The Savings Bank of Port Phillip is reorganised as one of the Commissioners' Savings Banks.
1853 Apr.	The Oriental Bank Corporation, founded in India in 1842, starts in Australia. In 1857, it sets up in New Zealand to become the colony's second trading bank.
1854	An onerous gold-prospecting licence fee and its harsh methods of collection lead to a diggers' revolt in Ballarat known as the Eureka Stockade.
1856 Jan.	The Moreton Bay Savings Bank opens in Brisbane.
1856 Apr.	The Colonial Bank of Australasia is set up in Melbourne.
1858 Oct.	The National Bank of Australasia opens — forerunner of the National Australia Bank.
1858–77	Sydney, Melbourne and Adelaide are linked by electric telegraph in 1858. By 1872, there is a direct cable link to England, but Perth and Adelaide are not connected until 1877.
1861 May	Gabriel Read discovers gold at Gabriel's Gully in the Clutha River region of South Island, New Zealand. For 10 years, gold comprises half of all New Zealand's exports.
1861 June	The Bank of New South Wales buys the New Zealand business of the Oriental Bank.
1861–74	Eight new banks operate in New Zealand, which has a population of 172 000 in 1864.
1861 Oct.	The Bank of New Zealand opens in Auckland.
1863 Sept.	The Western Australian Post Office Savings Bank is set up, following on the heels of the British Post Office savings bank legislation of 1861.
1865 Jan.	The Queensland Savings Bank takes over the business of the Moreton Bay Savings Bank.
1865 Sept.	The Victorian Post Office Savings Bank opens to tap the savings of the goldfields and supplement the savings banks in the state. Post-office savings banking is

	followed in all Australian colonies except Tasmania by 1871.
1865 Dec.	The Bank of Adelaide opens in Adelaide.
1866 Oct.	The Commercial Bank of Australia is founded in Melbourne.
1870 Dec.	The Married Women's Property Act is passed. A married woman's deposits from her earnings, are now hers alone and cannot be withdrawn by her husband.
1870s early	The Privy Council decides that banks have a legal claim on land that is used as security for a loan.
1871 Sept.	The Government Savings Bank of New South Wales opens. It operates from many post offices and agencies, alongside the Savings Bank of New South Wales.
1872 June	The Queensland National Bank opens in Brisbane.
1872 July	The Bank of New Zealand opens its first branch in Australia, in Melbourne.
1880 Sept.	The first Australian telephone exchange opens in Melbourne.
1883–1917	New South Wales and Victoria are connected by railway in June 1883. In January 1887, Victoria and South Australia are connected; and in January 1888, the rail link joins New South Wales and Queensland. Not until October 1917 are South Australia and Western Australia linked, when the Kalgoorlie to Port Augusta stretch is complete.
1882 July	The Tasmanian Post Office Savings Bank opens.
1884	The Bank of Australasia introduces electric light in its head office, with 50 Swan lamps each of 20 candlepower.
1886	The Bank of Australasia introduces the Remington typewriter. With its special desk it costs 31 pounds. The bank also hires the first woman in any Australian bank. Miss M. E. Swifte works as the superintendent's typist for 34 years before retiring in January 1921.

1888	A general depression begins. Wool prices fall by a third from 1884 to 1891. Melbourne land prices and the building boom collapse by the end of 1888.
1892 June	The Oriental Bank reconstructed as the New Oriental Bank in 1885 closes in Australia.
1893	Panic results at the end of a speculative mania in Victoria, in land and buildings and the stock exchange. With the increase in interest in Britain, deposits from Britain do not flow into the Australian banks. Wheat, silver, wool are at a low. Land and mortgage banks and buildings societies crash. Melbourne, the largest city and banking centre in Australia, suffers the most.
1893 Apr.	The Commercial Bank of Australia closes, precipitating a banking crisis. By mid 1893, 54 of the 64 deposit-taking institutions that call themselves banks, close. Most reopen but freeze deposits for a number of years. This marks the end of the freewheeling and pioneering period of Australian banking and adds to resentment against private banks.
1893	Savings banks increase their share of deposits.
1893 Apr.	The Victorian state government guarantees the funds of the Commissioners' Savings Banks in Victoria.
1893 June	Paddy Hannan discovers the first gold in Kalgoorlie, Western Australia. In the first decade of the 1900s, Western Australia produces four-fifths as much gold as the famous diggings of Victoria in the 1850s.
1894 May	The Commissioners' Savings Banks in Victoria start giving long term mortgages based on freehold land.
1897 Sept.	The Victorian Post Office Savings Bank is taken over by the Commissioners' Savings Banks.
1901 Jan.	The Commonwealth of Australia is inaugurated in Melbourne's Exhibition Building, and the federal capital remains in Melbourne till 1927. The population of Australia in 1901 is 3.8 million. NSW is now the most populous state, but Melbourne is the largest city. Part of the policy framework is to provide uniform banking laws for all except state banks.

1901 Aug.	The Bank of New South Wales opens a branch at Suva, Fiji.
1902 July	The Tasmanian Post Office Savings Bank is renamed the State Savings Bank of Tasmania, and starts business.
1910 May	The Bank of New South Wales opens the first bank in Papua-New Guinea.
1910 Nov.	A Commonwealth note issue replaces notes issued by banks and the Queensland government. The sole power to issue and reissue notes is now vested in the federal Parliament.
1911 Dec.	The Commonwealth Bank Act 1911 creates the Commonwealth Bank of Australia, the first national government bank owned and guaranteed by the federal government.
1912 July	The savings bank department of the Commonwealth Bank opens for business. The Commonwealth Bank becomes the first bank to do both savings and general banking business in Australia. It takes over post office savings from the State Savings Bank of Victoria.
1912 Sept.	The Commissioners' Savings Banks combine into the State Savings Bank of Victoria.
1913 Jan.	The Commonwealth Bank starts its commercial banking business in the capitals of the six states, Townsville, Canberra and London.
1913 Jan.	The Commonwealth Bank takes over the State Savings Bank of Tasmania.
1914–18	The First World War.
1914 Apr.	The Government Savings Bank of New South Wales amalgamates with the Savings Bank of New South Wales.
1914 Oct.	The Commonwealth Treasury requests the banks to provide 10 million pounds worth of gold in exchange for notes. This gold is to finance public works.
1915 July	Notes increase in circulation, taking over from gold coins as the chief form of currency. Because they have

	to be backed by 30 per cent of gold, export of gold is prohibited except with the consent of the Commonwealth Treasurer.
1916 Dec.	The Queensland Savings Bank is renamed the Queensland Government Savings Bank. In 1920, its business is transferred to the savings bank department of the Commonwealth Bank of Australia.
1917–21	Bank mergers reduce the number of private trading banks in Australia and New Zealand from 22 to twelve.
1918 Nov.	The National Bank of Australasia absorbs the Melbourne-based Colonial Bank of Australasia.
1920	A four-member Notes Issue Board takes control of note issue from the Treasury. The governor of the Commonwealth Bank chairs the board, which is administered by a department of the bank yet is formally separate from it.
1920 Dec.	The Commonwealth Bank takes over the Queensland Government Savings Bank.
1922 Feb.	The National Bank of Australasia merges with the Bank of Queensland, but similar talks with the Commercial Banking Company of Sydney founder on the choice of headquarters for the bank.
1923	The Primary Producers' Bank of Australia Ltd is promoted in Queensland as a farmers' bank.
1924 Oct.	Control of note issue is transferred to the board of the Commonwealth Bank, giving it some of the functions of a central bank. The bank is now managed by a board instead of by the governor alone. The governor is a member of the board but not its chairman.
1926 Oct.	Western Australian Post Office Savings Bank changes its name to State Savings Bank of Western Australia.
1927 Mar.	The Bank of New South Wales takes over the Western Australian Bank and so controls almost two-fifths of the state's business.
1928 June	The Commonwealth Savings Bank of Australia begins operations as a separate entity. It was established as

	separate from the Commonwealth Bank of Australia by the Commonwealth Bank (Savings Bank) Act of 1927.
1929 Oct.	The Labor Party wins its first federal election since the First World War.
1929 end	The Commonwealth Bank compulsorily acquires all the gold of the trading banks. It marks the end of a period when Australian banking was based on gold and gold was seen as the universal means of exchange.
1930	Melbourne is linked to London by telephone.
1930 Oct.	The sterling exchange rate worsens gradually from 101.6 pounds Australian to 100 pounds sterling at the end of 1929, to 108.5 pounds Australian to 100 pounds sterling in October 1930.
1930s	The Depression. Wool prices halve between 1928 and 1930. In 1931/32, national income falls 34 per cent below that of 1927/28. Unemployment is 30 per cent. Mid 1932 is the period of deepest depression in Australia.
1931 Jan.	The Bank of New South Wales offers 115 pounds Australian to 100 pounds sterling. Other banks follow.
1931 Apr.	The Government Savings Bank of New South Wales, the second-largest savings bank, does not open, as 25 per cent of its deposits have been withdrawn. This reduces confidence in the banking system.
1931 Aug.	Despite a loan of 145 000 pounds by the Commonwealth Bank, the Primary Producers' Bank of Australia Ltd suspends payment.
1931 Sept.	The Government Savings Bank of New South Wales is reconstructed and opens for new business.
1931 Oct.	The State Savings Bank of Western Australia merges with the Commonwealth Bank.
1931 Nov.	The Commonwealth Bank determines the rate of exchange.
1931 Dec.	The Government Savings Bank of New South Wales fails and amalgamates with the Commonwealth Savings Bank.

1933 July	The Rural Bank of New South Wales is formed primarily from the rural bank department of the Government Savings Bank of New South Wales.
1934 Aug.	The Reserve Bank of New Zealand begins operations.
1937 July	The Royal Commission set up in 1935 to investigate the Australian banking and monetary system after the Depression, issues its report. Much of the blame for the problems of the Depression falls on the unregulated banks. The report of the Royal Commission recommends strengthening the central banking powers of the Commonwealth Bank, but it maintains that a system of private banks is desirable.
1939 Apr.	Robert Gordon Menzies is elected Prime Minister of a conservative coalition government.
1939 Sept.	The outbreak of the Second World War leads to war-time banking regulations. Exchange controls are introduced.
1941 Oct.	John Curtin is elected Prime Minister of a Labor government. J. B. Chifley is his Treasurer.
1941 Nov.	National Security (Wartime Banking Control) Regulations are introduced, making for greater government control over banks. Banks are required to deposit their increase in deposits from August 1939 with the Commonwealth Bank. Banks have to be licensed and are subject to policy direction from the Commonwealth Bank on interest rates, investment and lending policies. Banks accept these controls to wage war efficiently.
1942 July	The Bank of China begins operating in Sydney.
1944 July	The International Monetary Fund and the International Bank for Reconstruction and Development are set up as a result of the Bretton Woods Conference in the United States. Australia joins after much discussion.
1945 Feb.	The Rural and Industries Bank Act 1944 establishes the Rural and Industries Bank of Western Australia.
1945 July	Joseph Benedict (Ben) Chifley becomes Prime Minister after the death of John Curtin.

1945 Aug.	The Second World War ends.
1945 Aug.	The Banking Act 1945 is passed to continue the wartime regulations in peacetime and, for the first time, to provide national legislation on banking. Section 48 requires public bodies to do their business with the Commonwealth Bank. The problems of Depression together with the effective functioning of the economy with the wartime controls lead to another 40 years of highly regulated banking.
1945 Aug.	The Commonwealth Bank Act 1945 directs the Commonwealth Bank to expand its general banking business and compete with the other banks. Its independent board is dissolved by a Labor government, which sees it as an instrument of business and rich farming interests. It is replaced by an advisory council of bank officials and public servants.
1947 May	Two hundred local authorities are told to stop dealing with private banks and to transfer their business to the Commonwealth Bank by 1 August 1947.
1947 Aug.	The High Court of Australia rules that section 48 of the Banking Act 1945 is invalid. States, government authorities and municipalities can bank wherever they wish.
1947 Aug.	Prime Minister Chifley announces that his government will nationalise private banks. Their staff and business are to be taken over by the Commonwealth Bank.
1947 Nov.	The Banking Act 1947 to nationalise banks becomes law but is not proclaimed, and its validity is challenged by the private banks.
1948 Jan.	The National Bank of Australasia takes over the Queensland National Bank.
1948 Aug.	The High Court rules that vital sections of the Banking Act 1947 are invalid.
1949 July	The Privy Council dismisses the government appeal of the High Court ruling.
1949 Dec.	The Labor Party is defeated in the elections. A major issue is the nationalisation of banks. The Menzies government is re-elected.

1951 Mar.	The Australia and New Zealand Bank Ltd (ANZ) is formed by merging the Bank of Australasia and the Union Bank of Australia.
1951 Apr.	A general election returns the Liberal Party with a majority in both houses and a mandate to reform banking.
1951 July	The Commonwealth Bank Act 1951 reconstitutes the bank's board, but with the governor as chairman.
1953	The private trading banks push into the hire purchase business through subsidiaries, the first being the English, Scottish and Australian Bank (ES&A).
1953 Apr.	The general banking division of the Commonwealth Bank becomes the Commonwealth Trading Bank of Australia. This is to separate the commercial banking functions of the bank from its central banking functions.
1955 Mar.	The National Bank of Australasia absorbs the small Ballarat Banking Company.
1956–62	Private banks operate savings bank subsidiaries on the condition that 70 per cent of their assets at least are held in cash, Treasury bills or government or semi-government securities. Savings banks then handle the banks' housing business.
1956	Three major trading banks start restricted savings-bank activities through subsidiaries.
1957	The private banks approach the federal government to separate the Commonwealth Bank's trading and regulatory central-banking functions.
1958	The Bank of New South Wales enters the unit trust business.
1958	The Bank of New South Wales enters the superannuation field, with Wales Superannuation Ltd. It is to be the fastest-growing sector of financial business in the late 1980s.
1959 Feb.	The official short-term money market starts when the first authorised short-term money-market dealers start operations. This is one of the first steps from a regulated economy to a market situation.

1960 Jan.	The Reserve Bank Act 1959, the Commonwealth Banks Act 1959 and the Banking Act 1959 come into operation. The Commonwealth Bank splits into the Reserve Bank of Australia and the Commonwealth Banking Corporation. The latter comprises the Commonwealth Trading Bank, the Commonwealth Savings Bank and the Commonwealth Development Bank. The Banking Act 1959 sets out the structure of the regulation of banks through the Advance Policy, exchange controls and interest rates.
1962 Apr.	The Reserve Bank of Australia institutes a term loan scheme to provide bank credit for a fixed 3 to 8 year period. This is to finance capital expenditure for rural and secondary industry and to produce capital goods for export.
1962 July	Treasury notes are issued for the first time.
1966 Feb.	Decimal currency is introduced, with a pound equal to $A2.
1967 Nov.	The Australian dollar does not follow sterling when sterling depreciates. It is the first variation in the exchange rate of Australian currency against sterling since the 1930s.
1970 Oct.	The Australia and New Zealand Bank Ltd and the English, Scottish and Australian Bank join to form the Australia and New Zealand Banking Group Ltd.
1971 Aug.	The US dollar is not convertible to gold.
1971 Dec.	The Australian dollar is linked to the US dollar.
1973 Jan.	Britain joins the European Economic Community. It changes the trading patterns of Australia and, to a lesser extent, of New Zealand.
1974	Banks introduce part-time employment.
1974 Aug.	The Financial Corporations Act 1974 provides for the collection of statistics from non-bank financial corporations. Part IV of the Act, which has not been proclaimed, enables the Reserve Bank to exercise direct control over some aspects of these corporations.

1974 Aug.	The major trading banks launch Bankcard, the first bank credit card in Australia. It changes the way in which customers relate to banks.
1974 Sept.	The Australian dollar's link with the US dollar is discontinued, and the Australian dollar is valued against a trade-weighted basket of currencies.
1975	Women and men get equal pay in banking.
1975 Nov.	The Governor General dismisses Labor Prime Minister Gough Whitlam. Malcolm Fraser becomes a caretaker Prime Minister of a Liberal/Country Party government.
1975 Dec.	Malcolm Fraser is elected Prime Minister.
1976 Nov.	A managed exchange rate is introduced with a flexible link between the Australian dollar and the trade-weighted basket of currencies.
1979 Jan.	The Liberal government under Malcolm Fraser sets up the Campbell Committee of inquiry into the Australian financial system.
1979 May	The Reserve Bank of Australia orchestrates the first Australian bank rescue when the Australia and New Zealand Banking Group agrees to buy the Bank of Adelaide.
1979 Dec.	Treasury notes are offered at tender for the first time.
1980 May	The Bank of New South Wales is the first bank to introduce automated teller machines (ATMs) to Australia.
1980 May	A trading bank is allowed to hold up to 60 per cent of a merchant bank. The previous limit was 33.3 per cent.
1980 Aug.	The Treasurer tables the interim report of the Campbell Committee in Parliament.
1980 Sept.	The Australian Bank is given permission to operate. When it opens in 1981, it becomes the first private bank to open in 58 years.

1980 Dec.	Trading and savings banks are permitted to offer deposit rates without a ceiling set by the Reserve Bank. This is an important step in the deregulation of banking.
1980 Dec.	The State Savings Bank of Victoria is renamed the State Bank of Victoria.
1981 May	The Bank of New South Wales announces its merger with the Commercial Bank of Australia to become Westpac Banking Corporation. The National Bank of Australasia announces its merger with the Commercial Banking Company of Sydney to become the National Australia Bank.
1981 July	The Rural Bank of New South Wales is reconstituted as the State Bank of New South Wales.
1981 Nov.	The Campbell Report is tabled in Parliament. It becomes the blueprint for the subsequent deregulation of the Australian financial system.
1982 Mar.	Savings banks are allowed to accept fixed deposits.
1982 June	The Reserve Bank announces the end of quantitative bank lending guidance.
1983 Jan.	The Closer Economic Relationship (CER) Agreement between New Zealand and Australia comes into effect, to develop a single market between Australia and New Zealand by 1995.
1983 Jan.	The Treasurer announces that the government will allow ten new banks, including foreign banks.
1983 Mar.	Labor wins the election to form the government under Prime Minister Bob Hawke.
1983 May	The Labor government commissions the Martin Review Group to re-examine the financial system and the Campbell Report. The report is published in December 1983, arguing for the need to make the financial system more efficient.
1983 Dec.	The Australian dollar is floated. Financial deregulation in Australia is popularly seen as beginning at this point. Most exchange controls are abolished.

1983 Dec.	Westpac announces it will introduce the world's first national Electronic-Funds-Transfer at Point-Of-Sale (EFTPOS) system in March 1984.
1984 Apr.	Banks, merchant banks, life insurance companies and other finance groups are permitted to hold up to 50 per cent of a stockbroking company. Overseas financial institutions may hold up to 15 per cent.
1984 June	The Australian Payments Council is established to oversee the development of Australia's payments systems. It is chaired by the Reserve Bank of Australia and includes representatives of the finance industry and one representative from the consumers' groups.
1984 Aug.	Trading banks may hold 100 per cent of the equity of a merchant bank.
1984 Aug.	All remaining controls on bank deposits are removed. Banks are able to offer interest on call deposits and short-term fixed deposits.
1984 Sept.	The 30/20 rule requiring life insurance companies and superannuation funds to hold at least 30 per cent of their assets in government and semi-government securities is abolished.
1984 Sept.	The Australia and New Zealand Banking Group buys Grindlays Bank for $A282 million and has to inject another $A168 million into its capital. It becomes the most international of Australia's banks, with representation in 45 countries.
1985 Feb.	The Treasurer announces that foreign corporations have been invited to apply for banking licences.
1985 Apr.	Lending rates are freed, other than for loans for owner-occupied housing for less than $A100 000.
1985 June	The New South Wales Building Society Ltd becomes the Advance Bank Australia.
1986 Feb.	The Royal Bank of Canada and the National Mutual Life Association of Australasia form a joint venture and own 50 per cent each of the National Mutual Royal Bank.
1986 Apr.	The interest rate ceiling on new housing loans is re-

moved while keeping the old housing loans by banks at a fixed 13.5 per cent interest per annum.

1986 July	Foreign Investment Review Board regulations are relaxed, so that foreign investment in property is freely possible without the necessity of previous government permission or an Australian joint venture partner.
1986 Nov.	The Cheques and Payment Orders Act 1986 is passed, providing for new cheque-like instruments called payment orders.
1987 Mar.	The United Permanent Building Society merges with the National Mutual Royal Bank.
1987 Apr.	Domestic financial institutions can hold up to 100 per cent of a stockbroking house.
1987 Sep.	The Launceston Bank for Savings amalgamates with the Tasmanian Permanent Building Society to become the Tasmania Bank.
1987 Oct.	World stockmarkets crash.
1988 Aug.	The distinction between trading and savings banks is phased out, as both have to keep to the same regulatory ratios. The Statutory Reserve Deposit (SRD) ratio is replaced by 'non-callable deposits', which apply to all banks. The Reserve Bank of Australia issues guidelines for the capital adequacy of Australian banks, generally consistent with those of the Bank for International Settlements.
1989 Jan.	The State Bank Victoria buys 100 per cent of Australian Bank. Its plans to back Tricontinental Holdings Ltd, its 100 per cent owned merchant bank, into Australian Bank are aborted in May 1989.
1989 Mar.	A nationally linked Electronic-Funds-Transfer at Point-Of-Sale (EFTPOS) system is announced, but stalls as negotiations founder on the issue of fees.
1989 Apr.	Westpac announces the appointment of an ombudsman to look at customers' complaints.
1989 May	The Australian Bankers' Association decides to appoint a banking ombudsman, funded by the banks but independent of them.

1989 July	The Australian Payments Council sponsors an independent investigation of security standards in financial institutions' systems for retail electronic funds transfers.
1989 Sept.	The Reserve Bank pays a closer to market rate on banks' non-callable deposits. The rate moves from 5 per cent to 5 per cent less the Treasury note rate. At the same time the major banks agree not to raise housing lending rates as long as general interest rates remain at existing levels.
1989 Nov.	The Banking Legislation Amendment Act 1989 removes the distinction between savings and trading banks. It gives the central bank explicit powers in respect of prudential supervision of banks. It also formally replaces the Statutory Reserve Deposit requirement on trading banks with the new non-callable deposit requirement applicable to all banks.
1989 Dec.	The Reserve Bank of New Zealand Act 1989 makes fighting inflation the sole function of the central bank. It comes into force in February 1990.
1990 Feb.	The National Australia Bank acquires Yorkshire Bank.
1990 Feb.	The Reserve Bank of Australia announces a change in the Prime Assets Requirement for banks. Instead of holding 10 per cent of their assets in high quality, readily cashable assets, the banks will be required to hold 6 per cent of their total liabilities in these assets by May 1990.
1990 Apr.	ANZ and the National Mutual Life Association of Australasia announce their intention to merge, with ANZ buying 51 per cent of National Mutual for $3.4 billion. If approved, the merged group would become the largest and most international and diversified financial institution of Australia. ANZ buys the National Mutual Royal Bank from National Mutual and the Royal Bank of Canada for $400 million, on the understanding that the National Mutual Royal will revert to National Mutual if the merger does not go through.
1990 May	Treasurer Paul Keating vetoes the merger because it is 'contrary to the national interest'. The status quo of four large banks and two large life offices is to be preserved for effective competition.

	A non-mutual life office is allowed to own a bank subject to certain conditions. The conditions prompt National Mutual not to buy back the National Mutual Royal, but instead to sell it again to ANZ. A banking ombudsman is appointed to look into consumers' disputes with banks.
1990 June	The second largest building society group in Australia — Pyramid, Countrywide, and Geelong belonging to the Farrow Corporation — closes its doors. The loss of confidence in the non-bank sector flows on to cause a run on the Bank of Melbourne.
1990 Aug.	State Bank Victoria is to be sold to the Commonwealth Bank of Australia. The Commonwealth Bank is to be partially privatised to fund the purchase.

1 Banking today and yesterday

Monday at a branch

The counters at a Westpac Banking Corporation branch in Melbourne look virginal at 9 a.m. The day begins with the clanging of steel grey cashboxes opening as a teller slides the covers back so that they stand upright. The back office staff can then read the warnings written on each cashbox. One reads: 'Oops! Take a little extra care. Avoid false alarms.'

Stella Chacholiades, 20, and Fay Lavos, 20, start organising the two cashboxes, with notes ranging from $100 to $5 and coins, rubber bands and pins in smaller compartments to the side. In front of each teller is a monitor, half the size of a regular personal-computer monitor. The senior teller is on leave, and the second teller, Betty Pattas, 25, checks the figures from the day before.

At 9.30 a.m. some regular customers come in with white bags of coin. Monday sees a lot of them coming to deposit their takings over the weekend. Betty is at the counter now, and at 9.42 Fay, who is really the enquiry clerk, places a wet sponge next to each teller to aid in note counting. There is a fair trickle of customers till 10.30. The constant sounds at this time are the clanging open of the cashboxes and the whirring of the proof machine, where Patricia Potenzi, 20, the batch clerk, encodes the cheques so that the computer at the clearing house can read them. She also sees that every debit has a matching credit.

Peter Wolfe, the manager, says that 40 per cent of this branch's business is commercial and that it averages roughly 230 customers a day. This is one of the top branches in terms of profit. In some ways, though, it is an old-fashioned branch, for it is not yet functioning as a supermarket of financial services. Wolfe says that they average only one enquiry a week about the superannuation, insurance, advisory or broking services.

It is also a traditional branch, in that it still works with tellers dealing with the cash and cheques and with a separate enquiry counter and overseas desk. Some branches that have gone 'network' have only one category of counter staff, called customer service officers; they deal with everything from enquiries to overseas drafts. The branch is old-fashioned also because the back office processing has not yet been centralised. That is why Patricia is still doing the proofing in the branch itself and why the tellers also have to keep track of fixed deposits and standing instructions.

The hour from 10.30 to 11.30 is easy. The counter staff do some of their back office duties and have a cup of coffee. The coffee area is a make-do space in the storage room, with large stationery racks and remnants of Christmas decorations in one corner. There is a knack to the hot water tap; you have to turn it slightly to the left to prevent it from dripping.

Going to the toilet is something of a problem, for the toilets are outside the branch in the corridor. You have to first open a heavy door with two large latches at the top and bottom of the door, one lock and a chain. Somebody then has to lock this back. In the ladies' toilet, the fluorescent light flickers. To get back into the branch, you have to knock hard for somebody to open the door for you again.

At 11.30, Betty and Fay go off for lunch. This is a sandwich and some fruit at the coffee table in the store. Lunch lasts 45 minutes exactly, for Stella, the third teller, is waiting to go off, and soon the rush will start.

The lunchtime crowd queues up. The priority now is to get the queue down. The accountant, Mark Griffiths, 30, steps in at the tellers' counter. The assistant manager looks after enquiries. The manager answers the telephones.

At 2.20 p.m. it becomes quiet again. The manager switches the television on, for Australia is playing the West Indies in cricket. 'It's for the customers,' he says. Everyone laughs; but sure enough, the customers also wait to check the score before doing their banking.

The next rush comes just before closing at 4 p.m.

By 4.05 everyone gets very busy, for the faster they work, the quicker they can go home. After the customers leave comes the time of reckoning for the tellers. Stella finds that she is out by $6000. The accountant steps in, and they check and counter check. They look at the clock; it is 4.21. Finally they remember a cheque placed with the ledger clerk, Peter Weickhardt, 17, for collection by a customer; he never arrived. The calculations go on, and they find themselves short by $5.39. That is allowed, for there is a $10 float to account for shortage in coin.

At the other cashbox, Betty and Fay are checking; it doesn't balance. 'Use the other adding machine,' says Betty. 'This one is no good.' Fay moves over to the other machine, and soon after they shout, 'We're balanced' — to the last cent. The accountant says, 'Bloody time too.' It is 4.33 p.m.

Some of them turn their attention to Patricia, the batch clerk. They help her to complete the proofing. The others heap the trays of cash on the tellers' chairs and wheel them to the strongroom. The file trolleys are put away. Computers are turned off. Mark, the accountant, wedges the coffee-cum-storage room open with a black bristle brush, 'so that the security staff can look inside'.

It's the end of a day at a branch.

Today's tellers

A customer walking into a similar branch in the early 1960s would have seen some remarkable differences. There were no computer screens at the counter. The latest mechanised gadget was the ledger machine. Instead of eight to ten people in the branch, there would have been thirteen or fourteen. The tellers were men, at least 21 years old and predominantly Anglo-Saxon. Women did the typing or the ledger work towards the back of the bank, facing away from the counter.

In 1989, however, three-quarters of tellers are women. A third or half of tellers work part-time, and most part-time tellers are women. Also, tellers are younger, ranging between 17 and 22 years of age. There is also a greater ethnic mix at the counter. It is hard to give a percentage to this mix, as banks do not ask for the ethnic category of their employees; but of the 25 tellers interviewed in branches chosen by the banks in Melbourne in January 1989, less than a third (only eight) were of Anglo-Saxon descent. It is now unremarkable to be served by Australians of Greek, Italian, Spanish, Chinese, Vietnamese, Cambodian, Malaysian, Lebanese or Indian descent.

The main difference is that, till the 1960s at least, tellers and bank officers saw themselves as distinctly middle class, a cut above other working people. Tellers were conscious they were beginning a 40 year career at the same bank. If things went well, they expected to retire as branch managers. In 1989, however, some tellers join knowing they are going to leave. Some join thinking they will 'give banking a go'. Only a few join knowing they will make it their career. Today, every year, one teller in five expects to leave banking altogether. For them, banking is not an avenue of social mobility.

This is tied with the downgrading of the teller's position in the bank. Tellers themselves have a low image about their job. One teller praised the accountant at her branch by saying, 'He does not mind serving at the counter, even doing the degrading jobs.' Talking to tellers gives the overwhelming impression that they see themselves in an ill-paid and dead end job. Though tellers do move — Westpac's

Jodie Harrison, Westpac general hand (Moshe Dinor, courtesy BRW)

average in early 1989 was 6 years and 4 months to make a general hand — this perception of immobility persists.

Jodie Harrison's story is fairly typical of a teller, or customer service officer as they are now called. Jodie left school after Year 11 because she did not like it. She applied to banks because some of her friends worked in banks and because her teachers also said that it would be a good job. What clinched it for her was a very pleasant 2 weeks' work experience at the Australia and New Zealand Banking Group. Moreover, she said, 'I wanted a secure job.'

Like all 16-year-old starters, she began at Westpac at the proof machine, at $140 a week, encoding cheques. Then she worked at the enquiry counter and from there moved on to telling. The formal training was a 2 day course, learning how to address customers by name and smile a lot. After that it was a matter of the people at the branch training her on the job. She is doing well at the bank in January 1989 in Melbourne. Within 4 years she has moved up, becoming a general hand at the district operations centre, which processes the back office work of a number of branches. As a general hand, she is one step above the tellers, but not yet one of the appointed officers. Now 20, she likes her job and the people with whom she works, but the bank as a wider entity has little meaning for her. Like many other tellers, she does not know the name of the bank's chief executive.

The next step up for her is to become a signing officer. This would be a big jump, for it would take her from the ranks to the appointed officer category. She is unsure when this will happen or whether it will happen at all. She sees two factors working against her: being female and not being a graduate. From her perspective, the males have it better, and the graduates are on a fast track in the bank, even when they do not know as much as those who joined from school. There is a strong feeling in the branch that graduates come on 'tour' and then make out that they know it all. Jodie said, 'I know a girl who has a BA, and within six months she was getting paid more than a person with six to seven years' experience in the bank.' However, she does not want to study further to increase her prospects in the bank. She said, 'The bank encourages you to study at night, but I was glad I got out of school. I enjoy my social life too much.' Right now, she cannot see herself as a bank manager. 'I won't be around that long,' she said. 'An accountant perhaps. I'll bide my time.' Pausing, she added, 'I am not sure what I'd like to do. After 4 years, I am making $19 200, and even that is better than my other friends in the bank, who at 20 are averaging $18 000.' She sees herself as having a two-way bet: she's doing well in the bank; and if she does quit at some stage, having worked in the bank, she feels, can only be a plus.

Jodie's story is repeated many times in the banks today, but there are the other two ends of the spectrum also. There are some like Patricia Potenzi, the batch clerk at the Westpac branch, who clearly said in January 1989, 'I don't want to be here for the rest of my life. My ambition is really to be a graphics designer.' She sees herself leaving after she has worked as a teller for a while. She joined the bank after Year 12 because her fiance was with Westpac. She said, 'It is a bit hard trying to sort things out. I need a secure job to get married, and it is better to be in a bank than being unemployed.'

Then there are those like Stella Chacholiades, who aims to move from being teller number three to being a general hand in the overseas department. After doing her Higher School Certificate, she said in January 1989, 'I didn't want to study further. My dad was a bank manager overseas. One of my cousins is a bank manager, and two other cousins are in banking. So it is in the family.'

What is clear, though, is that not many tellers join the bank knowing that they are going to stay. Many stay, but quite a few leave. Though the turnover rate in the banking industry in 1988 was 17 per cent, it was greater at the counter level. For the Commonwealth Bank of Australia, the overall exit rate for 1988 (including retirement) was 15 per cent, while that of the general classified staff (which includes counter staff) was 20 per cent. In December 1989, Kevin Scott, federal secretary of the Commonwealth Bank Officers' Association, said in a telephone interview in Sydney that this rate may have slowed down a little, but it has not turned around in the metropolitan areas.

One reason why one in five tellers leave the bank every year is that they see their job as being ill-paid for the amount of responsibility it carries. The starting wage for a teller in early 1989 was $8732 a year. Till age 21, the teller is on junior wages, which are based on age. After this, wage goes by performance, and even this came into effect in the major private trading banks only in 1987.

The Commonwealth Bank of Australia wages in February 1989 started even lower, at $8166 for a 16-year-old with a Year 10 qualification, with less than 1 per cent extra for performance — and it went by age till the person was 27. This linkage of salary to age was only abolished in May 1990. However most full-time tellers are in the two junior grades which are age-determined. The cheaper loans that go with a bank job also do not count for much at this level. At a net $140 to $250 a week, it is hard to afford a housing loan even with a subsidised rate of interest. Though these wages are competitive with the shop-awards wage scale, which starts at $8725 for a 17-year-old, they are a major cause of dissatisfaction. This goes all the way to the accountant/supervisor level. After 13 to 15 years in the bank, the person can look forward to some $25 000 a year.

For the part-time teller, the position is even worse. Barbara Oxworth, who works at the National Australia Bank, receives $430 a fortnight for 27 hours of work a week in early 1989. At $8 an hour, she gets paid less than a cleaning woman, whose rates are $11 an hour. So why do people come to work in a bank? Barbara Oxworth, for instance, accepted nearly half the pay she was getting in the medical records department of a major hospital, because she wanted a clean break from her previous job. She opted for more flexibility and personal contact with customers.

Angela Cerritelli, 25, who works for the Australia and New Zealand Banking Group (ANZ) as a securities clerk, for $19 500, said in Melbourne in January 1989, 'I was getting more when I was 18 and a secretary with a law company.' What she likes about the bank is that it is a bigger working environment, not just two people.

Betty Pattas, of the Westpac branch, came to the bank after she sold out as a partner in a city boutique. She said that, when she was at the boutique and spending well, she could save more than $20 000. In 1989 she gets approximately $18 000 a year. She joined the bank because she 'needed some security and wanted my weekends free. I am going to get married in a year. At the bank, I can walk out at 5 p.m. or 6 p.m. At the boutique, I had to pick up materials, or drop off patterns, or go to the cutters after 9 p.m. There was no spare time to myself. I was exhausted.'

Contact with customers and an amenable working environment are the pluses of working at a bank. Many tellers, like Betty Pattas or Jodie Harrison, also mentioned 'security of job' as one reason why they joined. This is particularly interesting, as it is a perception that is a carryover from the past. Len Hingley, federal secretary of the Australian Bank Employees Union, said that today there is less security of tenure in banks than before. In January 1989 in Melbourne, he said, the union 'takes one unfair dismissal a week to the commission. They are mainly women dealing with the transaction processes of banking.'

Moreover, with banks closing or restructuring branches, there are fewer people in branch banking now. Hingley strongly feels that technology will have its repercussions on employment, especially in the teller category. Though the number of full-time bank employees in the trading and savings banks has risen (from 96 731 in 1975 to 129 705 in 1987, the latest available figures), Hingley is apprehensive of the future.

So the teller's job has less security than it had before. It is seen as an ill-paid job. It is also seen as a dead end job; the increasing use of part-time tellers, who do nothing but serve at the counter and have no hope of doing anything else, contributes to this perception. The faster promotion of graduates also is seen as playing havoc with opportunities for advancement.

Stories of the past

One of the main differences between tellers today and those who were tellers more than 20 years ago is that banking used to be seen as a good way up the social ladder and as a means of making something of yourself.

Sir Bede Callaghan's career typifies the kind of mobility possible through banking in Australia going back to the 1920s. Son of a teacher, he started as a junior at the Commonwealth Bank of Australia in 1921 and retired as the managing director of the Commonwealth Banking Corporation in 1976. He left school after 9 years, because his eldest brother was going to university and family finances dictated that only one of them could study; the other had to go to work. Speaking of it in February 1988 in his house in Gordon, Sydney, Bede Callaghan said that he did not mind leaving school, because his 'academic record was mediocre'. So he started work as an office boy in an engineer's office in Newcastle. There was a branch of the Commonwealth Bank of Australia in the same building; and when he heard that they were looking for a junior, he applied.

The manager interviewed him, and he had to supply references. His family had no relationship with the Commonwealth or any other bank, as his father did his banking with a building society. 'I started at 80 pounds a year,' he said, 'which was better than what I was getting as an office boy.' He had the basic qualifications of a junior: good handwriting, ability to add columns of figures fast and correct English composition. After that, it was a matter of learning on the job from your seniors. As a junior:

> I would be dressed conservatively. I wore a suit, coat and tie and wore a hat until after the war — a felt hat. The suit had to be grey or blue, virtually never brown. Black shoes. The tie was generally blue, straightforward and cheap.
>
> My first duty was to collect the cheques, sort them out according to the different banks. The inkwells had to be filled with blue-black ink, nibs

Bede Callaghan, managing director, Commonwealth Bank of Australia 1965–76 (courtesy BRW)

> changed as necessary, the blotting paper changed. The handwritten ledgers would be taken on a trolley from the strongroom and back again. There was always something to do, and I just watched what was going on. After 6 months I was doing the records for the teller, writing down the number, name, amount of deposit and final balance.

Every banker now in his 50s and 60s can tell much the same story of social mobility through banking. Bob White, for instance, joined the Bank of New South Wales (now the Westpac Banking Corporation) at Echuca in 1940, aged 17, after finishing school. He retired as managing director of the bank at the end of 1987.

His father had sheep on an unviable 750 hectares of dry mallee land in the south-southwest of NSW. Talking about it in his Westpac office in Sydney in October 1987, he said, 'My father had no desire, and neither did I, that I should be a farmer, because of the recurrent hardships.' Behind him were the experiences of Depression and drought. The Second World War had just started. Though he had a scholarship to go to university in Sydney, his father decided that White should go to the bank. 'The bank represented a secure opportunity,' White said.

Like White, many boys of 17 must have seen a bank as an opening to an exciting world and being a bank manager as a definition of status and wealth. White said, 'When I reported to start work at Echuca, the manager had just taken delivery of a new Chevrolet, a navy-blue

Chevrolet sedan, 1939 model.' Even after 47 years, his voice went silky as he said:

> Just imagine owning something like that. I loved motorcars, ever since I was so high. Because we lived in a very isolated environment, motorcars were very much a part of my life. We had a Dodge and a Ford round the farm, but the big wealthy graziers always had the large American or European cars.
>
> And, of course, the manager lived in a big residence at the top of the bank. This was an old-fashioned bank built in the latter part of the century — a big stone facade, big high bedrooms. It was just so different from our modest timber house in the country.

Joining a bank was one way of getting all this. For White, the dream of the navy-blue Chevrolet was supplanted by a Jaguar. Now he is on his third Jaguar, a beautiful deep red maroon.

Banking was seen as an avenue to a prosperous and respected position, a way of moving up in the world. Most successful banking stories in Australia tell how the sons of teachers, farmers, clergymen and tradesmen started at the bottom as juniors and rose to head the banks. Because the bank paid while the school leaver learned the profession, banking has been an unparalleled avenue of social mobility for more than 100 years. Will Bailey, head of ANZ, the second-largest bank in the country (in terms of assets) is son of a tradesman turned farmer. Nobby Clark, managing director of the National Australia Bank, the third-largest bank in the country, is son of a travelling tradesman. Don Sanders, managing director of the government-owned Commonwealth Bank of Australia, is son of a school teacher. Stuart Fowler, head of the Westpac Banking Corporation, Australia's largest bank, is a bit out of the mould, for he is son of a professor of psychology at the University of Western Australia; but he too joined as a junior and worked his way up the banking hierarchy.

Women at the bank

Australian banking is a story of how men got to the top. The difference in the opportunities available to men and women in banking is illustrated most dramatically by the career of Miss Tennyson Beatrice Miller.

In 1898, Miss Miller became the first woman employed by the Bank of New South Wales. She was 16 and employed at the bank's head office at a salary of 80 pounds per annum. Though there was a precedent — the Bank of Australasia, later to be part of the Australia and New Zealand Bank Ltd (ANZ), had hired a woman in 1886 to do typing for the superintendent on a Remington typewriter — it was still seen as unconventional to have a woman working in the bank. The wives of bank officers protested at this, so the bank put Miss Miller and another woman colleague in a separate room away from the general banking work and had them work slightly different hours from the men (*Bankers' Magazine of Australasia*, Oct 1972). Miss Miller was hired to work on the typewriter and was called a 'lady typewriter'. After 42 years, she retired as a lady typewriter. Her brother Denison Miller joined the Bank of New South Wales in 1876 when he was 16. In 1912, he became the first governor of the Commonwealth Bank of Australia.

The position of women in Australian banking, of course, has to be seen in the wider context of the position of women in Australian society. More particularly, it has to be seen against the economic status of women. In the 1880s, as Blainey and Hutton (1983) in *Gold and Paper* note, it was seen as perfectly normal for Grey Smith, head of the National Bank of Australasia (now the National Australia Bank) to wonder whether he should even accept deposits from women. The view was that women were too subject to panic.

This did not sound absurd at the time, for, until the Married Women's Property Act was passed in 1870, a married woman could not open an account without the written authority of her husband. The money in her account would belong to her, but only if it was determined that the money deposited came from her own wages and earnings and not from those of her husband. Otherwise, the husband had to authorise the withdrawal of her money. He, however, could withdraw the money in her account without her permission. So with women not seen as bona fide customers of banks until after the 1880s, hiring women in the bank was a major step.

The number of women in banking slowly crept up. In chronicling the feminisation of the banks, the important reference points are the First World War, 1914–18, the introduction of equal pay for men and women in 1969 and the introduction of part-time employees in the banks in 1974. The First World War marked the first large-scale entry of women into banking. The number of women in Australian banks increased from 45 in 1911 to 1882 in 1921. After the war, many of the women left. However, the trend was set. In 1945, women were 24.4 per cent of the workforce in banks. In 1975, women were 42.1 per cent of the full-time bank employees. By 1987, women had become 51.9 per cent of full-time employees and 96.8 per cent of part-time employees in banks.

However, this increase in numbers was not accompanied by an equivalent increase in opportunities. In the main, women took over the mechanisation of bank work and became the 'lady typewriters' of subsequent generations. Till the 1960s, at least, the view was that a woman at work takes a job away from a man. So it was the practice, unquestioned for the most part even by women themselves till the 1960s, that when a woman married, she quit the bank. This, of course, made it impossible for women to think of banking as a career, unless they chose not to marry.

Eva King, working as an operations supervisor at the National Australia Bank (the top non-management position) joined ANZ in 1962. At the time there were no women tellers. Women did the background work, as ledger operators, batch clerks and typists. She got married 2½ years later and resigned, as was required by bank policy. She herself did not question the policy; that was the social norm. 'In the 1960s, a working woman was seen as a witch with a broom outside her door,' she said in Melbourne in January 1989. She came back to banking part-time in 1976 as a teller with ANZ. In 1983, she moved to the National Australia Bank, also as a part-time teller. In 1986, she started full-time work again with a bank. For all practical purposes, her career prospects were frozen during her 10 years of part-time work. Hence, after 4½ years of full-time work and 10 years of part-time work, she still has not made it to the appointed staff position.

This legacy has meant that a woman chief executive of even a small bank in Australia is still a fair way down the track. There are no women even in the second tier of the major trading banks. It is still so unusual to have a woman in a top managerial position that Westpac issued a press release in February 1989 announcing the appointment of its first woman general manager — and she too decided early on in her career that she would have to remain single if she wanted to move ahead in banking.

This is not to minimise the great attitudinal change that has taken place in Australian society and banks. Marie Mariniello, in her late 20s, a lending officer with the National Australia Bank in Melbourne, is very much a woman who knows that she is going ahead. Wearing a light purple lipstick and a loose black designer blouse, she said in January 1989, that she has been with the bank for 9 years. In the beginning she found discrimination against women, but she does not now:

> I am not going to let it make a difference. No way. There are still some old managers who are anti-women, but most of the women I know want to get ahead. I know I am heading for a bigger branch or for the accountant's post.
>
> In the beginning, I was not really ambitious, but you get involved in the job. Perhaps knowing I could get ahead did it. Even if I got married, I would still want to go on.

Women accountants and managers are not uncommon, but still noticed. Bankers easily trot out the numbers of women who have made it to these posts, because they are aware that women are under-represented in the senior positions in banks. In some cases, this awareness is raising the ire of men who feel that they were qualified for a job but a woman got it 'because she's a woman'. Moreover, banks are so in need of competent personnel that they cannot afford to overlook suitably qualified people.

Though the significance of women in these mid level positions cannot be under-rated, it still remains true that women dominate at the lowest-ranking jobs in the banks. As Ann Game and Rosemary Pringle (1983) show in their book *Gender at Work*, at every stage, more women in a banking job has meant less status for that particular position. When women came to operate the ledger machines in the early 1950s, ledger keeping stopped being the first step in a banking career. Ledger machinists were kept deliberately away from customers, at the back of the bank with their faces to the wall. The same kind of job degradation is noticeable in telling. Claire Williams, who wrote *Blue, White and Pink Collar Workers in Australia*, says in a telephone interview in Adelaide, 'The teller category is being used as a way of bringing in new technology. Now it is an almost nothing category.'

Banking as an avenue of social mobility

One reason why it was possible in Australia for a man to join a bank at the bottom and arrive at the top was that Australia has no family-owned banks. The first bank, the Bank of New South Wales (now the Westpac Banking Corporation), was set up in 1817 by Governor Lachlan Macquarie under a charter he was not authorised to issue. The reasons for the bank lay not with family business but with giving the new colony a uniform currency and financial stability. Banks after this were formed mainly as partnerships and later as joint stock companies. An exception was the Commercial Bank of Tasmania, established in Hobart in 1829 by John Dunn. However, it too was converted to a partnership in 1832.

The absence of family-owned banks has gone a long way to ensure that there has been no 'banking caste' in Australia, for the distinction between the shareholders who owned the bank and the people who managed it was clear from the start. It was only in the 1970s that the chief executive of the major private trading banks, and often his deputy, sat on the board. So in Australia the family linkages, if any, are found at the non-executive board level. Sir Rupert Clarke, chairman of the National Australia Bank, is the third generation of his family on the board. The Gibbs family also goes back several generations on the board of ANZ.

This is very different from the British tradition of family-owned banks. It is also different from the family-owned banks that have played important roles in banking in Hong Kong, Thailand, Malaysia and Singapore.

As a career, banking took off only after the 1850s. Before that, even the Bank of New South Wales had only one branch, with eight men on its staff. The British banks, referred to as the Anglo-banks, first came to Australia in the 1830s, when the economy boomed because of wool. Many of them are now part of ANZ. They set up branches in small country towns, but they preferred their clerks to come from England.

It was only with the gold rush in 1851, and later the expansion of farming lands, that banks began to open branches prolifically.

In the 1850s, the banks recruited people from the more well-off sections of society, as they paid no salary for the first probationary 3 to 6 months and also needed a guarantee for any loss over 500 pounds that was suffered because of the employee. However, by the 1870s, with the new banks opening up, there was a need for more staff. Sons of teachers and clergymen began to receive a small allowance for boarding away from home.

Though no special connections were needed, managers would ensure that the boy came from a respectable family and had a good character. In the country, the bank manager would often know the family, and so the boy would be interviewed with his family. Interestingly, few sons of labourers made it into banking. It was a middle class phenomenon. As such, bankers were drawn mainly from the Anglo-Saxon Protestant majority. This has been so much an accepted part of the private banking tradition in Australia that Bill Gurry, 42, chief executive of the National Mutual Royal Bank, is deeply conscious that he is a Catholic boy who has made it.

It was so ingrained in Australian banking culture that a person started as a junior at 16, after leaving school, that even in the 1950s banks were reluctant to take in university graduates. Dr Herbert Cole (Nugget) Coombs, one of Australia's best-known bankers, who retired as governor of the Reserve Bank of Australia in 1968, told in Sydney in April 1988, how Sir Robert Menzies, Prime Minister of Australia for 1939–41 and 1949–63, tried to place one of his relatives who was studying at university, in a bank. This was in the 1950s, and Sir Robert Menzies mentioned it to a chief executive of one of the big banks. He was told, 'No. We don't take in any graduates. We like taking them as juniors after school.'

Graduates, however, had been hired before, but as economists rather than bankers. In this regard, it was Sir Alfred Davidson, head of the Bank of New South Wales from 1929 to 1945, who broke new ground when he hired the noted economist Professor Edward Shann from Western Australia as a consultant in 1930. This set a precedent that the Commonwealth Bank of Australia felt that it needed to follow, so it recruited Sir Leslie Melville from Adelaide University. Melville then recruited Dr Nugget Coombs in 1935. However, in itself this did not open the door for graduates in the mainline branches of banking.

The prejudice against graduates was so fundamental that, when Bob White of the Bank of New South Wales enrolled as a part-time student in the University of Melbourne in 1947, his branch manager gave him a choice: bank or university. White chose the bank, but he has spoken of it on numerous occasions with a lingering regret that policies were so short-sighted.

The Commonwealth Bank was the first to encourage its officers to go in for part-time study. Vern Christie, who retired as managing director in 1987, and Bob Johnston, governor of the Reserve Bank of Australia for 1982–89, were among the first few who studied part-time while working with the bank. This part-time degree is typical of the curriculum vitae of many senior bankers today. This is how Don Sanders of the Commonwealth Bank, Nobby Clark of the National Australia Bank and Bill Moyle of the State Bank Victoria, obtained their tertiary education.

The other move to supplement on-the-job training with a more conceptual approach came with the establishment of the Banking Administrative Staff College in Mount Eliza in the 1950s. This was a joint venture by the major banks, at the initiative of Dr Nugget Coombs, who at the time was governor of the Commonwealth Bank of Australia. The Commonwealth Bank till 1960 was both a trading bank and a central bank. Coombs said in April 1989:

> We were formulating the policy of the Reserve Bank in accordance with Keynesian economics. But when I talked to the general managers of the trading banks, they didn't know what I was talking about. I don't mean they were stupid. They just had not had that kind of analytical training. They'd spent their lives looking around for deposits and lending money.

So in a move to enable the bankers to criticise the central bank from an intellectual point of view, the college took the second rung of bankers and helped them to place banking in the wider context of the economy and social policy.

Gradually the educational profile of a bank's senior executives changed. The merchant banks that were set up in the 1960s and 1970s attracted the highly educated. It became not unusual for the merchant bankers to have postgraduate degrees, with a small Harvard network emerging. When these merchant bankers moved to the new trading banks in the 1980s, it marked the emergence of a different kind of banker, like Mark Johnson, the first chief executive of the Australian Bank.

About the 1970s and 1980s, the trading banks also started looking for graduates to recruit. ANZ, for instance, is not unusual in having half of its top 120 executives in 1988 with tertiary qualifications, counting both banking and accounting studies. Today it is recognised that it will be very difficult to reach the top without a tertiary degree. However, it is not impossible, as the National Australia Bank succession demonstrates. Don Argus, who is slated to take over from Nobby Clark as managing director in 1990, has only a high school education without university degrees. However, it is going to be difficult for future chief executives to repeat this pattern.

Because banking is now seen as more complex and sophisticated, banks see graduates as a good investment. However, because the introduction of graduates so threatens the traditional banking hierarchy, graduates often find that they are given a specially tough time on the banking floor. Brandon Camfield, a graduate trainee with ANZ in Melbourne said in January 1989, that when he first started with the bank in 1987 the tellers 'did not talk to me for a couple of weeks. They would say, yes, no. They'd ask me to get the milk and bread or photostat things. All the rotten jobs. When they found I would do anything, they eased up.'

Banking used to be a long slow slog to the top, going up step by step. White was 40 and had been with the bank for 23 years before he received his first managerial appointment. Today, some have become managers before age 30, with less than 10 years at the bank. The turning point in White's career, as for many of the chief executives today, was a posting to London. In banking terms, it signalled that the officer was marked for higher office. Moreover, going to London in the 1950s and 1960s was also an intensely emotional experience for Australians, a kind of homecoming. More than 30 years later, in October 1987 in Sydney, White described it 'as the greatest thrill of all times in my life. When I rang my wife to tell her, she couldn't answer. She just lost her voice. That's an indication of how important it was to us.' It is hard to say what would be the present day equivalent to White's posting to London. A job related to technology would have to be an essential to make it to the top, but it does not have the same emotive implication as a posting to London in the 1950s.

It is also no longer necessary for a chief executive to have started in the same bank as a junior. People from outside the bank are being inducted not only into the expert fields, like data processing, economic research and personnel management, but also into the retail area, which has always been seen as core banking. ANZ's head of retail, Don Mercer, is a trail blazer in this regard. He came to banking from the oil industry in the early 1980s, and in 1988 he became the bank's director, Australian retail services. What is seen as core banking is also changing, so that in time it is possible that technology experts will be seen as the quintessential bankers. Because of this, it is likely that, in the 1990s, Australia will have one of its major banks led by a person who did not start with a bank at 16 as a junior after finishing school.

This will indeed be a big change for Australian banks. When Don Sanders became chief executive of the Commonwealth Bank of Australia in 1987, one of the points raised against him was that he was an outsider — despite his having started in the Commonwealth Bank as a junior. However, he had served the last 27 years in the Reserve Bank of Australia, which separated from the Commonwealth Bank in 1960, so he was no longer an insider.

One element that is common to the stories of the older bankers and tellers of today is that banking often was not a first choice. Few of the bankers who head banks in Australia today set out to be bankers. Some of the older bankers tell how they went into the bank because they could not afford to go to university. Others say that they entered banking because their families opted for security. Another refrain is that they thought they were not smart enough to follow the other two upwardly mobile professions and become doctors or lawyers. So banking was the residual choice. This strain continued even when entry was via university for the merchant bankers in the 1960s: the smart ones studied law or medicine and the others studied economics. It is unusual to come across any bankers in their 40s who say that they chose banking as a career because they wanted to be bankers. Bill Gurry, of the National Mutual Royal Bank, and Mark Johnson, the first chief executive of the Australian Bank, for instance, both went into law first and then happened onto banking.

This does not sound very different from the tone of William Moffat's 1921 book, *A Banker's Letters to his Son*. Hearing that his son wants to switch from medicine to banking, he laments that he thought that his son would be more ambitious. 'You want to be a Banker — there are worse professions and there are better,' he says. 'I would have liked you to stick to Medicine when you had the chance,' he says. 'If you don't want Medicine I prefer you should go into business.' He goes on to ask his son to consider the rag trade. 'Most drapers come out on top in the end,' he tells his son. What about hardware? he pursues. The son, however, persists with banking and no doubt acquires his carriage and a house with 12-feet-high ceilings and marble mantlepieces (pp. 11–16).

The boardroom

Though banking has been a spectacular avenue of social mobility in Australia, the boardroom remains a microcosm of the establishment. This is where the old family connections, the right school tie, the old boys' club still work to perfection. This is where the power of the banks is interlinked with the power of the corporate world.

Old family connections are rated highly in the major trading banks. A member of the Clarke family has been on the board of the National Australia Bank for three generations. The chairman, Sir Rupert Clarke, 70, has been on the board for the past 35 years. D. C. L. Gibbs, of ANZ, also has a family connection with the bank going back more than 120 years.

The major private banks particularly like knights of the realm on their boards. Knighthood has not been conferred in Australia since 1983 by the Commonwealth government, nor by the states of NSW, Victoria, South Australia and Western Australia. Tasmania stopped in 1988 and Queensland in 1989. Yet, one–third of the directors of the major trading banks are knights (including one dame). Westpac is in the lead, with six of its fifteen directors having the knighthood in 1989.

Solicitors and chartered accountants make regular appearances on the boards, as do people with extensive pastoral interests. The curriculum vitae of the directors often includes schooling at Melbourne Grammar or Geelong Church of England School or Eton, followed by the University of Melbourne, Sydney University, Oxford, Cambridge or Harvard. Most of them list as their clubs at least one of the following: Melbourne Club, Australian Club, Athenaeum, Royal Sydney Golf Club.

Many of the directors also meet each other at their favourite public organisations. The Walter and Eliza Hall Institute of Medical Research, the Baker Medical Research Institute, the Australian Outward Bound Foundation and the World Wildlife Fund occur frequently in their lists of interests. The board of the Graduate School of Management of the University of Melbourne also provides an informal meeting ground. Some interests, though, are more characteristic of one bank; the ANZ board has more opera lovers than any other bank, for instance.

A bank board with its interlocking directorships most resembles the marital alliances of kings of old, who used them to cement strategic relationships. ANZ's fifteen directors in 1988 represented 66 public companies; Westpac's fourteen directors were on the boards of 37 public companies; and the National Australia Bank's thirteen directors were also directors of 41 public companies. These public companies included some of Australia's biggest companies and therefore some of the biggest borrowers from the banks.

The directors have been chosen to represent a wide range of interests covering the business and geographic sectors important to the banks, but their range is not as great as the numbers suggest. Together, they represent slightly less than one-third (32) of the top 100 listed companies. Most often, the directors represent companies that have performed well in the past rather than companies of the future, as the major banks have kept away from entrepreneurial companies. This spread of interests is further narrowed because there are many instances where two or more directors sit on the same boards. Further, although customers are now more than ever seen as the key to profitability, there are no directors who have particular expertise in consumer and labour affairs.

The old boys' club nature of the boards of the main private trading banks is more apparent when one looks at what the boards do not represent. They do not include the new rich who are running corporate Australia. No postwar migrant makes it to the boards. That rules out Hungarian-born Sir Peter Abeles of TNT, Estonian-born Sir Arvi Parbo of Western Mining Corporation, Latvian-born John Spalvins of Adelaide Steamship and South African-born Robert Holmes à Court. Nor do the boards include women. Dame Leonie Kramer at ANZ is the only woman on the boards of the main private banks.

Though banking in Australia has changed at an unprecedented pace, the boards of the major private banks have been semi-feudal in the length of service of the directors. Unlike company directors, who retire at 55 to 60 years, bank directors stay until they are 72, unless they die earlier or leave the country. A position has been known to last anywhere from 11 to 35 years. Resignations are so rare that it made quite a stir when directors of the Australian Mutual Provident Society (AMP) and National Mutual Life Association left bank boards in 1984. This was to avoid a conflict of interest, as AMP and National Mutual had become 50 per cent owners of Chase AMP and the National Mutual Royal Bank respectively. Their resignations made it possible for younger chief executives of major companies to be appointed to bank boards. These new appointees have contributed much to the banks' response to deregulation; but if these directors, who are now in their 40s and 50s, stay their term, they may be on the board for about 25 years.

In the mid 1970s, though, a major change took place in the way in which the boards and the management relate to each other. This is when chief executives, and occasionally their deputies, began to sit on the board. Before this, the board made the policy and the management executed it. Sons of traders, teachers and farmers found that they were now part of the establishment. They were now users of the opulent boardroom, resplendent with large polished tables, crystal and silver, paintings on the walls and portraits of past presidents staring down at them.

The bankers and the directors, each group in its own way, have participated in the enormous changes that have taken place in the banking industry since 1817: the setting up of a national network, unbridled competition in banking followed by a banking crash, the subsequent era of conservatism, attempted nationalisation and regulation. It is these events that have given Australian banking its particular flavour and set the stage for deregulation and the beginnings of electronic banking. These, in turn, have propelled banking into the fastest period of change in its history.

2 The historical framework

The major Australian banks have extensive national networks, with more than 5500 branches spanning the whole country, unlike the USA and Japan. Malaysia and Australia have roughly the same population, but any one of Australia's major trading banks has more branches than the whole Malaysian banking system. These branches reach deep into the rural hinterland of a highly urbanised country. So, unlike agricultural economies such as India, rural access to credit has not been a problem in Australia.

Setting up a national banking network: 1817–90

Though a national branch network is now the hallmark of the main Australian trading banks, it was not a feature of early Australian banking. The Bank of New South Wales, the first bank to be established in Australia, was a one-branch operation in Sydney from 1817 to 1850, partly because the population was not dispersed and was concentrated in Sydney, Hobart and Launceston. Also, the banks did not need branches to garner deposits, for they were not keen on deposits and even considered charging a fee for keeping them. They left small deposits to the savings banks, specifically opened for that purpose. The money lent by banks came from their issue of notes to serve as paper money and from their shareholders' capital. The notes in effect were like interest-free deposits, especially if they circulated for a long time before being presented to the bank for repayment. So, as S. J. Butlin (1961) notes in his history, *Australia and New Zealand Bank*, apart from a brief experiment with branch banking in Tasmania, branches were virtually unknown before the British banks first opened in Australia in the 1830s.

The Bank of Australasia, later part of the Australia and New Zealand Banking Group (ANZ), opened in Sydney in 1835. Like the other British banks that followed, it was planned as a group of branches, answering to a chief executive in Australia, who in turn was responsible to the board in London. Branches were needed at this time in Australia, for the boom in wool exports had helped to open up half the Australian continent and had unleashed a demand for capital. Deposits became more important for the banks. The Commercial Banking Company of Sydney (CBC), now part of the National Australia Bank, started offering interest for deposits in 1834. When the British banks opened, there was a scramble as banks tried to mop up as much of the savings as possible. During the boom the local banks, called colonial banks at the time, did open a few branches, but these soon closed when hard times came. So in 1851, according to Butlin, the eight trading banks had only 25 branches.

The banking network in the nineteenth century expanded in three great bursts: with the gold boom of the 1850s, the opening of wheatlands in the 1860s and the suburban expansion of the 1870s.

After the discovery of gold near Bathurst was announced in May 1851, for a while bankers sat in their head offices waiting for the diggers to bring the gold to them. Then in December 1852 the Bank of New South Wales opened an agency three miles from Castlemaine at Forest Creek, with Mr James Larnach as its agent. His office and home were an uncomfortable tent. He wrote to the bank nearly 4 months after he arrived, saying:

> The winter is now setting in and the tent is getting very cold and uncomfortable in the evenings. I will feel obliged if you will cause a small stove to be purchased and sent up before the roads are impassable. Let the pipe be sufficiently long to carry the smoke clear of the tent say 12 feet (Holder (1970) pp. 192–93).

Nothing much happened, and nearly a year later, in November 1853, he presented what must have been a clinching argument: 'I would have sent you a remittance of cash but found impossible to keep the notes on the table, the wind blowing furiously in the tent' (Ibid. p. 193).

Larnach was not alone in his discomfort. Getting to the goldfields in the first place often meant riding, walking, fording rivers, and could take more than 10 days. Once there, accommodation was a tent or a shanty roofed with corrugated iron or bark shingles. Goldfields bankers had to arrange for bed and food, find a safe place to keep the gold and transport it. The office was often divided from the living area by a suspended sheet. When the inspectors came, chairs would have to be borrowed from a store nearby. These concerns were related again and again by bankers of the goldfields in the 1860s.

George Preshaw, an official with the Bank of New South Wales in 1860s, was told to go from Castlemaine in Victoria to the gold rush town of Kiandra in the Snowy Mountains of NSW. Kiandra was 50 miles from the Cooma goldfields. The journey took him 18 days. He went by a Cobb and Co. coach from Castlemaine to Melbourne, then by steamer to Eden, then rode a horse, for the first time ever, to Kiandra 150 miles away.

Preshaw came to a bank in a calico tent. Writing of it in *Banking under Difficulties or Life on the Goldfields* (1888), he says that the man who was to be his assistant 'was perched on a piece of bark which rested on two logs, a stream of water running under him; in fact right through the building' (p. 54). This was caused by melting snow at the back of the tent. A piece of calico with a sapling at the bottom served as the door. The counter was four saplings stuck into the mud with a few rough boards on top.

There was no safe. They kept the notes and gold in two pairs of saddlebags under the commissioner's bunk in the police camp. Every morning he and his assistant would walk the three-quarters of a mile to the camp and bring back a pair of saddlebags with the notes and coin required for the day. The rest they left in the other pair of saddlebags. At the end of the day, they would take the bullion they had purchased back to the saddlebags under the commissioner's bunk.

Cooma attracted its share of bankers. About the same time as Preshaw, in 1861, Thomas Dibbs went to Cooma, taking his wife with him. They had to cross seven flooded rivers to arrive at Cooma. They set up the bank in two rooms of a hotel, and for 6 weeks, until the safe arrived, they slept with the moneybags and barricaded the bedroom door by placing the washstand and the toilet service against the door. From 1882 to 1915, Dibbs was to be chief executive of the Commercial Banking Company of Sydney (Griffiths, 1955).

Conditions of banking in the goldfields of Western Australia in 1894 were such that one banker calling himself T. H. wrote in the *Bankers Magazine of Australasia* in September 1918, 'Looking back at it is the best part' (p. 28). T. H. wrote that he went to open a branch of the Western Australian Bank in White Feather, later known as Kanowna. He tells a story of food too terrible to eat, being coated in dust, not enough water, typhoid, sleeping on the counter. After Kanowna, Kalgoorlie had more comforts, but it meant working from 8.30 a.m. till past midnight. If the work did not get you, then typhoid did. Later, when the work lightened as more clerks were sent, it was drink at the hotels that posed the greater danger (T. H. 1919).

In the east though, from the 1860s, the banks followed the farmers as they opened up wheatlands. Between 1850 and 1890, 21 new note-issuing banks opened, most of them in Melbourne, trying to cash in on the boom years. Competition among the banks meant that a sure way of winning was for a bank to be physically present to gain the business. Because the business was in the rural areas, for many years banks were under-represented in the cities and in suburban areas. *The Australasian Insurance and Banking Record and Statistical Register* notes that in

1877 the ten leading banks in Victoria had 300 branches and agencies. Six of these ten accounted for 240 branches. It says:

> When two branch managers become rival candidates for the patronage of three or four petty traders, we cannot help considering that branch business is overdone . . . The primitive Australian township consists of a public house, a general store, a smithy and a butcher's store. In the second stage of its development it is now an even chance whether the next good allotment finds its way into the possession of a bank or of a church committee' p. 284.

Expansion to the wheatlands also meant that banks now had to lend for land. This was a departure from traditional lending practice, especially for the British banks, for land was not seen as acceptable security. This was such a firm tradition that the British Treasury had it incorporated in the charter of the Bank of Australasia, so prohibiting it from accepting land as collateral.

The preferred way of lending by Australian banks in the early days was via the trade bill to finance overseas trade. In 1860, according to R. Holder's (1970) history of the Bank of New South Wales, bills counted for 82 per cent of all money lent by that bank. This was very much in the pattern of colonial banking everywhere. During the wool boom, the definition of a trade bill was widened to accept liens on stock. However, the British banks got round this prohibition on land in a number of ways. They were known to give the loan one day and take the land the next; or the business would be done through merchants, who would give the bank their bills and on-lend to farmers against their land.

Blainey and Hutton (1983), in their history of the National Bank of Australasia, *Gold and Paper*, say that it was the National Bank that first lent directly on the security of land in 1859, a year after it was founded. It was done via a 6 month promissory note from the farmer and subsequently renewed. It was only in 1894 that the Commissioners' Savings Banks of Victoria (now the State Bank Victoria) introduced the familiar long-term mortgage on freehold land in its credit foncier loan.

The bill business, however, remained an important part of country banking. It worked like this: an agent would sell livestock to a farmer and accept the farmer's bill; this was a note promising that the farmer would pay in 3 months' time. The agent, however, wanted the money immediately, so would cash this bill at the bank. He would receive the stated amount minus the interest on the sum for 3 months and the fee for the bank's service.

The bill business was such an important part of country banking that stories were told, half in jest, of how a country branch was kept in business by transactions revolving round the sale and resale of the manager's horse. Each time the horse was sold, the bill was brought to the bank for discounting. One day a man came buying horses for export. He bought the horse for cash, and the bottom fell out of the local banking business (*The Bankers' Magazine of Australasia*, 1893 p. 206).

The traditional stereotype of the sedate banker, a pillar of society, derives most directly from the country banker. However, in some of the more remote parts of the country, life was not quite so conventional. Blainey and Hutton (1983) describe how drink ruined some of the bankers who went to the pastoral branches in western Queensland. They tell how one previously reliable accountant, after 11 months in Adavale, spent a Saturday afternoon 'racing through the town in a half nude state mad from drink' (p. 126).

Lending for land in the cities picked up in the 1870s. Banks lent directly or via building societies and later through the land banks. As Michael Cannon (1967) describes in his book *The Land Boomers*, Melbourne was transformed from a comparatively small city surrounded by orchards and paddocks to a sprawling suburbia. In the 1880s Marvellous Melbourne changed from a modest city to a city where all things were possible. Land rose sharply in value. In Surrey Hills, for instance, land selling for 15 shillings a foot in 1884 sold for 15 pounds in 1887. Competition in the 1880s became frenzied. More than a quarter of the deposits in Australian banks came from London. By the end of 1891, Australia had 1553 bank branches.

Crash and transition: 1890–1945

The unfettered competition to lend money for land and the general depression of the late 1880s were the undoing of the building societies and the land banks. Wool prices fell by a third between 1884 and 1891. Melbourne land prices collapsed by the end of 1888. The failure of the building societies and land banks also brought down the more conservative banks in 1893, especially as there was no bank of last resort to prop up the banking system. As David Merrett (1988) notes in an unpublished paper, 'Two hundred years of banking', some of the banks had not sufficiently provided for the risks they were undertaking. They had borrowed short and were lending long. By the end of 1891, land prices had fallen so far that allotments in any suburb could be had for 10 to 100 pounds, according to Cannon (1967). In 1893, 54 of the 64 deposit-taking institutions that called themselves banks closed their doors. A whole generation of people had their savings frozen for long periods, with some of it being forcibly converted into preference shares.

Though no depositors technically lost their deposits, the banking crash of 1893 firmly entrenched the image of the big bad private banks, uncaring of the ordinary person. This view was reaffirmed by the fact that the state-owned savings banks had remained unscathed in the crash and had increased their share of deposits. A. L. May (1968) notes in his book *The Battle for the Banks* that J. B. Chifley, Prime Minister of Australia from 1945 to 1949, thought of this period as one where local farmers were 'desolated and grief stricken at the closing of the banks. They had no guarantee of ever being repaid their deposits.' It became a folk memory, that a whole generation had lost its savings. Nationalisation of banks entered Labor policy debates. It also led to renewed calls for a publicly owned people's bank; this was to result in the establishment of the Commonwealth Bank of Australia in 1912.

The banking crash also began a long period of conservatism in banking. The banks now depended mainly on local deposits, as UK depositors walked away from the Australian banks. Merrett (1989) in his typescript of an article entitled 'The 1893 bank crashes: the aftermath', notes that some banks declined these UK deposits even when they were offered. Dividends were cut and greater provisions made for bad debts. The banks that remained trimmed the opening of new branches. As Merrett notes, bank mergers took place reducing the number of privately owned trading banks from 20 in 1917 to nine in 1931. Only two small new banks were formed between 1893 and 1981. Competition between banks gave way to an industry cartel on deposit and lending rates. Liquidity ratios in banks rose from 18 per cent before the crash to 25 per cent in 1903 and 34 per cent in 1913.

This conservatism was only reinforced by the First World War and the Depression of the 1930s. The Depression in turn strengthened the feeling against the banks in the Labor Party. It was felt that the banks had tightened the screws so that conditions for the ordinary worker worsened. In 1934, nationalisation of banks was a major plank in the Labor federal election campaign. The 1935 Royal Banking Commission, set up to examine the banking system, reinforced this anti-private-bank attitude, for it concluded that trading banks must bear some responsibility for the extent of the Depression. Moreover, it had some pointed strictures against the Commonwealth Bank. Its delay in devaluing the Australian pound, the Commission said, had increased the hardship of the exporters.

The Commission, however, did not recommend nationalisation, though Ben Chifley, who was a member of the Commission, dissented in favour of nationalisation. However, before the recommendations of the Royal Banking Commission could be translated into legislation, the Second World War started in 1939. This in turn led to a period of greater control, as the Commonwealth Bank began acting more and more as the central bank. This macro framework set the scene for attempts to nationalise the banks in 1947.

The nationalisation saga: 1946–49

Sir Leslie McConnan, chief manager of the National Australia Bank, then known as the National Bank of Australasia, had been worried about increasing bank regulation since 1944, when he heard of government plans to introduce the Banking Act 1945. However, it was only in

1947, after the government had announced its plan to nationalise banks, that the whole banking industry rallied to the fight.

The sequence of events was as follows. The Chifley Labor government (Chifley had become Prime Minister in July 1945) introduced the Banking Act 1945. This extended the wartime controls on banking on a national basis for the first time. The Act stopped short of the nationalisation of banks. However, section 48 of the Act sparked a furore, for it told government bodies that they must bank with the Commonwealth Bank. The Melbourne City Council, which did its banking with the National Australia Bank, challenged section 48 in court. The High Court ruled on 13 August 1947 that section 48 was invalid. Two days later, Chifley announced tersely in one sentence that legislation was being prepared to nationalise all banks other than state banks.

Dr Herbert Cole (Nugget) Coombs, who was governor of the Commonwealth Bank of Australia from 1949 to 1960 and the first governor of the Reserve Bank of Australia from 1960 to 1968, talking of it in Sydney in April 1988, said that Chifley was 'really a fairly moderate person', but his thinking was dominated by his experience of the Depression and by memories of the banking crash in 1893. Coombs added, 'Chifley felt that unless you can control the creation of credit, control could be taken away from the hands of the central bank or the government.'

The story behind the terse statement nationalising the banks, according to Nugget Coombs, was that Chifley asked the chairman of the Associated Banks, Sir Leslie McConnan, for an assurance that the banking control sections would not be challenged. The banks were not intending to challenge these but went to their lawyer. He said that they had a really powerful weapon in those sections and advised them not to give it away. So then came the statement nationalising the banks.

The government's case was hurt by Chifley's short arrogant statement. The banks rallied their staff and customers to oppose the nationalisation, saying that the government was putting its hands into the pockets of the household. The Catholic Church also pitched into the dispute; its views ranged from non-interference to dissent and would influence the large proportion of Catholic Labor voters. The nationalisation case was also not helped by some members of Chifley's Cabinet suggesting that bank employees would be made redundant and that this was the first step to the government's taking over home and church.

Bankers became openly political to a greater degree than before, to turn this legislation around. Bob White of Westpac at the time was 24 years old and had just returned from Darwin, where he was stationed during the war. Thinking back on it in Sydney in October 1987, he said:

> I have a vivid recollection of walking down the street in Melbourne and hearing the newspaper boys cry out that the government had decided to nationalise the banks. I purchased the paper and there it was. I saw that as a threat to my whole future. I became very active in the staff organisation which was formed to fight against nationalisation. They were very exciting times. I actually knocked on doors all over Melbourne and other parts of the state and advocated that people should vote for Menzies to defeat this attack on their freedom.

It is interesting though that, even when the government was fighting the banks on nationalisation, there was little attempt to act against individual banks. In January 1947, when McConnan, head of the National Australia Bank, was leading the fight against the government, the National had applied to Chifley for approval to merge with the Queensland National Bank. Blainey and Hutton (1983) quote McConnan as writing:

> I am a bit anxious about the Treasury people, but here again I am inclined to think Chifley may not be difficult. He is a peculiar mixture — he can be brutally pig-headed, but I have known him to be broad-minded and generous, and in spite of political differences he has always acted fairly towards me (p. 237).

On 1 January 1948, the merger went through, and the National Australia Bank became the second-largest bank in Australia and the largest bank in Queensland and Victoria.

On the nationalisation front, the banks took their case to the courts. On 11 August 1948, the High Court ruled that some important sections of the Banking Act 1947 were invalid. The government appealed. Coombs, who had become the governor of the Commonwealth Bank of Australia on 1 January 1949, said in Sydney in April 1988:

> I was sitting there at the bank with the possibility that within the next few months the banks might be nationalised. It would have been my job to give effect to this. We set to work. I had a little planning committee with Bede Callaghan as its chairman. I said at the time that I'd never really thought it was important who owned the banks. It was important what they did, what the policy was. But the legislation provided for the incorporation of all the banks into one bank. I went to Chifley, and said that was impossible. You can't have a situation where the bank manager has absolutely the last word and his customer has no alternative. Let all the banks be owned by the government or the people. But there must be somewhere else to go if the manager says 'No' if I go to him for a loan. All the plans that we prepared were on the basis that there would be five banks, I think from memory, all publicly owned, but separate and competing.

However, on 26 July 1949, the Privy Council dismissed the government appeal of the High Court ruling. In December 1949, Chifley lost the elections. For the next 23 years, Labor did not return to power.

Nationalisation was no longer a threat in 1949 with the defeat of the Chifley government, but the debate left bankers more politically aware, and the schism between Labor and the banks became even more pronounced. Bob White said in October 1987 in his Sydney office at Westpac, 'Mr Hawke made a comment once that the banks destroyed the last three Labor governments in Australia.' These were the governments of James Scullin during the Depression, the Chifley government and the Gough Whitlam government, sacked in 1975. White doubts that the banks brought down the Scullin government, and with the Chifley government they were fighting for their very survival. With the Whitlam government, White says, 'Banks inevitably were involved in that exercise to the extent that there was a suggestion that bank finance might have been used to overcome the government's lack of supply.'

According to Coombs, however, in 1949 the banks were very powerful political institutions. He said:

> The war had been won. People were sick and tired of restrictions, tired of constraints, and having the whole place run by regulation. They identified the control over the banks with the general tendency for everything to be controlled for the purposes of the war.

When Menzies came, the whole structure prepared for nationalisation was very quickly broken down. Coombs said, 'I think he got a bit of a scare for the rate of inflation jumped from 2.5 per cent to about 20 per cent in 1950–51. There was the Korean War also. But it did frighten the man and took quite a lot of time for the last constraints to go.'

Though Menzies returned to power on the back of the banks, according to Coombs, he was bored with economic matters. Coombs quoted Menzies as saying, quite early, 'I leave it to Fadden [Arthur Fadden, the Treasurer]. I don't know banking. But if you are worried and think I should know about it, ring me up.' Though the banks had won the battle against nationalisation, they had to accept stringent control over nearly every aspect of their business for more than 30 years.

It is against this historical backdrop that we can look at some of the important central bankers of Australia, to see how they helped to steer the banking system.

3 The central bankers

The central bank of Australia had a hazy birth. In 1912, when the Commonwealth Bank of Australia was established, one of its aims was to be 'the bank of banks'. The 1893 banking crash had emphasised the need for a central bank that would help to stabilise the banking system.

During the First World War, the Commonwealth Bank conducted more government banking business and helped to manage the government's finances, but it was not until 1924, when note issue came directly under the Commonwealth Bank, that it came of age as a central bank.

Its regulatory powers came most directly with the Second World War. The private banks, which earlier had resisted controls, now had to be licensed, to have their profits controlled and to have their lending policies and interest rates determined by the Commonwealth Bank, in its role as the central bank. These wartime controls became part of the Banking Act 1945, the first Banking Act that applied to all banks in the country, except state banks.

However, there remained an inherent conflict in the two roles of the Commonwealth Bank: as a central bank and as a commercial bank. So in 1960 the Commonwealth Bank of Australia separated into the Reserve Bank of Australia and the Commonwealth Banking Corporation.

In the postwar period when these changes were taking place, Nugget Coombs was the banker at the centre of the scene of action. He was governor of the Commonwealth Bank of Australia from 1949 to 1960 and the first governor of the Reserve Bank of Australia, from 1960 to 1968. He was a product of the Depression, and in his world view we can see how the Depression influenced the thinking of bankers and the banking system for decades. More than that, as an individual he has been one of the most influential and unusual bankers of Australia.

Nugget Coombs, governor, Reserve Bank of Australia, 1960–68 (courtesy Reserve Bank of Australia)

Nugget Coombs: a banker with social responsibility

Nugget Coombs, 84, is dynamic, with too few hours in the day. He is short and slight, so nicknamed Nugget, and wears his spectacles hung with a strap. Meeting just after Easter in 1988, at the University Club in Sydney — a very British experience — he was dressed in a grey jacket with brown pants and wearing a conservatively striped tie; he looked more like an academic than a banker.

He stands out among the bankers past and present, for banking has been only part of his life. It is hard to duplicate, even among younger bankers today, the versatility and breadth of interests of Nugget Coombs. Unlike other bankers who have spent their whole life in banking, usually one bank, Coombs has been an outstanding civil servant, an educationist, a patron of the arts. At the time of interview he was closely involved with Aboriginal welfare. He was working on a project at the Australian National University, detailing the effects of mining and tourism on the Aborigines of the Kimberley region.

Talking of himself, Coombs said, 'I saw being a banker as the use of intellectual understanding for social purposes. I was a banker, not because I was interested in money — my wife used to say, any knowledge my husband has of financial matters is strictly theoretical.' Some of his closest friends 'were at the central bank. I had friends in universities, friends who were artists. I don't think I had a close friend in any of the other banks.'

Though Nugget Coombs has been one of the most influential bankers of the country, he has remained suspicious of bankers as a category and of what they represent. This harks back to his education and working experience.

One of the five children of a country railway stationmaster, Coombs won a scholarship that enabled him to go to Perth Modern School, then the only government high school in Western Australia. He went on to teach school and first became interested in Aboriginal affairs. While teaching, he did his BA in economics part-time from the University of Western Australia. In 1933 he received his doctorate in economics from the London School of Economics, his thesis being on central banking. It was in London that he met Leslie Melville, the economist for the Commonwealth Bank. This meeting led to Coombs' joining the Commonwealth Bank as an assistant economist in 1935. However, this lasted only 4 years, for in 1939 he moved to the Treasury as an economist. During the Second World War, he became more directly involved with the war effort as Director of Rationing. From 1943 Coombs was the Director-General of Post-War Reconstruction. It was with this background that, in 1949, he became the governor of the Commonwealth Bank of Australia.

Much of his approach to banking, however, came from his mother's influence:

> My mother had a big influence in almost every way. She was very well read and intelligent and had a wide range of interests. She introduced me to real literature. I think she also had a profound influence on me socially and politically. She was not exactly a devout Christian, but she took Christianity seriously. She believed you had an obligation to other people.
> I think that was the beginnings of a socialist or humanitarian approach which is at the back of my political beliefs and what I have tried to do.

It was this socialist and humanitarian approach to life that made him want to keep a distance from bankers, the establishment and the offered knighthood:

> It was part of my political prejudices, I suppose. Someone was writing a book about Australian financiers. I told them I was not a financier. My job was controlling financiers. In a way, I share [Labor's] distrust of the power of the banks. I'm not a fanatic about it, but I became very conscious of it while I was living amongst bankers and big businessmen. I saw others who shared the social views I had, who almost became identified with the big banks. I didn't want that to happen. And also it is a terribly narrow intellectual field. I felt I needed other things to think about in self protection.

He sees that the sense of social responsibility has lessened today among bankers, operating in a deregulated world:

> It is an old-fashioned view that, whether you are in a public or private institution, you have a social responsibility. And I don't see that bankers any longer do. Not even to their clients. In the old days, if a farmer was a good farmer, he may have a number of bad years, but there was a kind of tradition, that if you were a good farmer, you supported him. You didn't grind him down. It was your job to know whether he was a man worth supporting. That is a social function. I think bankers don't care now. It is just a question of they've lent you money, and they want it back. Even the days when we were having arguments on nationalisation, I did believe that you could talk to the bankers about their responsibility for the state of the economy, not just their profits. I believe that by and large they accepted that responsibility. I think there was a sense of sharing in the business of your clients, provided they were competent. That was characteristic of Australian banking.

The Depression of the 1930s also deeply influenced the way in which Coombs thought. The haunting images of this era were of the unemployed wandering the countryside looking for work: 'There was scarce a family in Western Australia that did not have children between 15 and 30 out of work.' A hangover of these Depression years, he says, was to work economic policy so that such unemployment could be prevented. Success was identified with full employment: 'When we were devising postwar institutions, including financial ones, that objective was in people's minds. It was the dominant feeling not only in the Labor Party or trade unions, but right through the community.' That is how the central bank of Australia remains unusual: it is written in its statutes that one of its responsibilities is the maintenance of full employment. Objectives have changed, however: 'We used to be concerned to create conditions where there would be a demand for labour. Now we set out to create conditions in which investors will invest their money and bankers will lend.' Though the two objectives could overlap, even till the 1960s, it was the first attitude that prevailed.

It was the Depression again that at first made Coombs oppose the separation of the Commonwealth Bank of Australia into the Commonwealth Banking Corporation and the Reserve Bank of Australia in 1960. The nationalisation debate of the 1940s had made it preferable for the two to separate:

> I saw some advantages in it. It had become an obstacle to reasonable relationships between the central bank and the private banks. But I opposed it for two reasons. Like economists of my time, I did continue to have this fear of the return of the Depression. I was always terrified we would encounter the kind of conflict there was in the thirties between the government and the central bank.

This was when the Commonwealth Bank refused to lend more money to the government and so prevented the government from attempting to spend its way out of the Depression:

> In a way, . . . [the bank and the government] were sabotaging each other. Being able to put into effect the kind of policy you need in the Depression, the control of the central bank should be effective. And to be effective, you need to be able to use the Commonwealth Bank.

This was very much the way in which the 1935 Royal Banking Commission had argued for the two to remain one institution.

Coombs was just as much influenced by his experiences of reconstruction after the Second World War. Not only did they lay the basis for his interests in theatre and education, but they also led him to propel Australian banking towards the region in the 1950s, as a buffer against too great a dependence on the USA, UK and Europe.

As Director-General of Post-War Reconstruction, Coombs had to advise the government on the strengths of the British and the American economies, when the issue of joining the International Monetary Fund (IMF) came up:

> We had great argument, bitter argument, in Australia as to whether we should join the International Monetary Fund. Many people in the Labor Party saw the Monetary Fund as another form of international finance domination. And they are not far wrong.

Coombs was uncertain about Australia's joining the IMF:

> I conducted the first negotiation with the Americans. We owed them money for the war effort. There was an argument as to how much Australia owed them and how we should pay them. What became apparent in this argument was they weren't interested in the money. They wanted access to the Australian market for their cars and aeroplanes. They wanted to run the air services in Australia.
>
> There was the same kind of argument with Britain. They were the world's creditors before the war. By the end of the war, they'd lost all that. I can remember writing letters to Chifley at the end of those conferences, where I certainly said, we must not allow ourselves to become dependent on the British economy.
>
> It was very clear that Britain and Europe were in a state of absolute economic collapse. Finally, I recommended, somewhat unwillingly, that we go into the IMF, because I could see that [without American goodwill and scientific expertise] we could find our export markets deteriorating. We were substantially in debt, so it was highly likely that sometime in the next 20, 30 years, we would need to borrow.

So Coombs turned towards Southeast Asia to strengthen Australia's economic independence:

> I also did believe that the big expansion was going to come in Asia. I didn't have much to do with the Japanese, but I was very impressed with the way they had reorganised themselves. And I had great hopes for India, and they seemed to have very able civil servants. I did have ideas of some kind of

> regional trading group in Southeast Asia. We had negotiations with New Zealand, and it was talked about, but it wasn't historically possible at that time.

What did emerge from Coombs's regional concerns was the formation of SEANZA in 1959, a grouping of Southeast Asian, New Zealand and Australian central bankers:

> The Bank of England used to have periodic meetings of central bankers from the Commonwealth. One of the things we used to talk about was training. The promising young men were sent to the Bank of England and later to the Federal Reserve. I became convinced that sending an Australian or an Indian to work at the Bank of England was not going to do any good. The Bank of England is part of the City of London and the London market. At that time there was no Commonwealth country which had a money market like that.

So he suggested to the other central bankers of the Asia-Pacific region that, instead of learning from Europe and America, they should learn from each other. Each central bank would take turns to run the course. Accordingly, SEANZA became the first grouping of central banks in the region, and it remains active today.

From regulation to deregulation: 1950–83

The 1950s were buoyant self-satisfied years for Australia. The war was over. People did not want to accept controls on where they banked, and attempts to nationalise the banks failed. However, people had little faith in the markets. They saw market intervention as the answer, for they had won the war with the help of a very regulated system. The memories of the Depression remained and legitimised the regulation of banks, and through it all ran a strong sense that bureaucrats, politicians and businessmen should serve the national interest.

A major vehicle of this regulation was the Advance Policy administered by the Commonwealth Bank of Australia, in its role as the central bank. This policy stipulated how much banks could lend, for what purpose and at what rates. For instance, banks could not lend for speculation or imports if the balance-of-payments situation was bad. This meant that banks became rationers of funds instead of competitors in harnessing savings and lending them out.

The regulations multiplied through the tenure of governors John Phillips, 1968–75 and Harold Knight, 1975–82. Despite some moves towards a more open banking system, the regulated banking structure remained substantially in place. Don Sanders, deputy governor of the Reserve Bank from 1975 to 1987, speaking in Sydney in February 1988 commented on this period of regulation: 'You had a book of regulation and case law on issues or decisions which ended up being 1 to 2 inches thick. It was a thriving little industry for a while.'

This detailed regulation had the seeds of its own demise, however, Sanders said:

> The first time people ask you how much banks should lend in a week, you are pretty flattered that they think you ought to know. So you work away at it and come up with a number and put various justifications for it. After you have done it a few times, you realise you don't know how much they should be lending. Then you start arguing against it. But unfortunately these horses aren't so easy to get off.

The regulation grew more unwieldy. Nobody could police it. The pressure of regulation on banks only led to the establishment of more non-bank financial institutions. In the early 1950s, banks entered the hire purchase business through subsidiaries. In the late 1950s, banks went into unit trusts and superannuation. The first merchant banks came up, and building societies and credit unions took advantage of the ceilings on bank deposit rates. Thus the scene was set for the multiplicity of financial institutions that distinguishes the Australian scene today.

The central bank itself was going through a change. The private banks had remained suspicious of the Commonwealth Bank of Australia in the aftermath of the attempted nationalisation. Moreover, they saw its dual roles — as a regulating central bank and a competing trading bank — as conflicting. As a result of the push from the private banks, the central bank separated from the Commonwealth Bank in 1960.

By this time, within the central bank, many of the regulators were moving more towards operating through the markets. In 1959, the official short-term money market began. However, despite this move towards a greater market orientation, there still remained people who had faith in regulation. As Sanders said: 'Behind the Financial Corporations Act of 1974 was the idea that the only reason we were not succeeding with regulation was that we were not regulating enough.' However, the regulators themselves knew 'damn well they couldn't regulate', what they had. So 'it was useless trying to regulate the lot'. Others felt that, at the very least, the Act would deliver better statistics. However, the spectre of complete regulation of the financial system, banks and non-banks, only spurred the move away from regulation. 'It's often very good to have very intensive regulation because it brings out the nonsense quicker,' Sanders said, laughing. So the regulators became open market supporters. In December 1979, Treasury notes were offered at tender for the first time. Trading banks were allowed to own more of the merchant banks. In December 1980, the ceiling on deposit rates offered by trading and savings banks was removed.

By the time R. A. (Bob) Johnston became governor of the Reserve Bank of Australia in 1982, the sentiment within the central bank had shifted perceptibly towards deregulation.

Bob Johnston: the central bank in a deregulated era

Dressed in a dark blue suit, sitting in a small conference room at the Reserve Bank of Australia, in Sydney, in April 1988, Bob Johnston reflected back to the work of the Campbell Committee of Inquiry into the Australian financial system. This was set up in January 1979 and was to lay the foundations for the deregulation of the financial system. Johnston, who was involved with the last phase of its work, said that the Campbell Committee Report 'is a splendid document. But I've maintained that the Campbell Committee didn't tell us anything we didn't know. Maybe it codified a great deal and it is internally consistent. But we practitioners knew all those things.' He said that the Reserve Bank itself would have come out with a similar report, but perhaps nobody would have listened. 'You have to get outsiders to tell you what you already know.'

Because the central bank was moving along the same path, the changes recommended by the Campbell Committee went smoothly: 'We knew what we were doing, what we wanted to do. It wasn't somebody imposing it on us. Because we were in tune with it, financial deregulation went like a charm. There have been no real foul-ups at all.'

The Campbell Committee, however, stopped short of positively and unequivocally favouring the float of the dollar. Johnston said that this was despite the fact that, within the central bank, they had been advocating it for some time. Some years before 1983, 'We had come to the view that it was inevitable. But officialdom was really shaking their heads and saying "Yes, but not now." We had an ally in John Howard, then the Treasurer. But he wasn't able to persuade his colleagues.'

When Labor came to power in March 1983, Treasurer Paul Keating also had come to the view that floating the currency was the wise thing to do. The trigger point, Johnston says, was speculative money flowing in and pressuring the Australian dollar upwards in 1983:

> Unless we could somehow introduce massive capital controls, there was nothing for it but to float. The main issue then was whether we have an open float or whether we remove some of the controls piecemeal. But the government decided to abolish virtually all of the controls. It was a very bold decision to make.

This was unfamiliar territory, but:

> In terms of pure theatre, floating the exchange rate was the greatest thing that ever happened in the monetary sphere. The day before the float, there were some who said the exchange rate will rise. Others said it will fall. Very learned people were divided as to what would happen. It was an exhilarating period, for everything went so marvellously well for quite a while. We floated the dollar, and it did not collapse. The rate went on merrily for a year or so.

Bob Johnston, governor, Reserve Bank of Australia, 1982–89 (Gary Ede, courtesy BRW)

On the human front, it meant that nearly 200 people of the Exchange Control Department at the Reserve Bank had to be retrained. Johnston recalled, 'I had to come back from Canberra and assemble all the people here and tell them that their work was abolished. They said, "Suspended, you mean?" I said, "No, it is finished." It was very hard for people to grasp that it was over.'

The next step was the licensing of the new banks. Even the governor of the Reserve Bank was surprised when sixteen were licensed, as the common belief was that there might be six. It was hoped that the new banks would set up retail operations and successfully compete with the established banks. For the most part that has been unsuccessful. With deregulation, the central bank also had to lay greater stress on prudential supervision; it had to learn new techniques to deal with the deregulated markets.

Looking at Nugget Coombs, who directed the regulatory system from 1949 to 1968, and Bob Johnston, who presided over its deregulation, the thing that stands out is the complete contrast in their world view. Johnston himself remarked on it:

> Dr Coombs is totally unrepentant and does not favour floating exchange rates. He thinks it is within the wit of man to manage these things and not leave it to the markets. That is a result of the Depression years, and he hasn't seen fit to change his mind.... [In a deregulated system] you have to

> believe that market forces will allocate resources to the best use. I was never much of an economist.

What affected Johnston deeply was the injustice of the regulatory system, with bureaucrats telling the community what they should do with their money: 'We suffered that 40 years after the Depression. I just thought it was abominable.'

The other major difference between the two men is their view of banks. Dr Coombs still remains suspicious of their power, but Johnston said:

> I don't think the banks have hidden power. There are no powerful wealthy individuals, slinking around, manipulating government policy. The banking industry here in the last few decades has been more of a public service kind of organisation. They don't have any particular rights of access to ministers or governments. They don't make or break governments. They speak out because that's really the only way they have of being heard.

It is a fact of life, he said, that 'Nobody loves banks. Governments don't love them. Oppositions don't love them. The man on the street doesn't love them.' Nevertheless, his experience has been that the Australian banking system has been 'wholesome, open, pretty competitive and honest. There is very little in the way of corruption in Australian banking, because they are all employees, not owners.' The statistics they provide are believable, he said, speaking of the banks that the central bank supervises.

Whatever the differences between Coombs and Johnston, they agree that the trading banks do not have a deferential relationship with the central bank; both men laugh at the suggestion that this might be so. Johnston said, 'We're very good friends. They are rude to me and I am rude to them. We understand each other very well.' This has much to do with the fact that Johnston shares a common career pattern with many senior bankers: he joined the bank at age 16, then went to the Air Force, came back and worked for his degree part-time. For Johnston, 'The great thing Dr Coombs did was to break down the stiffness of the financier. A great deal of irreverence has crept into the system.' Explaining this further, he said:

> You don't pull rank in this country. I would never order anybody, or expect precedence. People are polite and give you the benefit of doubt, but you don't want to presume on it. . . . [I] expect to be able to talk to the chief executives man to man without much formality, without obsequiousness or fear that, if they offend him, he'd do something terrible to them. There is nothing I can do. We don't control anything any more.
>
> If Westpac says that the Reserve Bank are a pack of idiots and it is terrible what they are doing to the country, what can we do about it? I can only write a stinging response to the chief executive, but I can't punish them. It is a free society. It is a very open system.

Compared to many other central banks in the region, the style of the Australian central bank is extremely open and informal. At the annual press conference in August 1988, conducted on first-name terms between senior bank officials and journalists, the Reserve Bank frankly admitted that many times in 1987 it had wrongly read the signals of the economy. In 1989, this was common wisdom, but it is important that the Reserve Bank was freely admitting to it in 1988.

Despite this informality, the central bank remains very much a central bank. Bob Johnston may modestly believe that he and the commercial bankers talk like equals. However, bankers speak wryly of telephone calls in the late afternoon if they have a large exposure, and, uncharacteristically in Australia, relatively few from the financial world are willing to criticise the Reserve Bank on record. So, though everyone is on first-name terms, there remains a distinct line separating the central bankers from the commercial bankers.

However, even the appearance of a free and easy personal relationship between the chiefs of the banks and the central bank is changing. The increased competition, Johnston said, has moved them:

> . . . into an era of increasing legalism. It isn't enough simply to get the chief executives together and give them a few hints as to what they should be doing. The banks are in competition with each other, with non-banks and with the rest of the world. So we are driven increasingly to being very careful in our phrasing of things and making ourselves clear and our requests known to everybody. . . . People are looking at the letter of the law rather than its spirit.

This has resulted in the Banking Act 1959 being amended in November 1989, so that the Reserve Bank has explicit powers in relation to the prudential supervision of banks.

'Reserve Bank independence and all that'

In September 1989, B. (Bernie) W. Fraser, 48, took over as governor of the Reserve Bank of Australia, after being Secretary to the Treasury. Coming after Treasurer Paul Keating's statement that at the Reserve Bank 'They do what I say,' (*Financial Review*, 8 March 1989) this move brought to the fore the question of the independence of the Reserve Bank of Australia.

The Reserve Bank has had outsiders as governors before. In 1938, Harry Sheehan, Secretary to the Treasury, was appointed governor of the Commonwealth Bank of Australia, which at the time combined the functions of central bank and commercial bank. This outside appointment came soon after the Commonwealth Bank had been criticised sharply by the Royal Banking Commission in 1937, for failing to adjust the exchange rate of the Australian pound during the Depression of the 1930s. However, as economic historian, Boris Schedvin, points out,

Bernie Fraser, governor, Reserve Bank of Australia (courtesy BRW)

Sheehan's appointment had more to do with the government's desire to bypass the deputy governor, H. T. Armitage, because he was seen as a Labor man (Personal communication, 1989).

Dr H. C. Coombs was also seen as an outsider. Technically, however, he was not an outsider, for he had joined the Commonwealth Bank as an economist but then been seconded to the civil service and served in a variety of capacities. Though Leslie Melville was the senior economist and was seen as next in line for the job, Labor Prime Minister Ben Chifley trusted Coombs and put him in as governor. It was a political appointment to start with, but this political dimension was defused, as Coombs continued to serve under the succeeding Liberal Prime Minister, Sir Robert Menzies and his successors.

Governor Bernie Fraser too is likely to serve under more than one government. As he was 48 years old in 1989 when he became governor, he could have two terms before him. What is not so clear in Fraser's case is why the Treasurer felt it necessary to go over the head of deputy governor John Phillips, who in 1989 had been with the bank for 43 years and was respected in both the bank and the financial markets. That is why the move has been seen in some circles as an attempt by the Treasurer to rule the Reserve Bank. Another interpretation has it that Fraser's appointment had more to do with the internal manoeuvrings within the Treasury, so that Deputy Secretary Chris Higgins could move up to the Secretary's position. It is also said that Fraser wanted to move to Sydney for personal reasons. So there could have been a match between what the Treasurer wanted and what Fraser saw as being good for himself.

The question that was being debated in 1989 was whether this move will be good for the central bank. Bernie Fraser as governor is not expected to be a yesman, and he is respected both within the central bank and outside it, but his term in the Treasury has left him with a 'can do' tag. His first eight months with the Reserve Bank have not diluted this perception.

It is not possible from the outside to get a sense of Bernie Fraser, the man. He is reclusive and most often declines requests for interviews. Paul Kelly of *The Australian*, however, obtained at least one interview. In a series of articles on the Treasury in April–May 1989, Kelly said that there are three keys to understanding Bernie Fraser. The first is his background of rural deprivation and poverty. He comes from Junee, NSW, where his father was an unskilled worker who was periodically unemployed. Bernie Fraser was one of seven children, and often his family could not afford books for his work or boots for football. He won a scholarship to university and did his Bachelor of Arts in economics at Armidale. While working at the Treasury, he studied for his Master of Economics at the Australian National University. This background, Fraser told Kelly, has left him 'more concerned about unemployment, perhaps, than some other people have been' (1989a, p. 21).

The second point about Fraser is that he is a practical man. Fraser, with his years in the Treasury, saw that often the Treasury was not 'prepared to shape advice within the general framework' of the government. 'That's what I've been prepared to do, perhaps more than some others have,' he said. He saw this as a pragmatic approach, whereas some others have seen it as wimpish or too sycophantic.

The third aspect about Fraser, according to Paul Kelly, is that 'Fraser is self-effacing, accommodating and responsive' (1989a, p. 21). However, he has also been willing to give his deputies a great degree of autonomy, to enable them to present their points of view.

Though Fraser's appointment has helped to fuel the present debate on the independence of the central bank, this question of independence has been an issue from the very beginning. When Denison Miller accepted the job as the first governor of the Commonwealth Bank of Australia in 1912, he accepted it on condition that he would not be subject to any political interference in the running of the bank. So he ruled the bank alone, answerable to no board or member of the government.

However, the kind of independence Denison Miller enjoyed at the Commonwealth Bank until 1923 ended with him. Miller died on 6 June 1923, and on 13 June 1923 a Bill was introduced bringing in an eight-member board. The governor of the bank and the Secretary to the Treasury were ex officio members. In sharp contrast to Miller's independence, the governor of the bank was not the chairman of the board.

Government control over the Commonwealth Bank through an appointed board did not always make it a pliable institution. The Labor government during the Depression found the banks — including the Commonwealth Bank — unwilling to go along with government plans to increase spending. The Commonwealth Bank, which was Labor's 'baby', was held as contributing to the failure of the Labor government in 1931. So after the Second World War, instead of following the recommendations of the 1935 Royal Commission into the monetary and banking systems of Australia, that 'the Governor should be Chairman of the Board by virtue of his office' (1937, p. 275), the Labor government of Ben Chifley removed the board altogether. It was seen as too independent of the government and serving the interests of rich businessmen and large farmers. The board was replaced by an advisory council, which could be commanded by the Treasurer. The governor presided over the meetings but the council itself included the deputy governor, the Secretary to the Treasury, two other bank officers and another public servant appointed by the Treasurer. Dr Nugget Coombs was on the council till he became governor in 1949. The Commonwealth Bank Act 1945 also stated that, in case the bank and the Treasurer could not agree on a point in dispute, the bank would have to implement the Treasurer's policy but the government would accept responsibility for it.

When the Chifley government was defeated in the 1949 election and Robert Menzies returned to power, the government tried to bring back the board of the Commonwealth Bank, but this time with the governor as chairman. However, this move failed to pass the Labor-controlled Senate and led to a double dissolution of Parliament in 1951. The Liberal and Country Party government was re-elected with a majority in both houses of Parliament, and in August 1951 the Commonwealth Bank again had a board. This time round, Dr Nugget Coombs, governor of the bank, was also chairman of the board. The central bank still was subject to government control, but now in case of dispute it could have the subject raised in Parliament for a full debate. The tradition of governor as chairman of the board has continued with the Reserve Bank, though not with the Commonwealth Banking Corporation.

Nugget Coombs in April 1988 said that this provision of reporting to Parliament was not an immediate factor in the relationship of the central bank and the government:

> That's a confession of failure when you get to that. Generally speaking, you tried to compromise. For the government to introduce an Act in Parliament directing the bank to do something or the other, would have created a fantastic uproar. It was something that both sides wanted to avoid, but not to the point of always giving in. There were plenty of conflicts. The final

advice that went to him [the Treasurer] was joint advice. I think we both [the Governor and the Secretary to the Treasury] gave in to some degree.

Dr Coombs views the relationship of the central bank and the government as one of general congruence:

> The bank went its way and the government went its way. They kept one another informed. Generally speaking, there was a parallelism in their policies, but there was a degree of conflict always, even at the best of times. It was a continuous process, where themes were argued out between the Prime Minister and the Treasurer and the Secretary to the Treasury, and me or whoever was from the Commonwealth Bank. I used to talk to Chifley about it and remember saying, 'Someday maybe, I'd have to resign, because we might get to a point of disagreement where we can't reconcile.' He said, 'Doc, never resign.' I said, 'Why not? What if this conscience situation arises?' He said, 'While you're there, you might be losing the battles, but you're still fighting.'

Governors after Coombs have voiced similar sentiments. The key words used by Johnston in describing the relationship with the government are 'cooperation' and 'consultation'. In his last speech before he retired in July 1989, he clarified:

> But consultation does not imply domination — persuasion can cut both ways ... There is a pooling of views arising from looking at a problem from related but different angles. It would be nonsense to say that every little detail must be agreed. But it has been possible to reconcile views without doing violence to anyone's responsibilities. No matter of any consequence has proceeded without agreement' (1989, p. 18).

Johnston, speaking to Australian Business Economists in Sydney, said that he chose to influence government thinking by the 'private' route. He noted, 'As Coombs said, it is hard to be both private adviser and public critic' (1989, p. 19).

Bernie Fraser also chose to talk about the independence of the Reserve Bank in his first public speech as governor in November 1989. Speaking to the Committee for Economic Development of Australia in Sydney, he stressed the importance of cooperation but concluded by emphasising the bank's essential independence:

> It is possible for the Bank to be both independent and co-operative: a willingness to co-operate in partnership efforts to pursue changes of benefit to Australians should not be labelled a sign of weakness (or worse) (1989, p. 12) ... For the Bank's part, there is no lack of authority or 'independence': its performance — and hence its credibility — in the future, as in the past, will depend fundamentally on the quality of its analysis, its deftness in anticipating turning points, and its powers of persuasion (1989, p. 13).

Despite this emphasis on consultation, there have been many instances of disagreement between the Reserve Bank and the Treasury. Reserve Bank historians have pointed to the long and serious disagreement on interest rate policy between Coombs and the Secretary to the Treasury. There was a battle of dominance, and the Treasury very nearly did dominate the bank. During Harold Knight's term as governor from 1975 to 1982, the government's preferential treatment of housing interest rates, insiders say, almost led to a Section 11 reference. This is the section of the Reserve Bank Act 1959 that allows the board of the Reserve Bank to have its stand tabled before Parliament. However, with deregulation the independence of the Reserve Bank has increased, especially in its day-to-day operations with exchange rate management.

Perhaps the criticism most galling to the central bank is that it manipulates interest rates to serve political ends rather than the dictates of monetary policy. The opposition in particular has brought up instances when interest rates fell just before a state or federal election, only to rise after the election was over.

Bob Johnston, in his final speech as governor in July 1989, referred to these allegations of interest rate manipulation: 'These were scurrilous suggestions and showed little understanding of the realities of the financial system' (1989, p. 18). He said that problems that had arisen with monetary policy, referring especially to the easing of monetary policy soon after the October 1987 share-market crash, were due to misjudgement; and for that the Reserve Bank accepted responsibility, for monetary policy is its particular sphere.

However, allegations of political manipulation surfaced again with Bernie Fraser's first major decision in the central bank. The central bank increased the interest rate on non-callable deposits (the deposits that banks have to keep with the Reserve Bank) from 5 per cent to the Treasury note rate minus 5 per cent. At the same time, the major trading banks agreed that they would not raise mortgage rates within the current interest-rate environment. At one level, raising the interest rate on non-callable deposits was a logical step in a deregulated environment; but at another level, the timing of the arrangement got Labor off the hook, by temporarily at least capping the mortgage rate at 17 per cent. Shadow Treasurer John Hewson said in an interview with Paul Kelly of *The Australian*, in October 1989, that this decision showed 'very bad judgement'. He said:

> The Treasurer sat down with the governor and other Reserve Bank officials to negotiate the deal with the senior executives of the four banks involved. One does not suggest the governor should not discuss interest paid on non-callable deposits; but to link that issue explicitly to a '. . . political short-run, one-off deal' . . . to hold down mortgage rates is disgraceful (1989d).

It is interesting that, while this debate on the independence of the central bank was taking place in Australia in 1988 and 1989, in New Zealand legislation was enacted to make the central bank more accountable to Parliament and government direction of the central bank more transparent. The Reserve Bank of New Zealand Act 1989 makes fighting inflation the sole function of the Reserve Bank of New Zealand. Following that pattern, there have been calls for the Reserve Bank of Australia to focus more on fighting inflation. Within the central bank, media reports have deputy governor John Phillips as leading the anti-inflation faction, suggesting that there is some difference of opinion on this issue.

The Reserve Bank Act 1959 gives the bank a three-pronged role, saying that it should exercise its powers 'in such a manner as, in the opinion of the Board, will best contribute to the stability of the currency of Australia; the maintenance of full employment in Australia; and the economic prosperity and welfare of the people of Australia' (Reserve Bank of Australia (1989) p. 1).

Both John Phillips and Bernie Fraser in their public statements see these three objectives as complementary. The difference is in emphasis. The deputy governor thinks that the central bank should concentrate on fighting inflation, for once that is done, it will ensure the other two objectives. The governor recommends that we do not throw the baby out with the bathwater, for we have to keep the other two objectives in mind for the attack on inflation to be sustainable.

John Phillips, in April 1989, addressing the Australian Society of Corporate Treasurers (Victorian Chapter) in Melbourne, said that the end objective of monetary policy 'remains non-inflationary sustainable growth' (1989a: 19). Again in September 1989, he told the Overseas Bankers Association of Australia that full employment and the economic prosperity of the Australian people cannot be achieved if 'inflation runs rampant. So one has to see the battle against inflation as the key longer-run objective' (1989b, p. 15). He did not say that this can be achieved through the use of monetary policy in isolation from other government policy, but stressed that 'It is the key objective for the Bank's monetary policy because it is important to the long-term health of the economy and because fighting inflation is what monetary policy does best' (ibid., p. 15).

Fraser, in November 1989, as if answering this particular point, said:

> Fighting inflation might be what monetary policy does best but, however good it is at that, monetary policy alone will not beat inflation in Australia, other than at extremely high costs in terms of output and employment foregone' (1989, p. 13)... There can be no certainty that decreeing price stability as the sole objective of the Bank would enhance its capacity to fight inflation. Inflation has many causes and must be tackled in a way which coordinates fiscal, structural and especially wages policies, as well as monetary policies (1989, p. 12).

There have also been calls for the central bank to be more accountable and open. Peter Jonson, who left the Reserve Bank in 1988 as head of research to become deputy managing director of stockbrokers James Capel Australia, in a speech to the Economic Society of Australia in 1988, said, 'It is appropriate in a democracy that government have the final say. But citizens are entitled to know if the central bank has a view which differs from that of the government' (1988, p. 3). He saw no reason why the board papers could not be published 6 weeks after its meetings to allow people to understand the basis of the Reserve Bank's monetary policy. The discipline of having to explain the policies would only make them better, he said.

Bob Johnston addressed these charges in July 1989, by pointing to the increase in the amount of information provided publicly by the central bank. He said, 'Obviously, the Bank cannot say much about its near-future policy actions as this is very sensitive market information,' (1989, p. 19) but he pointed out, information about immediate past policy action has been published even faster than the proceedings of the Federal Reserve Open Market Committee, for they appear in the *Reserve Bank of Australia Bulletin* in 'a couple of weeks or so after the close of a month' (1989, p. 19).

Some of this opening-up of the central bank has been because of Johnston's personality. He has done more explaining of monetary policy since any governor since Nugget Coombs. Bernie Fraser has signalled changes in monetary policy more clearly. But in his first six months his speeches have been guarded. It is still unclear how the more reclusive personality of Bernie Fraser will affect the style of the central bank. What is certain is that his view of the relationship of the central bank to the government, the importance of fighting inflation and the accountability of the Reserve Bank will help to shape the central bank and influence its relationships with the banks.

4 Australia's Western Pacific bank: Westpac

Stuart Fowler, 59, laughs a lot and he laughs heartily. Interviewed in February 1988, 6 weeks after he became managing director of Westpac Banking Corporation, he said, 'I'm at full flight. I've reached my pinnacle.' When he first learnt that he would head the bank, his reaction 'was one of humility. We operate the largest financial institution, with 40 000 staff. We are the oldest public company in Australia and the first bank. To be told you are going to head it up — unless you're very obnoxious — you'll be humble.'

Two themes run through Westpac: it is Australia's first bank, and it has been Australia's largest bank for at least 124 years (Butlin, Hall and White, 1971: 131). This is a central part of the self-image of Westpac; but as its name suggests, its status as a Western Pacific bank is now equally important. Like all the major private trading banks in Australia, Westpac's strategy for growth has been to consolidate at home, to keep its status as the lead bank, and then expand internationally. What is special about its plan is that it has sought to expand on a trade-driven niche basis, mainly in the Western Pacific region. This is the story of how the strategy was chosen and how it has worked out so far.

First bank in Australia

The Bank of New South Wales, as Westpac was previously known, was the first bank to be set up in Australia, in 1817. Governor Lachlan Macquarie encouraged its formation, supporting it with a charter of incorporation so that the bank could stabilise the currency and help finance business enterprises. Though he later learnt that he had no authority to issue a charter, by then the bank was well established; it had a semi-official status, and its paper was accepted by the government as payment. In its early years, in 1826 and 1828, the bank nearly went under because of imprudent loans, especially to its directors. It was bailed out by loans from the government on the condition that it put its house in order.

Being number one is so much a part of the bank's self-image that its slogan remains 'First bank in Australia'. Stuart Fowler said in his Sydney office in April 1988, 'We've led in virtually everything that has happened,' pointing to its strings of firsts in savings banking, funds management and electronic banking.

Because it is the number-one bank, it is easy to look for and detect a kind of arrogance in its style. Its headquarters at the head of Sydney's Martin Place loom over the Reserve Bank of Australia. When Stuart Fowler sits in his office on the twenty-seventh floor, the panorama of Sydney Harbour lies before him. 'The best view in town,' he said.

Going up to the chief executive's floor can be a forbidding experience. Even with an appointment, for your first visit to the bank, you are halted at the brass-trimmed glass doors that guard the executive floor. It is swank with walls of black marble, a rust-coloured carpet and a matching leather suite. The security guard keeps you waiting outside while he rings for clearance. Everything is on a big scale — a globe to the right of the guard, and two tapestries on each side of him. There is a Big Brother atmosphere in the hall, as voices boom down from unseen people, even though it is just someone asking the time. Another two security guards come in; all three look at the black marble walls and the empty space outside the lifts. Though the style has softened somewhat since Stuart Fowler became chief executive, the message is stark clear: this is the office of the chief executive of the biggest banking corporation of Australia.

Stuart Fowler is not easily drawn on his feelings. He would not say what it feels like to be chief executive of Westpac. He fobbed off the question on two occasions, saying that it was too early to tell.

Robert (Bob) J. White lived with the experience of being managing director from 1978 to 1987. Six weeks before he retired, he said in October 1987:

> My life is the bank. Particularly when you are running an organisation like this, there is no escape. You don't stop being chief executive of the bank at 6 o'clock, or 8 o'clock when you leave the office. You just don't stop ever. When you are mowing the lawn, you're still the chief executive.

Even his wife had adapted, he said, and was totally interested in the bank:

> Whenever I ring up [from abroad], one of the first things she will tell me is the share price that day.
>
> One of my failings is that my total life is the bank. Maybe as one gets closer to retirement, you think you might have liked to have a broader base.

Stuart Fowler, managing director, Westpac Banking Corporation (courtesy BRW)

> Maybe I suffered for it, but it's still my life, and I wouldn't want to change it.

Bob White said he found that he was 'oversensitive. When the bank is criticised in public, as it is not infrequently, I take it personally. I do react very strongly, because I am very concerned about preserving the image of the bank. And it is difficult when it is such a large organisation.' However, behind it all is a sense of quiet pride: 'Occasionally I stop and look at this building and say to myself, "Well you know, I'm in charge of that." It's a good feeling.'

White's main relaxation away from the bank was gardening:

> I insist on cutting my own lawn. I've quite a big one, and it takes quite a while. The edges are immaculate. I think with the kind of life I live, if I did not have the discipline that forced me to do something like that, I'd probably work 7 days a week. My wife is a keen gardener, so we do it together. There is great satisfaction at the end of Sunday, of just looking at it.

How much of this experience as chief executive was due to Bob White's personality and how much to the demands of being chief executive of Westpac, Stuart Fowler himself will be able to tell in time. Interviewed soon after becoming head of Westpac, in February 1988, Fowler thought that he would have no difficulty letting go of the bank when his time comes. However, the feeling of being very much in the public arena had already hit him. Bob White pointedly said that his wife is a very private person, when asked whether she could be interviewd. Being chief of Westpac meant that a wall had had to be built around his private life. Though Fowler and his wife are both seen as more outgoing, to the surprise of people in the bank, including his communications chief, the same has happened with Fowler. He also seems most comfortable when the talk is of the bank rather than of himself. Asked a personal question, he laughed and turned it around, saying, 'I only have some claim to notoriety because I happen to be chief executive of Westpac.' So maybe the wall comes with the territory.

To differentiate between the bank and your own life must be hard if all your working life has been spent in it. Both Bob White and Stuart Fowler, like the chief executives before them, started as juniors in the bank. Fowler joined the bank in 1949 and has worked only in this one institution. Son of a professor of psychology at the University of Western Australia, Fowler joined the university to study engineering, but after a year he dropped out. He has no regrets on that score. Being a university dropout has also not hurt him in his career. Talking about it on a hot day in the Westpac offices in Melbourne in February 1988, his dark grey jacket slung on the back of a chair, a crystal jug of water on the table, he said, 'I was just not bright enough. My academic achievements at that time didn't suggest I'd ever be an engineer.'

Fowler did not say why he went into banking, but he quipped that, if one is to choose banking, then it's best to join the most prominent bank. (After Westpac had taken over the Western Australian Bank in 1927, it gained the dominant market share in the state.) However, another story he has often told is that he chose the Wales, as he calls it still when talking of the bank pre-1982, because his brother-in-law was with the National Australia Bank. He did not dwell on his early years in the bank. He was in the Western Australian branch-banking system for 4 to 5 years and then in the administration connected with retail. By this time a lot of his friends were coming out of university and going to London. So he too asked for a London posting, and got it, staying there from 1955 to 1959. He returned there in 1969 and became manager of the London office in 1974. With 5 years in New Zealand between 1964 and 1969, he had an unusual 15 years outside Australia.

As with all bankers of his time, London was a great experience for him:

> I wasn't particularly interested in history, but it would be impossible not to enjoy history in London, because you just see it around you. To be in London in the 1950s and to just see the names of the commercial houses was

> to create an interest in history. See the National Bank of India, the Standard Bank of South Africa and Grindlays Bank and Bank of London — you could see an enormous number of historical trade routes. Then, of course, the galleries, museums — I had no interest in them before I went to London.

Between his two tours of London, in 1960, he had three assignments as the bank's shipboard agency officer. The love-boat story ran true to form, and he met his wife working as a nurse on the liner *Oronsay*. This is how he first went to Tokyo, Seoul, Hong Kong and Singapore.

He came back from London in 1975 and joined the international division in Sydney, heading it from 1980 to 1986. This was the period of Westpac's major thrust into the international arena. Two years before he became chief executive, he returned to retail. In a way his career reflects the directions of the bank in the last 40 years.

When Fowler joined the bank in 1949, the bank had already built up a strong retail presence, especially in NSW and Western Australia. Being the first bank in NSW, it had a head start. However, its initial charter fixed the bank within very tight limits.

The general rules for the conduct of the bank said that no paper was to be discounted for more than 3 months. Loans against mortgaged property were not to be made for more than 12 months. No loans were to exceed 500 pounds, and interest charges were not to exceed 10 per cent. Interest was not to be paid on deposits unless by special agreement, when 3 months' notice of withdrawal was required, and any interest was not to exceed 8 per cent (Holder, 1970: 16).

Neither the original charter nor its subsequent deed of settlement of 1827 envisaged a need to set up branches. Only when the bank was reconstituted as a joint stock company in 1850 was it able to open its first branch, at Moreton Bay district (now Brisbane) in Queensland. Then, with brilliant timing, it moved to Melbourne, just before the gold rush of 1851. It became the first bank to send its agents out into the goldfields. Soon after, in 1853, it opened a branch in London. In the 1860s it grew with the opening up of farmland, and then with the suburban spread.

One of the boasts of the bank is that, unlike most other banks, it did not close its doors during the banking crash of 1893. The Bank of New South Wales expanded to Fiji and Papua-New Guinea between 1900 and 1910. It had gone to New Zealand earlier, in 1861, having bought over some of the business of the Oriental Bank Corporation. In the 1920s the bank grew by opening new branches and by amalgamations. In 1927 it absorbed the Western Australian Bank, and in 1931 the Australian Bank of Commerce.

When the bank was subject to increasing regulation after 1939, it expanded its non-bank activities. The most notable addition to its services was its entry into savings banking in 1956. However, it was the onset of deregulation that galvanised the bank. As Fowler said in February 1988:

> In the last 7 or 8 years, in Australia we've gone through a revolution. I don't think there has probably ever been a period of banking history that has changed so dramatically. We think it's great, but it has been an enormous change in the way we do things, in the product range, in how we expect our staff to respond. I think Mr White and his team created, from a relatively small business, an international bank of some standing.

Becoming a bank for the Western Pacific

Bob White said that, in a regulated environment, banking was boring. Talking of it in October 1987, he said:

> When I go back to the immediate postwar period, there was one interest rate. There was one set of charges for services rendered, and they were agreed between the banks. The most traumatic experience was to go to the meeting with the bankers' association to decide whether they'd be changed or not. From the 1890s till 1973, interest rates remained below 9 per cent. Despite a war, depression, heavy postwar inflation, the next time we got to 9 per cent was 1973.

He began to think in terms of deregulation when the bank had to make a submission to the Campbell Committee Inquiry, which tabled its report in Parliament in 1981. White said:

> So when deregulation arrived, there was no point putting up your hands in the air and saying we were not ready. One of the decisions we reached was that one of the best defences would be size. We looked at the banking structure then, which had come down to only five major private banks. Three of them were fairly large, and two were smaller. So it seemed obvious to us that the smaller ones were vulnerable. Yet there were three others, so we better be first. A lot of 1979 was spent in planning the merger [of the Bank of New South Wales and the Commercial Bank of Australia finalised in 1982].

White said that, after this merger, it would be difficult to 'go any further in the domestic markets. So the bank's future had to be increasingly in its international expansion.' However, the bank did not want to go just international. Of all the banks in Australia, it has most focused its thrust in the Asia-Pacific region. Trading relationships with Japan have been of long standing. After the Second World War, when Japan started to build up its textile industry, Australian banks were some of the first to lend to Japan. As Japan's needs changed, Australia moved from the export of wool to the export of iron ore and coal.

Other banking relationships in Asia were more personal. Stuart Fowler in February 1988 told of the special relationship between Westpac and the Oversea-Chinese Banking Corporation (OCBC) of Singapore. Before the war, they had the usual correspondent relationship; but during the war, Tan Chin Tuan, the managing director of OCBC, had to send his wife and family to Perth. The story goes that they were looked after by the branch manager, who lent them some money and extended other courtesies. After that, Tan Chin Tuan also arrived with nothing. He too was given the money he needed, and taken to see the state manager:

> We were doing this with a lot of people who came from the North during the Japanese Occupation. Like other banks, the bank slipped into gear and went out of the ordinary to help, and that happened to Tan Chin Tuan. But he never forgot. He came to Sydney and he set up his bank in our bank. He had a desk in what we then called the British and Foreign Department, and he used to have morning tea with the general manager. He became almost a part of the Wales in those days, and he bores his staff to the nth degree about how much he was looked after.

The relationship continues; today, Westpac's offices in Singapore are in the OCBC building.

However, after the Second World War, Westpac did not have a vision of becoming an important bank in Asia. Though Nugget Coombs had in the 1950s looked to the Asia-Pacific region, it was only when the UK joined the European Economic Community in 1973 that the umblical cord with the UK was cut. Then Westpac began to consider the region. Bob White was in London at the time. He explained:

> We as a bank were concerned about the implications for many of our primary producers in Australia and New Zealand. There was just no doubt in my mind that Australia's future was not in Europe. Nor was it on the other side of the Pacific. We were a part of Asia. We were geographically located here. We just had to meet the challenges of expanding to the Western Pacific zone. I suppose I was encouraged and given confidence there because of the prosperity of the Western Pacific zone as Japan was emerging.

Bob White recalled saying this to a gathering in Japan. In the ensuing discussion, a European banker said to him 'But how can Australia make its way in Asia, with its cultural background?' White commented:

> It just goes to show how little Europeans appreciate what's happening in this part of the world. You just learn to live with those cultural barriers progressively being broken down. And there's a tremendous amount of Asian immigration into Australia now. It would be head in the sand to say that we couldn't adapt in the cultural sense to living with, trading with, doing business with, the Western Pacific.

However, the bank's name, the Bank of New South Wales, was a hindrance abroad. White said that it sounded too parochial, identifying itself with just one state in Australia. When they tried the name Wales on their finance company in Hong Kong, people there saw Wales as referring only to Cardiff, UK. So on two counts — to express a brand new corporate identity for the merged bank and to project an international image — it was decided to change the name.

The bank projected its view of where it was focused in its changed name: Westpac Banking Corporation. 'Westpac', standing for Western Pacific, symbolised its thrust into the Asia-Pacific region. It became 'Western' Pacific because the bank wanted to retain the stylised 'W' that was its logo when it was the Bank of New South Wales. The logo had been very successful, so the new name had to go with that logo. 'We looked at "Australia Pacific", White said. 'You see it on tourist buses sometimes. We looked at "Asia Pacific". But we kept coming back to that logo, and that's how,' he said, they decided on the name Westpac.

Despite what the bank felt about its need to push out into the Asia-Pacific region, White said, the change of name:

> . . . is the single most traumatic experience I'd ever had in the bank. It engendered a degree of criticism and hostility that I would not have believed possible. From all strata of society — from customers, shareholders, from senior people who had a long association with the bank, even from senior people in the government. They just could not understand why this bank with this long tradition and proud part in Australia's history would forsake its name. This was not a matter of prejudice against the Western Pacific so much as it was a suggestion that we had forsaken our heritage.
>
> I suppose one other aspect of it that gave me courage to go ahead was the totally illogical nature of the criticism. First, people said the name was American. Others said it reminded them of a supermarket. A lady wrote to me saying it reminded her of a stubby and loafers. And I thought, How could she possibly draw that conclusion? I answered that letter, saying, I am a most conservative individual. I am very seldom seen without a collar and a tie and if that's the sort of image she was getting, it was totally wrong, because we were not like that in practice. I answered most of these letters personally. The chairman got quite a few, and he answered those. There were probably 200 letters.
>
> The stockholders' meeting lasted for 5 hours. It was attended by almost 1200 proprietors. The vote was favourable by a very narrow margin, and the vote required to change the name was 75 per cent. It was a very difficult period.

Out of this came the idea that, as a bicentennial gesture, Westpac would establish a museum reflecting its history.

The new name was launched with great flair in 1982, including fashion shows of the new bank outfits in Martin Place, Sydney, during lunchtime. As head of the international division between 1980 and 1986, Stuart Fowler was very much at the cutting edge of the action. The bank's international expansion, Fowler said in April 1988, was in the beginning 'driven by the enormous trade flows with Japan and

South Korea'. However, Westpac was not permitted to open branches there, because foreign banks were not allowed in Australia at the time. So the bank made do with a deposit-taking company in Hong Kong, an overseas banking unit in Singapore. The bank got to Tokyo only in 1986. In that year, Westpac achieved the troika: Tokyo, Seoul and Taipei. The bank bought some existing business in Taipei and Seoul, while in Tokyo it started from scratch.

The bank had already established a presence in the USA in the 1970s. Fowler said in December 1988 that initially it was to look after the unused balances of the bank there. However, with deregulation, he said, 'We got concerned that we might lose corporate business in Australia to the foreign banks, as much of the oil and motor industry was foreign-owned. So we went to the United States to get to base with the parent companies to protect our business in Australia.'

Westpac was trade-driven and followed a niche strategy. As Stuart Fowler explained:

> We can't be a Barclays in UK and we can't be a Citibank in New York. To try is very foolish, as the Citibanks and Barclays have found in this market. Foreign exchange activities have been a good product for us, and we do it well. So acquisition of the bullion business of Johnson Matthey was to us a logical extension of our foreign exchange activities. If you are dealing with deutschemark, Swiss francs and yen, you haven't got a full product range unless you have gold as well. That was a natural, particularly for a country which is a considerable gold producer.
>
> Again, we are quite large traders of government securities in our own market. It seemed to us that, if we were going to be a part of the international global wholesale market, then to be close to the comings and goings of the government securities market was important.

So the bank acquired the primary government securities dealer William E. Pollock in New York.

Westpac kept away from acquiring retail networks abroad. Fowler said in April 1988:

> It seems to me that the only way to make money is to have a critical mass in a market place. Wherever we are in a retail sense, we have a major market share — in New Zealand, Fiji, the Pacific islands. Look at the foreign banks that have come into Australia and their struggle to build up a retail base. HongkongBank wrote to its customers that, if you haven't got $10 000, we don't want to know you. Chase AMP is still struggling to find a niche. Citibank changes direction every time the wind changes. They are not quite sure where they are going. Bank of America has hardly started. Bankers' Trust is holding up a 'No cash here' sign. Really, the only foreign entrant that has established itself in a position to stay, in my view, is the National Mutual Royal Bank. They did that through acquiring two quite reasonably sized building societies.

Fowler said that they could not see any place in Asia where they could establish a large dominant network. Speaking at a pre-Christmas dinner in Melbourne in 1988, he said that there are only two banks that have networks in all Asian capitals: Standard Chartered and Hongkong and Shanghai Banking Corporation. 'Standard Chartered we did not want to buy,' he said, 'and Hongkong Shanghai is too big.' Earlier in April 1988, he had also said that, if the Bank of New South Wales had not merged with the Commercial Bank of Australia, 'I'm sure we would have reviewed the opportunity with Grindlays seriously. We had reviewed it on a number of occasions, but we came to the conclusion it wasn't for us.' Australia and New Zealand Banking Group (ANZ) bought the international Grindlays Bank in 1984.

However, this conviction about concentrating on wholesale banking and keeping away from retail banking abroad wavered in 1989. The bank's 1989 annual report said that part of the group's strategy would be the 'diversification of the group's funding base by acquiring a retail banking presence in major offshore markets . . .' (p. 8).

A matter of relationship

Westpac's major response to deregulation was to expand in Australia and overseas. However, deregulation also meant doing business differently. One difference was that, in a competitive environment, banking relationships had less significance. This came home to the bank over the case of Broken Hill Proprietary Ltd in 1986. The bank had a close relationship with BHP and had shared directors for many years. However, when Robert Holmes à Court was stalking BHP with a view to taking it over, Westpac lent Holmes à Court money. As Bob White commented:

> That was a very agonising time for me and many of my colleagues. Here we were faced with a situation where we had to make a decision to support one customer in a situation which would be seen as unfriendly or even hostile by another customer. But if this bank was going to remain alive and was going to be one of the leaders, then it must accept the risks involved. We had a customer here, who was an extremely valued customer and whose relationship we valued very highly, who had put to us a perfectly logical, legitimate, sound proposition. Were we going to say 'No' on the basis that it might cause some criticism from the other quarter? I would like to have avoided that decision like the plague. But it had to be made, and it had to be faced. It is public knowledge that I telephoned BHP's chief executive to tell him that. That was a traumatic experience also, but it had to be. I think, now that it has happened, that kind of change will increasingly be entrenched in the financial world of the future.'

However, White said, one unhappy result of the BHP matter was that it began to raise doubts in lots of other corporates as to where they stood in their banking relationships:

> I explained to them that the primary consideration in matters of this nature will be dictated by the prime nature of the relationship. If you have a

> long-standing prime relationship, then we would not put ourselves in a position of taking an unfriendly act. In the case of BHP, BHP did not have a major relationship with us to the same extent as it had with the ANZ and the National.

Nevertheless, however kindly White wanted to put it to others and himself, the days of the old type of relationship banking were over. Banks were competing for business rather than following old loyalties; and once the corporates had learnt to play the game equally well, they would go for where they got the best price and the best service. Any relationship aspects that remained would hinge on service rather than loyalty.

This change in customer relationships was not confined to the corporate area. In the rural sector, long-standing relationships with farmers also came under threat. In 1987, in the Victorian mallee area, some farmers referred to Westpac as Pressurepac. Though this may have reflected the feelings of a few farmers under threat, it did indicate that the bank manager was no longer always seen as the trusted adviser. In some cases he had become the liquidator. The sophisticated customer too has reacted to this change, moving from one bank to another, though not quite as fast as the corporates.

Westpac, like the other Australian banks, also became aware that, to maximise profits, it would have to get to know more about its customers. It would have to learn which categories of customer were the more profitable and also try to improve the profitability of customers by persuading them to use more bank services and products. In order to do this, the bank needed to set up a customer information system, so that it could design products to suit customer needs.

To do this, Westpac, unlike the other major trading banks, decided in 1985 to invest $125 million over 5 years in a tailormade technological system: the Core System 90 (CS90). Westpac's view was that it was better to have a system flexible enough to cope with the future instead of a system kept together by rubber bands. One main benefit of the CS90 project is that it will help the bank to respond to customers' needs faster and so increase productivity. It will also be able to analyse the way in which a customer uses the bank, so that it can address the gaps in the banking services through direct marketing.

Despite mutterings in the market that the bank had spent too much on a system that was too complex and untried, Westpac's investment in technology appears to have paid off. Having IBM market the CS90 system internationally has been a major boost and seems to confirm the bank's claim that it has led to improved productivity.

Keeping the lead

By 1986 the bank's resources were stretched by its expansion at home and abroad. Its major investments were yet to give a return. Housekeeping at home was not as tight as it could have been. Costs were

Bob White, managing director, Westpac Banking Corporation 1978–87 (courtesy BRW)

rising, particularly in the retail department. Profitability was down compared to the 2 preceding years. The bank's lead status in Australia was being threatened.

At the beginning of 1986, Stuart Fowler was moved to head the retail operations of the bank. This was part of the succession drama taking place at Westpac. In October 1986, Bob White was 63. Under the rules that applied at the time he should have retired, but at the end of 1985 the board extended his term for another 2 years. The two known contenders for the top job were Fowler and Warwick Kent, who was then head of retail. So in a definite move to test the candidates, their jobs were switched; Kent went to international and corporate and Fowler to retail.

In the retail arena, Westpac has often been a leader. It first initiated the private banks' move into savings banking in 1955, though when it came actually to starting the first private savings bank in 1956, both Westpac and ANZ opened on the same day. It was the leader in electronic banking in Australia, introducing automated teller machines (ATMs) in 1980 so making it mandatory for the other major banks to follow suit.

However, from the mid 1980s there was an imbalance in the retail department. Retail accounted for 39 per cent of the pre-tax income of the bank at the end of 1987 but for 60 per cent of the costs. So getting the costs down became a priority for Fowler.

Much of the corrective action being taken is commonsense, he said in February 1988: stressing courtesy, the personal touch, remembering the client's name, making sure that the premises are right:

> I've issued housekeeping checklists. If they can do it in McDonalds, we can do it in Westpac. I have a thing about our signage. We spent a whole lot of money on changing signs, on our neon signs. I go beserk when I don't see them on. I ring up the branch manager and ask, Has he noted his signage recently?

The other major change has been in how the bank attempts to use its extensive branch network. In April 1988, he said:

> Twenty years ago, we kidded ourselves that a full range of services was available at every branch; but with specialisation in the marketplace, that is just not possible. We still mean to be all things to all people, but not at one place. We will always be a universal bank in our home territories. All we are doing is streamlining the point of sales.

So there are the electronic delivery systems for the high transaction customer, to get the unit cost down:

> Local banking centres have been set up with personal banking, and district commercial banking centres really for the guy that is running a small business who could borrow up to half a million dollars. He requires a different range of manager to discuss the issue. We have the international banking centres where we've concentrated the expertise to serve the branches to lift the level of service. All this has been done in the past, but is still settling down. What we have done recently is put in the personal investment centres.

Fowler maintains that some of the problems in retail banking are a hangover from the bureaucratic practices during the days of regulation. In February 1988, he pointed out:

> Since 1939, we've been regulated as to the extent of the loans we can make; we've been regulated as to whom we can lend the money; we've been regulated as to the interest rates we can charge; we've been regulated as to the time of opening; we've been regulated as to the product range; we've been regulated by the need to fill in forms and do the exchange control. That breeds bureaucracy.

He said that Westpac is breaking this down, by using a regional manager structure:

> We have about 90 regional managers in Australia, and they have 25 to 30 branches in their area. As a result, the regional manager is closer to his

> branches than we've ever had in our history. We believe that is the best way to run our branch network. We believe we have senior people closer to our branches, than any of our competitors. Most of their regions are of about 100 branches. We have now delegated considerable authority to these regional managers to manage and to hire and fire staff.

The other initiative for increasing revenue vis-à-vis costs was the introduction of a user-pays fee for services. Fowler announced this soon after he took over as managing director of the bank at the beginning of 1988. Fowler said in April 1988:

> You have to look at the major dynamics of our business. On our savings bank side of the business, we have 54 per cent of our accounts with less than a $100, producing less than 1 per cent of the deposit base and something like 27 per cent of the transactions. It means that area is being cross-subsidised by other areas.

The motive behind this was also specifically to prevent businesses from using savings accounts as if they were cheque accounts. Introducing the user-pays system was a risk, turning around decades of practice. Internal estimates in the bank were that they could lose 300 000 customers. Instead, Fowler said, they were surprised to gain some. However, it is difficult from macro figures to see how far the fees have helped the bank's profitability.

Like other banks, Westpac is also stressing productivity. The back office function of branches is being separated from the counter work. Some branches now are purely service centres, with the office work centralised in district operation centres. Since July 1988, Westpac has been using the Alexander Proudfoot Company to look at ways of increasing the efficiency of its counter staff. The catchword in this is the 'three Ps', standing for people, pride and productivity. Though senior management has pronounced itself well pleased with the results, the reaction at the counter varies from acceptance to strong resentment. One Westpac teller complained in January 1989, 'Proudfoot is the worst thing that has happened to the bank. They even want to know if you go to the toilet, and how many phone calls you get' (Singh, 1989: 37).

In addition to the concern with costs, there was also a perception — hotly contested by Fowler — that the bank was losing market share in the domestic retail market in 1988. This was evidenced by the domestic deposits and loans: between October 1985 and December 1987, the National Australia Bank and ANZ had increased their share at the expense of Westpac.

In 1989, the bank changed tack and increased its assets faster than the National Australia Bank and ANZ. Having acquired a $1.4 billion Defence Services Housing Loan portfolio, it also emerged as the country's largest lender for housing in a difficult economic environment.

However, lax lending in a high interest and worsening economic environment hit the bank especially hard. There was a decline in asset quality, especially in corporate and merchant banking operations in March 1990. According to banking analyst Wilson Lee of A. C. Goode & Co. 'the nine biggest bad debt accounts accounted for $235 million of the $568 million charged against profit' (Lee, 1990). The international operations of the bank showed a greater decline in profitability than the bank's Australian activities.

The bad debts charged to the profit and loss account (that is, net write-offs and additions to the specific and general provisions) increased by 159 per cent for the six months to 31 March 1990 compared to the equivalent period in 1989. This was the highest increase in the bad debts charge of all the major private banks. As a result, its return on average equity plummetted from 13.4 per cent in March 1989 to 4.7 per cent in March 1990. Only through the injection of $198 million of staff superannuation fund surpluses did the returns reach a more respectable 10.64 per cent.

What had gone wrong? Ali Cromie writing in *Business Review Weekly* just before the half yearly results said Westpac's 'credibility is low with the Australian investment community, its main union and even its own staff. Analysts say its international strategy has stalled, its management does not inspire strong confidence and the banking group lacks clear direction' (Cromie, 1990: 48).

One of the worries is that the bank's international strategy has been unprofitable. None of its major foreign acquisitions has been a scintillating success. It calls itself Australia's world bank, but its wholesale, fee-driven strategy is not delivering the goods, and there are no retail initiatives on the horizon.

Its unprofitable international and merchant banking operations, together with fall-out from succession battles have resulted in a number of exits and entries at its senior management level. In an industry where the norm is for senior management to be home-grown, Westpac has been experimenting with outside talent. This may be seen as innovative but it has also been interpreted as a sign of trouble at the bank.

Wilson Lee said in Melbourne in April 1990, that in the last two to three years, 'The market has not felt totally confident about Westpac. It's been trading at a discount to its net assets and on a high dividend yield for quite a while now.' This is the price the bank pays for the market's discomfort with its performance.

This market perception must be most galling for Fowler. In July 1988 he told a collection of stockbrokers, fund managers and journalists in Melbourne, 'If stripping in David Jones' windows will get the P/E ratio up, I'll do it.' Fowler's window performance is yet to come, but what the market requires is a series of good results.

However, not all is doom and gloom at Westpac. The bank's success with CS90 and IBM's intention to market it worldwide has important implications for profitability. If Westpac can move ahead of other banks in the areas of 'knowing the customer' and having flexible bank products, the figures will improve. Westpac also has the strongest fund management and insurance operations among the major banks. This will be particularly significant as superannuation attracts a greater portion of the community's savings. Moreover the bank is aware of the negative market perceptions and is taking remedial action. The heir apparent, Frank Conroy, is highly regarded in the market and by his peers. But he will have his work cut out for him. Westpac remains Australia's first bank. It is also the country's largest bank. His brief no doubt will be to again make it Australia's leading bank.

5 Going international: ANZ

Will Bailey, 57, has a problem. He dislikes the hassles of flying but is the deputy chairman and group chief executive of the Australia and New Zealand Banking Group (ANZ), represented in more than 40 countries and the most international of Australia's banks.

Bailey also cannot take curry or spicy food. This makes for another tricky situation, for ANZ owns Grindlays Bank, the largest foreign bank in India.

ANZ stands out among Australia's major banks because it is the country's most international bank. Unlike Westpac, which expanded abroad on a trade-driven niche basis, mainly in the Western Pacific region, ANZ expanded its international network by buying Grindlays Bank in 1984. Also, unlike the National Australia Bank, which went in for regional networks in culturally similar areas in Scotland and Ireland, ANZ has a large retail network in India, where it is the biggest foreign-owned bank. It also has important representation in the Middle East and Africa, in addition to South and Southeast Asia.

Because of this, ANZ faces two significant issues: it has to ensure that ANZ's domestic strength gives its international network a distinctiveness, rather than have its global image dilute its presence at home; and it has to make sure that the cultural diversity of its international network remains a plus instead of becoming a minus.

Will Bailey: leading an international bank

In September 1984, when ANZ bought Grindlays, John Milne, the chief executive of ANZ, lay dying. He had fallen ill with hepatitis in April 1984, shortly after initiating hush-hush negotiations for the purchase of Grindlays. At this point there was no deputy chief execu-

Will Bailey, group chief executive and deputy chairman, Australia and New Zealand Banking Corporation (courtesy BRW)

tive, only two chief general managers: Bailey, in charge of domestic operations, and Reg Nicolson, chief general manager responsible for the international field.

In the 6 months that it took to complete the Grindlays' purchase, Nicolson supervised the deal, leading a four-man team. However, even when the deal was signed, there was no indication as to whether it was Nicolson or Bailey who would head the bank. The chairman of the bank, Sir William Vines, had been particular not to reveal the bank's preference in any way, so he himself led the ANZ team to the annual World Bank and International Monetary Fund (IMF) meetings at the end of September.

John Milne died in November 1984, and Will Bailey became the next chief executive. Sitting in his fifteenth floor office in the ANZ's Melbourne headquarters in October 1987, Bailey said that, when the chairman rang him up and asked to see him, 'I walked in the door thinking he is going to say, the other guy got the job. He didn't. I suppose that would have to be the ultimate highlight of my career.'

Bailey's career in its fundamentals has been like that of many other chief executives before him. His father was a tradesman and farmer, and there was a time when Bailey thought that he too would be a farmer. After high school his first choice was to study electrical engineering, but his family and an uninspiring school experience persuaded him to defer it for a year or two. He never did make it to university. He expressed no regrets for that, other than to remark wistfully that perhaps after he retires he may go to university to study geography.

Bailey went to work for a building company and started studying accounting, building construction and quantity surveying. Wanting to study accounting further, he opted for a bank. So he joined the English, Scottish and Australian Bank (ES&A) in Oakleigh, a Melbourne suburb, in 1950, when he was close to 17. ES&A, commonly known as 'Scottie', was the smallest and the most junior of the three banks that merged to form the ANZ Banking Group in 1970.

He enjoyed his early years, the move from clerk to ledger keeper, teller, bill clerk, then instructor at a training school. He had no problem with his addition, but his handwriting was not particularly good. Bailey said, 'Fortunately, ledger machines came in 18 months after I joined the banks. I was one of the first ledger machinists in the bank, male variety, that is.'

What stands out for him in the early years is his 6 month stint in the Navy when he was called up for national service, 12 months after he had joined the bank:

> Without doing that 6 months in the Navy, I wouldn't be sitting here today. I think the self-reliance and discipline made me a different person. I had more confidence in my own ability. For the first time in my life I swam into a pool of 400 people, most of whom I didn't know. They were from all walks of life in Australia. Some were truck drivers. Some were slaughtermen. Some were Queensland cane cutters. Others were stockbrokers, accountants, university students.
>
> I was put in charge of 20 of those people. I was selected by a very difficult process: I was the only one with red hair. You can laugh, but that made you different. They were looking for someone and said, 'Hey you, with the red hair.' That's right. Without that, I think I would have been a different person in my 20s.

Like many juniors of the past, he thought that being manager of a bank branch was the ultimate goal. What was dismaying though, Bailey said, was that 'You virtually had to be about 40 to be a manager.' Not wanting to wait that long, in the late 1950s he applied for the position of personnel manager for a large manufacturing company. He was stunned when told that he had the job. 'It was a difficult decision,' he said. 'I was 26; but after talking to a lot of wise gentlemen who had nothing to do with the bank, I decided to stay.' Four years later, at 30, he was appointed manager of the Bairnsdale branch in Victoria. 'That was an enormous thrill,' he said. Afterwards, he and his wife opened a bottle of champagne.

He moved up, and from 1971 to 1974 he became regional manager, New Zealand administration. That brought new problems: 'The first thing you had to realise is that New Zealand is a totally different country. I had to continually say to myself, "This isn't part of Australia, this isn't part of Australia."' As yet, his career was running true to type. A few more signals also pointed that he was on the way to higher things.

In 1977, he went to London. He was told that, before this, he would go to Harvard to do the Advanced Management Programme. He celebrated this major break in his career by getting the family all dressed up — black tie, long evening gowns — and going to the best restaurant they could find in Adelaide. 'It cost an arm and a leg, but we enjoyed the time,' said Bailey.

Though with each move it was a step up the ladder, Bailey's wife, Dorothy, said in January 1988, sitting in her kitchen:

> I didn't really like any of the moves and didn't like leaving the community either. I'm a reluctant starter and a reluctant leaver. For the children, it meant they have no old school chums. But they adjusted well.
>
> In a way, it is not that hard, for you know you're not going to be staying long. So it is not such a terrible drama. You have to be very positive about it. Still, there are times we have driven by one of our old houses and seen the trees we have planted, now really big. The good part though is that you do make friends. There is always a community ready to accept you. So being with a bank, you don't feel lonely.

For her the big price was that, when they moved to New Zealand, she had to give up teaching school. She said that she loved teaching the first 6 years of school. She was teaching when they married. Then the children came, and for 6 or 7 years she stopped; then she took it up again. However, she said, 'Will's career was the most important. Will has never stopped me teaching. It just became too awkward to get back to it.'

Asked what it feels like to be chief executive, Bailey said, 'When you walk in and sit behind the desk for the first time, it gives you a thrill. Then you recognise that now you have to prove that you are the person that should be occupying that particular job.' He added that it felt very much like being manager of his first branch in Bairnsdale:

> I had to prove to myself that I could manage the bank's affairs in a little country town, that I could satisfy the customers, make the business grow, that I could do it professionally and properly.
>
> When I became chief executive, initially I felt lonely, and at times I still do. It is completely different from being number two or number three or number four, because you have a responsibility to the shareholders for the totality.

Dorothy later brought this topic down to earth by saying, 'One person once told Will that now he is at a dead end job.' For her that has come as a relief, for she is now in her seventeenth house in 32 years: 'This is the third set of leadlighting I've had done for the home,' she said over a cup of tea. 'There'd be instant divorce if I had to move again.'

Trying to gauge the nature of the man who heads Australia's most international bank is a difficult exercise. Bailey's communications chief in 1988, David Butcher, said in October 1987 that Will Bailey is wonderful. Down to earth, intelligent, has a grasp of the wider issues and yet is able to translate very detailed technical material to its essential core. He is good with people and has a fantastic memory. Yet, at first and second meetings in July and October 1987, the overriding impression he gave was one of being hard to penetrate. In a sense, it is because he looks very open and is articulate, but it is as though he is assessing you all the time, to see how much he should reveal. He was the only chief executive interviewed who had somebody else sitting in on the interviews. Only at the third interview in March 1988 and subsequently did he talk alone. Interspersed right through his talk were wry remarks, yet something prevented laughter, so as to see what he really meant. Only towards the end of the second interview did he loosen up and talk of his wife and three daughters and how important they are to his life and work. He spoke of his farm, where he can reflect and get life into perspective.

His wife, Dorothy, told how he likes building things in the shed at the back, and classical music. Describing him, she focused on the enthusiasm he brings to what he is doing. She started to say that he is ambitious, but then checked herself, saying, 'Ambition is not the right word. He feels he can do things.'

Nevertheless, there was little in Bailey's earlier life to suggest that he would head a bank represented in more than 40 countries. In 1984, there were some in the market who were suggesting that, if Bailey had had full discretion on Grindlays, ANZ would never have bought it. And a few years earlier, there would have been few predicting that ANZ would go the international route. To see how and why the bank did choose this path, we have to go back to history.

The bank moves from London to Melbourne

ANZ's history starts in 1835 with the opening of the Bank of Australasia in Sydney. It was the first British bank to come to Australia. David Merrett, who has written a history of ANZ from the mid 1930s to 1985, says that wool was doing so well in Australia at the time that the directors of the bank felt that 'in no part of the world can capital be employed more advantageously and securely than in carrying on the business of banking upon sound principles in the colonies of Australasia' (Merrett, 1985: 10).

The 'Asia, as it came to be called, was soon followed by the Union Bank of Australia Ltd in 1837. In 1852, ES&A arrived.

The 'Asia became the first bank to open in Melbourne in 1838, when it directed David Charteris McArthur, a Scottish clerk, to move from Sydney to Melbourne. In later years, he remembered that at the time there were three brick houses in Melbourne, a solitary boat on the

Yarra river and 1500 inhabitants. He started his bank in a two-room cottage, with two mastiffs, a military sentry and a stout fence with iron spikes for security (Griffiths, 1955). Melbourne was to become the headquarters of the British banks.

Coming at the time of the wool boom, the British banks became noted for branch banking and actively soliciting deposits by offering interest for them. They also had a natural advantage in foreign exchange, with their head offices in London. They attracted the most experienced staff and provided the chief executives of the National Bank of Australasia for its first 40 years after it opened in 1858.

The Union Bank moved to New Zealand in 1839 to become the colony's first bank. As soon as one talks of the bank in New Zealand, the first image is that of 'Jacky Box Smith'. He was so careful of the bank's safe that, when the settlement had to move from the mouth of the Hutt River to the less exposed anchorage of present day Wellington, the bank's manager, Smith, sat on top of the 2 tonne safe when riding the raft. The Maoris called him 'Jacky Box Smith' after that. Though business was slow in the beginning, the Union Bank had the field to itself in New Zealand till the Colonial Bank of Issue was set up in June 1850 and the Oriental Bank Corporation in August 1857. The Union Bank, since 1951 part of ANZ, remained an important bank in New Zealand.

The head start in Australia and New Zealand stood the 'Asia and the Union Bank in good stead in 1893, when they remained open while 54 of the 64 deposit-taking banks closed. However, this experience made them so conservative and averse to risk that, from second and third position in 1890, they fell to near the bottom of the league of banks by 1939.

Their conservatism was further worsened by their highly centralised administration, with decisions being made in London. The directors had little personal contact with their executives in Melbourne and measured the health of their organisations by the extent of their international business and dividends. The directors injected little fresh capital and stood apart from the bank mergers between 1917 and 1931. The banks also lost out because they were seen as foreign banks. While business had moved from the rural areas to the cities, the 'Asia and the Union Bank branches remained concentrated in country towns. The two banks also failed to diversify into lucrative fields like hire purchase, for, as Merrett points out, they saw hire purchase as a 'grave and increasing menace' (Merrett, 1985: 37).

In 1929, the 'Asia and the Union Bank first started thinking that it would be a good idea to merge. Overtures from Australian banks were spurned, mainly because it would mean shifting headquarters from London to Australia. The directors of both the British banks saw great advantages to their institutions and themselves if the two banks merged. The merger finally came about only in 1951, and they formed the Australia and New Zealand Bank Ltd (ANZ).

The new ANZ was now second only to the Bank of New South Wales. However, it soon began losing market share as it took longer to cope with the post 1945 regulatory constraints. Profits fell, and in 1956 and 1957 the directors had to consider cutting the dividend. This jolted them into brushing up the local administration and opening a savings bank in 1956. Soon after, the bank cautiously moved into hire purchase. The 1960s were more profitable, and the board was willing to spend more to expand the business. The bank opened 127 branches in the cities and suburbs between 1961 and 1967.

Through the 1950s and 1960s, the ANZ Bank had looked at merging with ES&A. It was a good fit, for it was British. It was the second-smallest bank in Australia but had a profitable hire purchase business. ES&A in the meantime had been approached by the Commercial Banking Company of Sydney (CBC) and the Bank of New South Wales in 1961. It had refused both proposals to merge, for it would either be the junior partner or would be swallowed up and lose identity. Then the Chartered Bank approached it, wanting to use it as its vehicle to enter the Australian market. It was a good deal from everybody's point of view, so the directors agreed to go with the Chartered in 1962. However, the Australian Treasury did not give permission, for the policy at the time was against the entry of foreign banks. Though it would have been one British bank taking over another British bank, the government hesitated to establish a precedent. In the end, the only real suitor left was ANZ. However, ES&A exacted a good price and advantageous terms for its staff. It was more like ES&A taking over ANZ, rather than the other way around. Though ES&A was half the size of ANZ, it was the ES&A chief executive, H. McE. Scambler, who became managing director of the new ANZ Banking Group in 1970, and ES&A executives have been very visible at the top ever since.

The next important date for the group is 1976, for that is when the headquarters of the group shifted from London to Melbourne. A London headquarters was increasingly becoming a liability, as tax rates were higher in the United Kingdom. Moreover, with the falling value of sterling and inability to transfer it freely to Australia, the bank was being restricted in its operations. It had its capital in one currency and its business in another. Bailey said, 'After the war, these English-based banks were fighting with one hand tied behind their backs.' So in 1976, London became an outpost of Melbourne for the very first time. A further addition to the ANZ came in 1979 when it took over the troubled Bank of Adelaide, in a rescue orchestrated by the Reserve Bank of Australia.

Bailey returned from London in 1980 to become assistant general manager, branch banking. Talk of deregulation was already in the air, and local banks were preparing strategies to cope with a more competitive environment and the possible entry of foreign banks. For a while, it seemed that ANZ was being thwarted in every direction. In 1981,

ANZ first sought to merge with the Commercial Bank of Australia Ltd, but it lost out when the Bank of New South Wales increased its offer price for that bank; the two became Westpac Banking Corporation. Then ANZ made a play for the Commercial Banking Company of Sydney (CBC), but this bank went with the National Bank of Australasia instead, to become the National Australia Bank.

There were no more trading banks to take over in Australia, so it tried the international route. In 1981, Grindlays, at the time jointly owned by Citibank and Lloyds, was on the market. ANZ and Westpac both looked at it and rejected it. Then ANZ looked at banks in California, but judged them too expensive. It then made an unsuccessful bid for Dao Heng Bank, owned by Grindlays in Hong Kong.

So ANZ chose to expand its non-bank activities in Australia and acquired companies to go into the fund management business, nominee and trustee operations, broking and merchant banking. It pushed ahead internationally by increasing its representation to fourteen countries. Nevertheless, with deregulation nearly on the bank, it had to be bigger, to compete with the foreign banks.

Buying Grindlays: a lemon or a gem?

By 1983, ANZ was in a bit of a hole. Then Grindlays again became a consideration, for it had restructured with Citibank in control. John Milne, then chief executive of the group, and Paul Rizzo, then general manager, international, dropped in on Citibank while they were in New York, attending a banking forum. They found that Grindlays was for sale.

Secret negotiations started in the first quarter of 1984. Soon after, John Milne fell ill, leaving Reg Nicolson in charge of the international front. He led a team that included Paul Rizzo, David Craig, then financial controller, and Bob Townsend, senior manager, strategic planning. They made secret visits to London over the next few months, taking care to travel in separate planes and book in at the Savoy instead of their usual hotel, Grosvenor House. By June the decision was made: ANZ would purchase Grindlays.

One day before the bank had scheduled a press conference to announce the decision, *The Age* broke the story on 13 June 1984, headlining it 'ANZ's $1 billion bid'. So the bank hurriedly called a press conference for the same day and revealed that it had bought Grindlays for $A282 million. The bank also declared a rights issue to help to finance the purchase. The purchase was completed in September 1984. With this, ANZ again became the second-largest bank in Australia in terms of assets, a position it had held off and on in its history. It also acquired a presence in 45 countries, and the ANZ network represented 70 per cent of Australia's trading operations.

Though the bank saw the Grindlays purchase as an important strategic move, converting it to an international bank with a significant

Asian presence, the market felt that ANZ had purchased a lemon. Not only was ANZ doing something unusual, going out to buy an international bank, but also with this purchase it was going to be stuck with considerable third-world debt. Even though ANZ said that the exposure was 'modest', the share price fell by 25 per cent in the 6 weeks after the purchase. ANZ shares continued to trade below the banks' finance index for another 2 and a quarter years, till September 1986.

Bailey is one of the impassioned defenders of the strategic value of the Grindlays purchase. He cites the importance of having an international network for becoming a relationship bank to multinational companies in Europe. Senior executives give their own examples of how a branch in Europe feeds another in Africa, China or the Middle East. However, none of this translates into a figure that can be cited. Whatever figures are available show that Grindlays did not mean much profit for the group till 1987/88. Its international assets, for all their networking, yield lower returns than the bank's domestic assets.

Bailey said that they knew what they were buying in 1984 and that they expected some of the problems. Speaking in Melbourne in July 1987, he said:

> We knew Grindlays would be some pain upfront. We knew Grindlays had been through a difficult period, constrained by being owned by two other major banks [Citibank and Lloyds] with whom it was in competition. We knew that in the last decade of its operations it had made a number of acquisitions and one could question some of them. What we didn't know was that oil prices would drop as dramatically as they did. This had a savage impact on Grindlays' business in the shipping portfolio, and in particular the Middle East, and I suppose a follow-on effect on third-world debt.

The third-world debt has also proved to be more difficult than ANZ thought. The provisions for this debt have moved steadily upwards. In 1987/88, the bank provided for 37 per cent of its $1.4 billion debt to rescheduling countries and declared itself satisfied. In 1988/89, the provisioning rose to 61 per cent of the debt. In the first few years, this depressed the market value of the bank and reduced its profits.

From 1984 to 1987, the return on average shareholders' funds plumeted from 17.7 per cent in 1984 to 13.1 per cent in 1987. Only in 1988 did this start rising again, to reach 15.1 per cent. In 1989, it very much depends on what profit figure one takes. Post-tax profit before the third-world debt provisions of $221 million, which have been treated as an abnormal charge, give a return of 17.2 per cent. Deducting the abnormal charge, the return on average shareholders' funds in 1989 goes down to 12.3 per cent.

More than five years down the track, one can say that ANZ has profitably digested Grindlays. It is hard, however, to calculate what Grindlays has cost the bank in terms of lost opportunities. It is also hard to ascertain the net cost of the Grindlays' purchase. Because many of the Grindlays operations have not remained distinct, it is not possible to tell the costs from the published accounts.

But in March 1990 the strategic value of Grindlays' international network was clearly reflected in the accounts. Faced with rising bad debts in the worsening domestic economy, the bank's international assets, for the first time, were more profitable than its Australian and New Zealand assets. The international operations yielded 37.9 per cent of the banking group's profits, while accounting for 22.1 per cent of its risk weighted assets.

Walking the tightrope

All the major private Australian banks are now international in scope — this has been one of the results of deregulation — but ANZ is the only banking group that is trying to run an Australian international bank from Melbourne. This comes with two specific challenges: it has to use the pluses of its international network, and at the same time it has to have a strong base in Australia and New Zealand. To some degree this is true of every international bank; but alone among the major Australian banks, ANZ also has to deal with the spectre of cultural problems and inherited bureaucracies.

An Australian international bank is not a difficult concept, but on the ground, it makes for conflicting images. In the modern glass and steel headquarters of ANZ at 55 Collins Street, Melbourne, it is hard to detect the international reach of the bank. Its paintings, silver, and tapestries in the boardroom reflect its London connections. There is little to suggest that this is the group that owns the largest foreign bank in India, has the most extensive network of all Australian banks in South and Southeast Asia, and has significant representation in the Middle East and Africa. The senior staff at the headquarters, however, remain predominantly Australian, with a few from New Zealand and the UK.

It makes commercial sense to stress the local image of the bank in Australia, for in 1988/89 Australia and New Zealand comprised 77 per cent of the group's profit before abnormal items. In March 1990 this came down to 62.1 per cent. But Bailey is very aware that ANZ's legitimacy in the global market rests on ANZ's being a major domestic bank in Australia and New Zealand. He said in Melbourne in March 1988, that is what distinguishes ANZ from other international banks like Standard Chartered and Hongkong and Shanghai Banking Corporation: 'If we are going to be successful in the international network type of business we are after, we need to be very strong in Australian business markets.'

Traditionally, ANZ has been strong in corporate relationships. Bailey said, in March 1988:

> We still claim to be the prime banker to one-third of the major companies in Australia. On information we have, we are a close second in middle-sized business banking. We've got a very good share of the relationship type banking, with people of professional background. Our Achilles heel, you might say, has been mass market banking. Our national banking share is 21, 22 per cent, but our mass market share is about 15 per cent.

This represented a significant decline. Bailey said, if one takes all the four core banks of the group — the Bank of Australasia, the Union Bank, ES&A and the Bank of Adelaide — these banks had about 30 per cent of the market share of Australian banking:

> In aggregate, we probably would have had the biggest market share in Australia. Progressively over the next 20 years, we tended to lose market share. In fact, when we merged in 1970 with ES&A, it was generally accepted in the bank that we would lose 3 per cent of combined market share; but in a regulated environment, your ability to grow market share was dependent on somebody else losing it.

With deregulation, the beginning was made to grow market share. This has a cost in finer margins and less profit. 'We accepted that. From 1985 onwards, we have been successful in growing market share. We've got it back in balance now,' he said in March 1988, referring to the two different strategies of growing market share and maximising profits — for ultimately, the success of the bank will depend on the profits it makes. Will Bailey said, 'The fact we are growing in more recent times gives us confidence that we haven't got it all wrong. But I know full well, we haven't got it all right.'

In order to have all sides of the bank moving full steam, the bank was reorganised shortly after Bailey took over:

> I had one of the very senior people in the bank, totally responsible for looking after Australian retail banking. He had as much discretion in running that as my predecessor had in running the entire bank. It was the classic case of very sizeable delegation. His job was to grow our bank in Australia. Another colleague had the job of supervising the rationalising of Grindlays.

The same thing was happening to their stockbroking and insurance operations. This left Will Bailey looking at strategy 10 years ahead.

Bailey said that, when planning the strategy of the bank, one of the first things they did was to:

> . . . sit down and ask, What is our strategy? What is our culture? What do we do best? Knowing our culture, it is no good our saying we want to be the biggest mass market bank. We've got to build on our strengths and retain a balance between our domestic and international resources. We found that, because of our roots as a colonial bank from London, we have always had an emphasis on business and international banking. We did it well. So our culture and that of Grindlays, a colonial bank — they fit.

In buying Grindlays, ANZ also bet that South and Southeast Asia will be increasingly important to the future of the group. The jewel in the Grindlays' crown is the very profitable Indian operations. Speaking of it in July 1987, Bailey waxed eloquent on the importance of India:

> People get wildly excited about the future potential of China. They ought to start getting wildly excited about the future potential of India. It's got better infrastructure, better communications, better education, and it's got a lot of entrepreneurs in the country.

With the Grindlays network they are well positioned:

> . . . to be able to share in what happens to the country. Now that's an enormous advantage. We've got people who know the culture, know the people; indigenous staff who like working for us, and they are doing well for us. That's an invaluable asset. We've got it repeated in Bangladesh, we've got it in Pakistan, we've got it in parts of Africa like Zimbabwe. They are not fashionable countries from a Western cultural point of view, but there's going to be one awful lot of business going on there in the next 50 years. And we're there. I would prefer to be there, thank you, for the future of this organisation than trying to develop business in terribly mature markets.

Fortunately for ANZ, they have had to do little reorganisation in South Asia, the Middle East and Africa, the regions culturally most different from Australia and New Zealand. Because ANZ was not represented in these areas, the problems of merging branches and rationalising operations did not arise. These problems came up in London, New York, Canada, Tokyo, Singapore and Hong Kong. For the most part, South Asia, the Middle East and Africa were self-funding, with the Middle East being a net exporter of funds. So ANZ could afford initially to leave the status quo undisturbed. These regions are still administered from London.

In India, the bank continues with the Grindlays' name, profiting from the 150-year-old relationship. There is little popular perception that now Grindlays is owned by an Australian group, and Grindlays in India is still seen very much as a British bank. However, there have been a few tentative steps to introducing the ANZ corporate identity in India. The popular Grindlays' elephant that was the symbol of the bank has been replaced with the ANZ graphic logo. However, the cultural sensitivities are so great that the demise of the elephant is seen by some senior staff as a measure of Australian insensitivity to Grindlays' position in India.

There is also some feeling that ANZ is not devoting enough time to India. Akhilesh Mittal, adviser to Grindlays Bank in India, said in New Delhi in December 1988, 'We still have a ricochet type of relationship. We look to London, which looks to Australia.' He also made a point of mentioning that Will Bailey has visited India only once since 1984 and that there are no Indians in the group's top management echelons in Australia. At this, Will Bailey pointed out that his deputy, Reg Nicolson, has visited India many times — also that an Indian was offered a top managerial position at headquarters, but declined the move.

A positive aspect of ANZ's ownership of Grindlays in India has been that the group invested $24 million between 1986 and 1988 in modernising and computerising the branches in India. A software house has been set up in Bangalore to help to develop software for ANZ's global information systems.

The stickiest part of the merger throughout has been London. There have been regulatory restrictions that require Grindlays as a bank to remain open, but ANZ also want its name in the marketplace, so both ANZ and Grindlays have branches in London. There were union problems to be sorted out with the merger of the two banks. ANZ had to totally cut away the headquarters function of the Grindlays' London office. However, one of the sensitive points lay in history. Instead of London directing an Australian bank, it was now Melbourne telling a London bank what to do. Bailey said in July 1987, 'When you are from Australia, moving in on a bank based in London, a lot of people assume people from Australia don't know as much as people from London. I had no doubt that we could run the thing and that we would do it our way, but our way is different to the ways of London.'

What also made the situation in London more tricky was a change of policy as to how Grindlays was to be handled. When ANZ bought Grindlays Bank in September 1984, the idea was that Grindlays would continue to operate as a semi-autonomous unit from London. However, this policy changed when Bailey took over as chief executive in November 1984. By March 1985, the amalgamation of Grindlays and ANZ was in progress. Bailey said that, if he had been chief executive at the time of purchase:

> We would have still bought Grindlays when we did. But instead of waiting till the following March to really start to put ANZ's hand on it, we would have grabbed it in both arms and loved it to death very quickly. You look at the history of bank acquisitions. The ones that have been successful are where the new owner goes in quickly, puts his arms right around it, finds out what's there and really jumps straight in.

So there was a turnaround in policy with Grindlays. Instead of leaving it to operate as an independent unit, it operated very much as part of the ANZ group.

So interestingly enough, the problems with acquiring an international network have been more organisational than cultural. It is not that ANZ has been particularly astute culturally; it is more that it has been fortunate enough not to have to chop and change too much initially in the culturally different regions of its network. So with much less pain than anyone could have forecast, ANZ can advertise in Australia, 'The world is our workplace. But this is our home.'

However, the race is not yet over at home. The three major private banks are each investing in technology to give them an edge. With the other banks making great claims for their computer systems, which allow them to design their products and direct them to the most likely customers, for a while it seemed as though ANZ was lagging behind. However, the bank's technology people feel that their combination of the HOGAN system, and the Teradata specialised data-processing system, will be a faster and more flexible way of processing millions of records. The customer information system is expected to be completed in late 1990. At the very least, it gives them a base from which they can move ahead.

Chief executive of a financial services holding company

'I'm not a practising banker,' Will Bailey said in October 1987 in Melbourne. 'I am the chief executive of a financial services holding company.' His claim was technically true as the ANZ group included funds management, life insurance and stockbroking. But in 1987, 91.9 per cent of the group's operating profit came from its banking and finance company arms. In 1990, however, Will Bailey may have been able to make the claim with greater credibility.

On Monday 2 April 1990, Will Bailey and Eric Mayer, managing director of National Mutual Life Association of Australasia (the second largest insurance company in Australia) announced their intention to merge. The new group would become the largest financial institution in the country, with $91 billion in assets and $39 billion under management. It would be the most significant merger of banking and insurance in the world, creating the ANZ-NM Banking and Insurance Group Ltd, a group with about 60 000 staff and agents in more than 50 countries.

The bare bones of the deal were as follows: National Mutual would change from a company limited by guarantee to a company limited by shares and guarantee. It would issue shares representing 51 per cent of the company. ANZ would buy 51 per cent of National Mutual for $A3.4 billion, and would be the only shareholder.

On 2 April, ANZ also bought the National Mutual Royal Bank for close to $400 million. This bank was 50 per cent owned by National Mutual and 50 per cent by the Royal Bank of Canada. The agreement was that if the merger was disallowed, the National Mutual Royal Bank would revert to National Mutual.

The proposed merger took the market by surprise, for till then speculation had rested on possible bank mergers. In 1988, ANZ had publicly aired its interest in the Commonwealth Bank of Australia, when it was thought the Commonwealth Bank would be privatised. In 1989, it bought PostBank in New Zealand to increase its share of the New Zealand market. Moreover in the last quarter of 1989, after a fit of denials, both Will Bailey and Nobby Clark of the National Australia

Bank confirmed that they had been looking at the possibility of merging and revealed that the two banks had significant cross-shareholdings in each other.

While the public speculated about likely bank mergers, Will Bailey and Eric Mayer were already advanced enough in discussions of a merger between their organisations to mention the possibility to the Treasurer in September 1989. In October 1989, the Treasurer ruled out mergers between the four major banks. Though this did not kill all speculation about bank mergers, Bailey said in April 1990 in his Melbourne office that it did show that 'windows of opportunity for bank-bank mergers have disappeared for the time being'.

In mid-April 1990, Will Bailey and Eric Mayer were confident the deal would be approved by the regulatory authorities and the policy holders. However, on 23 May 1990, Treasurer Paul Keating vetoed the merger for it 'would be contrary to the national interest' (*Financial Review*, 24 May 1990: 4). He went on to effectively disallow any merger of a large bank or insurance company with another large bank or insurance company. The preferred option for growth was to take over the smaller players or grow the business from scratch. In Keating's scheme of things, the financial services industry could best be served by maintaining the status quo of four large banks and two large insurance companies.

Though the merger of ANZ and National Mutual has been disallowed, financial institutions will still have to cope with the structural shifts in the savings pattern and the selling of financial services that were propelling the merger in the first place.

Bailey spoke at length about these two structural shifts in April 1990 in an hour long interview. The key factor behind the changes, he said, was the 1986 wage settlement where the Treasurer and the Trade Union movement negotiated the establishment of superannuation funds for workers as a clear goal. 'Straight after that announcement,' he said, 'we had a think about this and saw that the savings patterns of Australia will have to change considerably in the next decade ... We perceived that if the Treasurer is nearly right — and there is going to be $600 billion in investments in fund management, life insurance and superannuation in the next 10 years, — being able to grow to the size necessary from a small start was beyond us.'

In an attempt to grow faster in these areas, ANZ first looked at the option of acquiring smaller life companies. But in May 1989, after hearing that National Mutual might be thinking of a relationship with a large bank, Will Bailey approached Eric Mayer. The timing was fortunate for, as Mayer said in Melbourne in April 1990, National Mutual had recognised it needed to merge with a major bank if it were to gain the capital necessary to become a significant, diversified and international financial services group.

With the savings pattern changing, Bailey said, banks had to think again about their role:

> Governments were takers from the system with deficits. They are now providers. Corporates have been takers for a long while. The household sector for banking were providers for funds. In a couple of years, they are going to be takers.
>
> Ten years ago, you got a pension, but it wasn't enough, so you had a nest egg to go with it. In the new equation you will be able to get a home loan linked to your superannuation. If your shelter is covered, health requirements are covered (with Medicare), the only thing (you) have to worry about is clothes, food and leisure. None of them really require much savings except the 12 month holiday. Savings patterns are going to change. People are going to accumulate for short periods of time then blow the lot and save again. People are (soon) going to be borrowing for their annual holidays and they don't even have to save for that.
>
> We ought to be thinking of how we tuck into the savings of the community. They are not in what was traditional banking. Whether this deal comes off or not, in the minds of the community and the institutions operating in the community, they are no longer going to focus on banking as banking, they are going to focus on financial services. The goal posts have changed. If we pull this off, I think the most exciting thing is we are going to be positioned in the main stream where the arbitrage of the savings takes place. We are staying where we always have been, between borrowers and lenders.
>
> As the aggregation of personal savings moves to superannuation, you'll find savings banks will hold less of the community's savings. That will mean savings banks will have less funds to invest in home loans. So savings banks may become packagers of loan products. In other words they will arrange a loan for the customer, have it securitised and sell the securities to the market.
>
> Now who are going to be the holders of those securities? The life companies will be the people with the money.

The merger would have positioned ANZ–NM Banking and Insurance Group Ltd at both ends of the spectrum. Though, to the parties, this was one of the most attractive aspects of the merger, the same point may have seemed less desirable to the regulators. For if a group is to be both buyer and seller, who is to protect the rights of the depositors and the policy-holders? Bailey did not see this as a stumbling block, for he said banks previously have successfully run insurance operations and insurance companies have satisfactorily operated banks.

If this merger had gone through, it would have resulted in a different kind of financial service. According to Mayer, the cooperation between a bank and life office would 'enhance the services' that each is providing its customers. He did not think this would translate into a financial supermarket:

> I don't see the one stop financial shopper. I think that is a nonsense. That is not how people are behaving. I think people react to high quality service. And I think this group is going to be able to excel in service across a very wide range.

A major cultural difference between the bank and the life company is that banks generally service their clients in the bank, whereas the life company sells through agents who visit clients at home.

Bailey said banks will 'have to come to terms' with using the external sales force of the life company.

> We will hopefully have National Mutual agents selling ANZ bank products, or certainly introducing to our bank, people who can borrow certain bank products. We have gone through a whole range of bank products which life insurance agents will find useful to sell in combination with life insurance.

He thought this injection of new sales methods will be good for banks, for 'banks are furiously trying to get their managers to be salesmen. And here we are talking of an organisation that has got a hell of a sales culture.'

Bailey thought this cultural change was achievable. Drawing on his experience as a branch manager in a Victorian country town trying to expand business 30 years ago, he knows that seeking reciprocity from the key insurance company people in town can be beneficial. He told the representatives of a life insurance business and a general insurance company that he would refer business to them if they would put their term deposits with the bank. This worked so well that his bank branch became the largest individual bank branch holder in Australia of the two companies' term deposits outside the major cities. Bailey said:

> This convinced me then there was an affinity. When someone came in and wanted a loan from me, I would ask them questions about their insurance on their farm or property. How would they handle it if they fell ill? In most cases, I was able to say, here's a gentleman, here's his card, you give him a ring and get him to look after you. The customers knew they were being protected ... It wasn't hard to work out that the customer won, the life company won, the general insurance company won and the bank won. My branch profits exploded.

Keating was obviously not impressed. His veto of the merger appeared to take both ANZ and National Mutual by surprise, revealing at the very least that they were not in tune with the political dimensions of their proposal. However, a week later, after some hitches, both institutions announced their second-best solution. ANZ bought the National Mutual Royal Bank and secured an increased representation in NSW. That is, National Mutual did not exercise its right to take the National Mutual Royal Bank back. In addition, ANZ bought National Mutual's banking operations in New Zealand.

ANZ further maintained connection with National Mutual by committing itself to buy 10 per cent of any future share issue by National Mutual. In addition it made available $550 million to National Mutual as subordinated loan capital. This will be convertible to shares, subject to regulatory approval. Moreover ANZ and National Mutual will investigate permissible cross-marketing options in Australia and New Zealand. This gives the bank a connection with superannuation and the life office access to some increased capital. Whether ANZ will succeed via this route in getting hold of superannuation savings and shaking up the selling of financial services remains to be seen.

If the merger had gone through, Will Bailey and Eric Mayer would have had to deal with the cultural differences between the two organisations and the management problems that emerge in conglomerates. They would also have had to ensure that all the anticipated cost savings and benefits actually did flow through. These factors have historically been the undoing of conglomerates. For the moment, both the advantages and potential problems of the merger have been shelved. But one wonders if the holiday Bailey had planned to take after the merger, ever did come through.

6 Going retail: the National Australia Bank

The National Australia Bank is Australia's most successful retail bank. In 1989, about three-fourths of its profits came from its retail operations. The bank has the lowest costs and the highest returns on average equity and assets. Slow at first to expand overseas, its international operations are based on retail networks, unlike Westpac; and differing from the Australia and New Zealand Banking Group (ANZ) its international expansion has been regional and in countries culturally similar to Australia. This emphasis on domestic and regional retail has been a winner with the markets. Though it is the third-largest bank in terms of assets and second-largest in terms of risk weighted assets in March 1990, it has regularly been priced higher than its major competitors.

A frugal culture

Nobby Clark, 61, the bank's managing director since 1985, thinks that a whole lot of little things go to make the retail bank efficient and keep the costs down. Dressed in a grey suit with a red tie and a matching red handkerchief, sitting in his office in Melbourne in April 1988 with a rooftop view of the city's suburban sprawl, he said:

> Our culture is frugal . . . I drive myself to work. I don't have a chauffeur. When I don't have a chauffeur, I'm setting a culture. The managers might be careful too. When I travel overseas, I travel on weekends. I have just a modest hotel room, not a suite . . . I always travel first class. A little bit profligate there.

In his personal style too, Nobby Clark and his wife are not ostentatious. In 1987, they lived in a comfortable house with a pool in Mt

Nobby Clark, managing director, National Australia Bank (courtesy National Australia Bank)

Waverly, about 20 minutes from the city. In 1987, when I visited, one of his neighbours was a plumber; another had a printing outfit. Talking of himself in his Melbourne office in July 1987, he said, 'We still live a very simple lifestyle. We don't go out much at all. We meet our social responsibilities. We go to the theatre occasionally.' After a 7 a.m. to 7 p.m. working day, he is usually too tired at the end of the day. 'The bank is what I've known for 41 years, but when I go home, I switch off. I'm able to enjoy my family. I don't have many friends. Mainly because I don't have the time to enjoy them. The last seven weekends for instance, I've been on bank business.' At their home in July 1987, his wife Peggy commented that, if Nobby hadn't been a banker, he would have been a builder. In his spare time, while leading the bank, he has laid tiles for the kitchen. He likes gardening, especially pruning trees with the recently acquired chain saw, and an occasional game of golf. He cooks very good Chinese food and likes making omelettes.

His life revolves around his work and family. Married with two children, Clark said bankers generally have strong family units. 'We usually come from reasonably common-garden-variety type of people, and we've had to travel together. We've had to uplift, break relationships with friends and neighbours together.'

Though Nobby Clark thinks of himself as a frugal simple person, in the bank his style is at times seen as flamboyant. He has projected himself and the bank very effectively on the national stage, often taking issue with government policy. As, Clark said:

> Perhaps I am a little noisier than the others, for I think that governments occasionally need people who articulate a reasonable criticism. The reason that I talk about things is that I believe we should debate issues more in the community. I just think we don't get enough debate going.

Nobby Clark joined the bank in 1946, aged 16 and a half. For Clark and his parents, the bank meant 'a good, safe, secure job'. His father was a travelling salesman who sold machines and had been through the 1930s Depression. Clark did not consider any other options: 'There wasn't much available in 1946. It was the end of the war, and many industries were required to take back those who had left to go to the war. It was only institutions like banks and insurance companies who were looking for young people.'

His first year in the bank, he remembers:

> . . . was like something out of Charles Dickens. Very structured, very formal. Everything was done in pen and ink. There was a lot of blue ink and red ink and blotting paper. The nibs and the blotting paper had to be changed in the banking chamber each day. Inkwells filled. It was the way banking had been done for probably 50 or 60 years. There were high ledger desks. People stood up or sat on high stools. They wore alpaca coats while they worked — alpaca is a shiny sort of material — and a dress hat. It was just part of the formal dress of the day. We worked on Saturday mornings. Even on Saturday mornings, even as a junior, one wore a suit. I didn't have to wear a hat being a young person. But the older people all wore hats.

It was a very formal environment: 'Everyone was called Mr so and so. I was Mr Clark.' He laughs at that now. 'Later, when the people came out of the services, it became less formal, less structured and more democratic.' It was then that he acquired his name Nobby, his wife explained. His real name is Neil Rex Clark, but now only his mother and relatives call him Neil. Everybody else calls him Nobby. The way it happened is that when the men came back from the war, they asked him what his name was. He said, 'Clark'. Traditionally in England, clerks had taken the name Clark or Clarke. As they were educated, they were generally the wealthy and the local nobs. Hence the common nickname, Nobby. So the response that day was 'You're Nobby' and it was Nobby from then on.

He lived at home in Bankstown, about 20 kilometres from Sydney, and travelled by train each day. 'I think I got about 30 shillings a week. It wasn't very much. I used to pay Mum a pound a week board. I don't charge my children board, but in those days it was usual. Mum would have been subsidising my living. One pound a week would not have covered my food and so forth.' After spending 5 shillings a week for the train ticket, he felt quite rich with the remaining 5 shillings a week:

> One learnt the job at the desk in those days. There were no formal training programmes. For instance, while I was a junior at York Street in Sydney, I wrote up the passbooks. So you learnt speed, writing figures underneath each other, adding up. It gave you accuracy in reading a figure and transposing it to another medium. That was really what it was all about. Then you understudied the ledger keeper, and he would show you how to dedicate the signatures, see that the cheques were regularly drawn and not

postdated. You take an interest in things. Somebody would ask, Do you want to learn this? And you'd say yes, and stay the half hour.

By 23 he was a ledger keeper, had acquired a hat and was earning probably 5 pounds a week, paying 3 pounds a week board. The next big step was to become an accountant in Haymarket, and later an accountant in Canberra. By this time he had a banking degree, for which he had studied on his own.

He was married before then, in 1956. At first they stayed with his parents, to save up for a house deposit: 'We bought a house in Sydney by the sea, a weatherboard house about twelve squares.' Peggy added that it did not remain twelve squares for long, for Nobby kept extending it. When they moved to Canberra, they were given a bank house meant for the accountant. Peggy said, 'It had wooden floors, so we finally bought a rug, always keeping in mind what would fit into our house in Sydney.'

After 2 years in Canberra, in 1962, 16 years after he had joined the National, Nobby Clark won his first managerial appointment: to become branch manager at Rabaul, Papua New Guinea. At the time, it was an Australian protectorate and belonged to the NSW division of the bank. Clark did not 'particularly' want to go. 'But in those days you didn't pop back your first management appointment,' he said, 'because if you did, you probably wouldn't get another chance. Not for a while.'

Though the procedures and currency were Australian, the customs were different. Indigenous customers:

> . . . usually banked 3 shillings. Things were very cheap. And a shilling was a good unit of saving, for it did not disintegrate with mildew and rot because of the wet weather and the very high humidity. And the old shilling had a hole through the middle of it. They could string it and wear it as jewellery round the neck, or put a shilling in each ear.
>
> I came from a more urbane, a more sophisticated environment and was not really prepared for this. But you get used to it. We had a small but diverse business. A lot of it related to the export of cocoa and coffee, timber and crocodile skins, mother-of-pearl and tortoiseshell.

Peggy still remembers after all these years that there were 48 kilometres of road in Rabaul and that was as far as you could drive:

> Every cocktail, you met people from the other banks, the insurance companies and the local chemist. . . . Adjusting to the houseboy and the wash-and-iron boy took a bit of getting used to, but I realised you must have them, for in that climate men changed shirts three or four times a day. But the houseboy was like another child in the house. I had to watch him all the time. He would take the lawn mower apart, the vacuum cleaner apart.
>
> I used to write to friends about all the small things that happened, but then I stopped, thinking they won't believe this. . . . You could always tell a new lady, because her legs would be bandaged as she had scratched her sandfly bites.

She had her second child in Rabaul. There was just a tin shed for a hospital and an old retired lady doctor. Peggy and Nobby think that she developed an allergic reaction to an antimalarial drug. Their daughter was born moderately retarded. Nobby said this without preamble, adding that she is a lovely person and an integral part of the family.

After Rabaul, he became manager of Newtown, an inner suburb of Sydney. It felt good to be manager in his home state. 'It was a nice little branch. You got to know your customers very well.' After 3 and a half years there, he moved on to staff jobs in Sydney.

In these 6 years he did his Bachelor of Commerce degree from the University of New South Wales: 'It was very difficult. My wife didn't see me for 6 years virtually. Three evenings a week you go to university, other nights you'd be studying.' Peggy also remembers it as a trying time: 'The worst was keeping the children quiet when he would go to the little cupboard he studied in.' Nobby said:

> I found that at that stage, bank work was not offering much challenge. While it was interesting and kept me busy during the day, I found that my mind wasn't being extended. The university certainly opened up my mind to new concepts, management theory and management accounting, and economics in a more extensive sense. It was very worthwhile. When I passed through that, the bank also took a greater interest in me. So to have done a degree in which I had very good results might have helped to identify me as a person with a high potential. Then I started to get a quicker progression.

In 1976, he was posted to Melbourne and put in charge of the bank's computer system. The bank's philosophy was that the computer system should be directed by someone who knew the bank's needs, rather than just the technical aspect of the computer. This exposure was to prove important to him when he had to make some of the technological decisions for the development of the bank. After 2 and a half years, he moved to South Australia and then, after another 2 years, back to Melbourne. Soon after, he became involved with the McKinsey & Co. restructuring of the trading bank into retail and corporate banking. Branches were given more autonomy, with marketing becoming more important. This too was hands-on experience, as bank officers worked together with the McKinsey staff in reorganising bank structure.

In 1980, Nobby was appointed the first assistant general manager, retail and financial services. 'I was stunned,' he said. 'I had no idea I would be that person. I loved it. I went home and my wife and I celebrated. We had a bottle of beer with our dinner.'

In July 1985, he became chief executive of the bank. Talking of this 2 years later, he paused for a while and said that what really moved him about becoming chief executive was that 'Mum, who is 79, told me 3 months ago, for the first time, that she's very proud of me.'

For Peggy, the appointment meant that she got to travel abroad for the first time since Rabaul. They went to Seoul together for the 1985 World Bank and International Monetary Fund meeting. She enjoyed it. There was a lady from El Salvador sitting next to her, who showed her the eelskin heels she had bought and told how much they had cost. 'Women are the same everywhere,' Peggy said. She herself bought a small celadon vase and a piece of silk.

Don Argus: 'sitting number two'

Nobby Clark is to retire in 1990. Don Argus, 52, who became executive director of the bank in February 1989 and chief operating officer of the bank and member of the board in November 1989, is the nominated successor.

Asked in December 1989 whether being a chief executive in waiting was a difficult or delicate situation, Argus replied, 'Not hard at all.' Sitting in his office on the thirty-fifth floor of the bank's Melbourne headquarters, dressed in a white shirt and a red tie, he qualified this response, adding, 'I am a sitting number two, but you can never be sure of things till the number goes up on the board.' He said that getting to the number two position, just 'seemed to evolve', with the exposure that he was being given. 'It just didn't happen overnight. Mr Clark doesn't like surprises and doesn't like surprising people.' Asked whether there had been any champagne or beer or a night out in town to celebrate his reaching the number two spot, Argus said:

> It's not my character. I have had a lot of setbacks I suppose with sport [referring to his experience with international hockey] . . . You learn to live with the highs and lows. Those things harden you a little. I suppose whatever will be will be. It was nice. I went home and had a meal with my family, which was something different. I don't get too many meals with my family.

Interestingly enough, both Don Argus and Nobby Clark live in Mt Waverly, a suburb not particularly known as a bankers' haunt. Argus said, 'We live opposite the park. It is the first house we found when we came down to Melbourne', which was more than 10 years ago. This was the thirteenth house they had lived in since getting married, and he said, 'My wife said, "Don't ask me to move another house."'

Argus, like Clark, is a career banker with all his experience in the National Australia Bank. He joined the bank in 1955 at 16 years old and did the retail circuit in Queensland. In 1978, he moved to corporate banking in Melbourne, going on to hold managerial positions in that area. His last two positions were as general manager of the bank's credit bureau and, after that, as general manager, group strategic planning.

Argus's career path has been even more traditional than Clark's, for he does not have a university degree. However, he did his Australian Institute of Bankers' course at the Royal Melbourne Institute of Tech-

Don Argus, chief operating officer, National Australia Bank (courtesy National Australia Bank)

nology, and in 1988 he went to Harvard for 3 months to attend its Advanced Course. Argus said, 'When I finished school, in Queensland, you only had one university. You didn't get too many Queenslanders who went on and did their tertiary degree. In those days, you weren't really educated to want to go on. The big thing was to go out and get a job as soon as you could.'

His father was managing editor of the *Gympie Times*, Gympie being a small town between Bundaberg and Brisbane in Queensland. Though Argus thought that he had a good command of English, his father dictated that he should not go into journalism, for there was no future in the newspaper industry. So with that avenue closed to him, he went with his other love — figures and mathematics — and went into banking in Brisbane.

During his early years in banking, he invested any spare cash he had in shares: 'I fancied myself as a bit of a player on the sharemarket. I remember one manager in Townsville telling me that you don't play the sharemarket unless you understand what the balance sheet is all about.' Though he didn't make a fortune on the sharemarket, the exercise started a long love affair with balance sheets:

> I'm a terribly balance-sheet-oriented person. I love balance sheets. There is a sense of history and geography in balance sheets. I make a point of reading something like 80 of the top bank balance sheets a year. And you'll find the theme of the bank, the culture of the bank in the chairman and

> chief executive's written addresses. You can learn a lot from reading those.... My wife thinks I'm nuts.

When the bank was planning to acquire the Irish and Scottish banks in 1987, Argus looked at their balance sheets:

> I can honestly say, I hadn't read too many of the Irish and Scottish balance sheets till then. I read the English clearing bank balance sheets, Midlands, Barclays and Lloyds. Those three in particular, you can get a real feel about what's happening in the economy, where the economy is going, from where they are generating their money. If there is something happening in a bank somewhere else in the world where they are generating income, then maybe you can relate that back to your own bank. You learn a lot.

This balance sheet grounding served him well when he was working in the bank's credit bureau in the mid 1980s. Commercial lending was based on the balance sheet, and the bank lent to the cashflow portion of a corporate's business. It wasn't security he was looking for. What was important was that the bank be able 'to corral a portion of cashflow'. He wanted to understand where this cashflow was going and the 'assumptions behind what was making these businesses all of a sudden cash rich when their history did not dictate that they were cash rich'. This philosophy stood the bank in good stead. Though its bad debts rose significantly in March 1990, they were below those of the other major private banks.

This emphasis on the balance sheet and cashflow meant that most of the entrepreneurs did not qualify. 'We couldn't corral a portion of the cashflow that they were generating or we couldn't see that cashflow,' Argus said. 'That strategy back in 1984, 1985 was a pretty severe sort of strategy to take. I used to get an awful hiding from the people in the field where they would say you don't know what you're doing.' That was also the time when the American merchant banks were coming in and lending very aggressively:

> They broke down the trust deeds and the covenants that we used to abide by to give some balance sheet gearing and comfort. They broke all those things down, because they were taking the front end fees and parking the debt on the bank's balance sheet. History has seen that some of the high leverage just cannot survive particularly on the type of balance sheets that existed in Australia.

The one seeming exception to this avoidance of entrepreneurs is the National's exposure to the Bond group of companies. Argus said:

> We were bankers to Castlemaine and we were bankers to Swan Brewery, and we were the second bankers to Tooheys. We were there anyhow.... Despite what the analysts would tell you, we didn't depart from what we try to put into our loan documentation. We like to corral cashflow, and we like to put covenants in there which will give us some strengths when a recovery is required. We will not lose money in the Bond group of companies.

At the end of May 1990, the National and the Bond group of companies have been in and out of court and are still to conclusively settle the issue.

In the bank, Don Argus's style is seen as lower key than Nobby Clark's. Argus agrees. He said that he probably is a more hands-on person: 'Mr Clark probably takes a higher profile on political issues. I don't think I'll get myself involved in political debate, unless there is criticism levelled at the bank. Then I won't mind having a good one for one.' This difference is probably not as great as is made out. Nobby Clark too at times has chosen to speak out only when it benefited the bank. In 1986 and 1987, he spoke out often about the injustice of having one regulated housing rate at 13.5 per cent for those who borrowed before April 1986 and a higher deregulated rate for later borrowers. He said that it was inequitable that those who had borrowed from building societies, for instance, would have to pay more than 13.5 per cent. What was also true was that the National had gone heavily into increasing its housing portfolio shortly before the rate was deregulated, so for the bank the pain was great. It is interesting, though, that in 1989, when the major banks entered into a mortgage deal with the Reserve Bank which effectively capped their home interest rate at 17 per cent, Nobby Clark was silent about the home borrowers with the building societies and the smaller banks.

The bank that missed the gold boom

For a strong retail bank, the National Australia Bank had an inauspicious start. Blainey and Hutton (1983), in their history of the bank entitled *Gold and Paper*, tell how the bank was conceived in pique by a St Kilda gentleman, Alexander James Gibb. He had promoted the Colonial Bank of Australasia in 1856, hoping to be its general manager. When that did not happen, he began promoting the similar-sounding National Bank of Australasia. With the help of a prominent Victorian merchant and another promoter in South Australia, the bank opened in Melbourne in 1858. Because of a dispute over the powers of the general manager, its shareholders unsuccessfully tried to prevent it from opening. Then for 2 years it tottered because its directors borrowed recklessly from the bank.

The bank had missed the gold boom, for gold exports from Victoria peaked in 1856, 2 years before the bank opened. So the bank opened its first branch in Echuca, a wool port on the River Murray. It failed and had to be closed down a year later, in 1859. Then the bank opened branches in the gold diggings. Few have survived. In 1859, it started an ill-fated branch in Mauritius, on the back of the sugar trade, but that branch closed with the manager making off with the money.

In South Australia, it was more successful with its branches in the coppermining towns, but its major growth was with the wheat farmers and selectors in the 1860s and 1870s, especially in South Australia and

Victoria. It became the first bank to lend formally on the security of land and houses in 1859. Before this, banks, following British practice, lent only on the security of trade bills.

It also opened in Western Australia in the late 1860s, becoming the first bank there to expand beyond Perth. However, it was bitten by bad loans connected with the railway and pulled out just 1 month before gold was discovered in Kalgoorlie in June 1893.

In 1885, it had made a token entry into NSW by opening a branch in Sydney. However, the National did not see itself as a national bank, for it had no branches in Queensland. The 1880s were years when the bank pushed out into the Melbourne suburbs and lent money to the building societies and land banks, which were fuelling the land boom.

Though conservative in its own banking policies, the 1893 crash closed it down temporarily, like most of the other banks, and put a brake on branch growth. The bank grew then first by amalgamation with Gibb's Colonial Bank of Australasia in 1918, then by merging with the Bank of Queensland in 1922. In the same year, though, it pushed back an offer to merge with the Commercial Banking Company of Sydney. There was agreement on all the material points, but the merger foundered because neither party wanted to shift headquarters. Though the mumbling in the bank was about higher tax in NSW, it had much to do with state loyalties. Blainey and Hutton note that, when Victorians crossed into NSW at Albury, they commented that even the pies in the railway car got staler.

The bank's next major move was to merge with the Queensland National Bank in 1948. With this it became the second-largest bank in Australia and the largest bank in Victoria and Queensland. It is the branch network built in its first 90 years, through expansion and merger, that provides the basis for its retail strength today.

Like all other banks, the National came under increasing regulation during the war; but in the ensuing fight against the nationalisation of banks, from 1945 to 1949, it was the National's chief executive, Sir Leslie McConnan, who led the private banks' assault against government encroachment.

In early 1981, the National Bank of Australasia had completed its internal restructuring and was in good shape to take on the challenges of the deregulation of the financial system. In May 1981, the bank announced that it was merging with the Commercial Banking Company of Sydney (CBC). The courtship first begun in 1922 was finally being consummated.

The 1981 merger was a drama in its own right. With impending deregulation and competition from foreign banks, the major banks scrambled to consolidate as much of the domestic market as possible. Westpac went with the Commercial Bank of Australia. ANZ, having lost the Commercial Bank of Australia, then bid for the CBC. Later it withdrew, when it saw that the CBC preferred to go with the National Bank of Australasia. For the National, the CBC was a particularly good fit. The CBC was strong in NSW, exactly where the National was weak. Also, as Nobby Clark said in July 1987, 'It was a good fit really in that we were both good retail commercial banks.' This more than anything else helped to make the National the strong retail bank it is today. 'Before the merger,' Clark said, 'we were just two small banks.' After it, they became second only to Westpac. When ANZ went with Grindlays Bank in 1984, Clark said, 'We were again tailing Charlie.' However, the merger had consolidated the National's massive retail network. At the end of September 1989, the bank had 1148 branches in Australia.

It was the CBC merger that gave Nobby Clark the final push to the top. He became general manager, retail and finance after the merger and then moved on to deputy chief executive in April 1985, 3 months before the previous chief executive, Jack Booth, retired.

In 1981, Nobby Clark was in charge of retail and so had to handle one of the most awkward aspects of the merger:

> I had the responsibility of putting the two biggest parts of the two banks together. We had to unify the operations of the two branch networks. Provide one set of services, have one set of systems, one set of computers. That was quite a massive job. In the retail bank we had probably 49 or 50 sets of things we had to do.
>
> There were some hard decisions to be made. We unified branches and merged business and made bigger branches. I don't think we closed many branches, if any, unless they were commercially non-viable. We still have 60 or 70 points of representation where we have two branches in the one locale. It will be another decade or 20 years before we get an opportunity to cure that.

The merger made the bank think more intensely about its computer systems. National had an IBM system and CBC had a Honeywell system. Because the CBC was a smaller bank and had computerised later, its system had better information on customers. By the end of the 1980s, it was clear much of the retail battle would be won or lost on the basis of the bank's customer information systems. Despite the greater sophistication of the CBC system, the decision was made to go along with the National's IBM system. This was because the CBC's system did not have the IBM's capacity to grow. Nobby Clark said, 'So CBC had to degrade themselves a little bit in terms of the things they had delivered to them by the computer, but commercially it was the right decision. Now, of course, we have caught up with providing all those things to them.'

The major human problem was that, with the merger, there was a loss of identity, especially for the CBC. For a while, the bank changed its name to the National Commercial Banking Corporation of Australia, but soon after it came back to the shorter National Australia Bank. As Nobby Clark said:

> Some people felt the new bank wasn't the old bank that they loved and had a relationship with for a 100 years. The discontinuity was felt more by the customers of CBC. CBC had a distinctively personal flavour. They were smaller and had probably taken the personal approach to a degree that we hadn't. We have tried to keep some of that flavour about us, but we haven't kept it to the extent that it was in CBC.

The branch framework was the basic ingredient for the bank's retail strength, but in that the bank was not unusual. However, it was more successful than other banks in decentralising its network to bring decision making closer to the customer. Westpac and ANZ have done that too; but Ian Donald, principal consultant at PA Consulting Services Pty Ltd, in Melbourne in May 1988 said, 'National Australia Bank has the flattest administrative structure, the least levels between Nobby Clark and the teller.'

This was achieved with help from McKinsey & Co., first in 1967 and then again in 1980 and 1986. At each stage, the bank's own officers also worked with McKinsey and thus became advocates of an efficient administrative structure. Clark is a prime example of this, for in July 1987 he was very excited talking of the organisational change that took place in the bank after deregulation:

> For management reporting we break the bank up in eleven zones. We have a general manager in each zone. We've made him virtually responsible for everything that goes on around his zone — personnel, properties, the lending, the bottom line — and we don't want to see very much from him at all. We want him to run that business as his own business. An average sort of figure for each zone would be 1300, 1400 people.

So the eleven zone managers report to the chief executive. Each zone manager in turn looks after six regions, and each regional manager looks after no more than eighteen branches. This reorganisation has done two things. Firstly, it has flattened the structure, so that instead of having seven layers there are only four layers of bureaucracy: branch, region, zone, chief executive. Secondly, it has made the line men responsible for the decisions. Clark said, 'The former bureaucracy, the service areas as they now are — properties and personnel, computers and so forth — they'll frame the decision, but the line man would make it. They might implement the decision, but the line man would overview it.'

Clark said that this structure has meant a greater freedom and independence in decision making. In 1987, he said, an experienced manager of a large National branch could lend up to $250 000 without the approval of the regional manager, and a regional manager could lend up to $500 000.

This contrasts dramatically with Nobby Clark's own experience as manager of the Newtown branch in NSW in 1966:

> I could lend $2 to a customer for 8 weeks. Two dollars, which equalled a pound. I had no discretion to lend you money if your account was overdrawn for more than a pound for 8 weeks. It was just a figure that was arbitrarily set. I had to then make a submission on behalf of the customer and send it to the state administration, who would vet it and approve it or decline it. Mostly they'd approve it, but occasionally they'd decline it, usually because we didn't have enough funds. In those days we had quantitative advance control, and the bank would have to quota its lending.

Talking of management, Nobby Clark waxed visibly enthusiastic: 'The management problem is more intense and diverse in a retail situation than in treasury, investment banking or broking. Retail is a lot of little things that aggregate.' So an efficient administrative structure is a great plus. Management information comes regularly, via the computer, to tell the volume of lending in the different areas. It also checks whether the funding strategy drawn up at the beginning of the year is being followed. 'We want the spread to be roughly in the proportion of what that level of economic activity is in the total economy,' he said. However, there are times when it seems that, at the head office, the senior executives must be spending all day monitoring activities via their computer screens. Nobby Clark said that, contrary to the impression, the zone managers now have constantly to visit the regional managers, and they in turn have to keep in touch with their branches. As for himself, 'I've my own network — people I ring up, old friends of mine who are still branch managers, young people I see at courses. I ask them questions. That's how I get the feel.'

What they are doing with management is successful, for the National managed to extract more profit per employee than any other major Australian bank between 1985 and 1989. Clark said, 'We spend a lot of time, money and effort to make our people better and to give them more enjoyment in their roles. We'll never eliminate routine work in banks, but we are trying to structure jobs so that people can have responsibility.'

Going international

The National Australia Bank's strength till the mid 1980s was in its domestic retail networks. Alone among the major private banks, it did not have an international culture. Going to London or even to New Zealand was not part of the grooming process of the bright young executives. Unlike Westpac and ANZ, it was a stay-at-home bank. Its most popular corporate image is a calendar that, since 1957, has depicted nineteenth-century Australian art.

Nobby Clark said, 'The first plank of my strategy was that you become as good as any other guy in the street domestically. Having got that, I said that we then look to have two significant representations in UK/Europe and North Americas.' In these locations, what he wanted was a domestic retail network, doing abroad what the bank did best at home. Elaborating, he said that what the bank was looking for was a dominant retail share, something like State Bank Victoria has in the Victorian market. 'A domestic network, I believe, is the way to go. I don't believe in all this Big Bang investment banking. I think the banks that have really done well around the world are the banks that have a good strong commercial base and branch networks.'

Trade finance would furnish other points of representation. This has been a strong point with the bank, even though the Mauritius venture in 1859 flopped. In 1922, the National sent its first business missions to Japan, Korea and China. Later, it went to India, North America and South Africa. It is strongly represented in Southeast Asia, and it has opened a representative office in India.

Clark said that this trade and customer route would give the National representational influence in Southeast Asia:

> We would be Australian dollar funders and we would be domestic currency funders for our own customers, but I couldn't see us having a domestic network in China, or Japan or in India. I believe we can't compete effectively in those so–different cultures. People don't worry me, but institutions and culture are very difficult for people like me to assimilate and understand and then compete. So I thought, leave those markets and go to the markets where the institutions and the cultures, the language, those sorts of things, are fairly common.

In July 1987, the National Australia Bank announced that it was buying the Scottish-based Clydesdale Bank, Northern Bank Ltd of Northern Ireland and Northern Bank (Ireland) Ltd of the Republic of Ireland. These used to be part of the Midland banking group of England. The National had seen parts of the Midland group as possible acquisitions, but the deal fell together in a particularly felicitous way. The chairman, Sir Rupert Clarke, and Nobby Clark were paying a courtesy call on the head of the Midland Bank, Sir Kit McMahon. Sir Rupert Clarke said in Melbourne in July 1988:

> I knew him, of course, but I was making my first call after becoming the chairman of the National Bank. It just happened to be that window of opportunity, for Midland Bank had decided they had to have a rights issue and had to sell some assets. Just the mere fact that we happened to go in at that time, the chief executive asked us, Would you be interested in buying a package of three banks? We said yes.

Nobby Clark said:

> The deal was done in 8 to 9 days. I flew back from London on the Monday, had a board meeting here on Tuesday, went to Sydney on Wednesday, got to the Reserve Bank, briefed some of our people in Sydney and up here. On Thursday night I flew out of Australia and got to England on Saturday morning. Got changed, went to work and negotiated through the day. On Sunday, we worked all day. We worked all day Monday. Tuesday flew to

> Glasgow for a press conference. From there, on a small aircraft to Belfast for a press conference. Then Dublin for a press conference, all in the one day. Spent the next day in Dublin. Flew to Glasgow. Had a full day there. Went to London. Had a full day there with politicians and others, and flew back to Australia. I had Sunday here and so was able to have a rest. Went back to work on Monday.

In the middle of all this, during the Monday to Thursday stint in Australia, he managed to prune the roses. Peggy said, 'The neighbours joked, he was the only person they knew who flew back from overseas to prune the roses and went right back again.'

When the deal was announced, most of the early comment from bank analysts was that the National had paid too much for three small banks. The price came to just over a billion dollars ($1049 million) when it was finalised in October 1987. This criticism rubbed Nobby on the raw. Having just returned from arranging the purchase in July 1987, he said:

> It just so happens that those small little banks in aggregate, after the first four banks in this country, will be the fifth bank in this country. So perhaps they are not so small. That's the first point. The second point is that we bought that network at the price that Scottish banks' shares are being sold on the stock exchange. This means we paid absolutely no premium for control of that institution. We've paid 1.2 times their net tangible assets. In the US, for the best buys, you'd be paying 1.9 times to 2.7 times net tangible assets. So I think the price is right. We've bought absolutely at the bottom of the cycle. Things will not get any worse in Scotland, because the economy is very flat. My notion is that we've bought countercyclical. We've got some upside. When oil comes good, and it looks that way, Scotland will be booming.'

The bank obtained exactly what it had wanted in terms of strategy. The Clydesdale bank in 1987 had 20 per cent of the Scottish market. Northern Bank Ltd of Northern Ireland had 55 per cent of its market. Moreover, the banks couldn't get any closer culturally. The annual general meetings are now peppered with references to the green fields of Ireland and how the dividends will be announced on St Patrick's Day.

The figures too have turned out better than Nobby Clark expected. In 1987, he thought that they could make this Midland deal work in 3 or 4 years; but within the first financial year, ending 30 September 1988, the UK/Irish banks contributed 16.1 per cent of the after–tax profit of the group. In 1989 also, they made a 16 per cent contribution to the profit and in March 1990, together with Yorkshire Bank (acquired in February 1990) they accounted for 26 per cent of the after-tax profit. These acquisitions, unlike ANZ's purchase of Grindlays Bank, have been all profit and no pain.

Argus said that he does not have the 'same heavy bias' as Nobby Clark has, against expanding in areas that are culturally dissimilar. In the early stages, though, he thinks, it is good to expand from a cultural base that is similar. However, he notes that nobody has quite got their Asian strategy right.

Argus and Clark are however agreed on the regional retail strategy, and Argus is enthusiastic about the benefits of networking for delivering financial service products like insurance and brokerage. He also agrees that Europe presents great opportunities that haven't been fully grasped yet. 'I don't think we can compete against the big German or French banks,' he said, 'but I think, as Europe starts to open up, there will be some tremendous opportunities for the type of banking that we do.' The National's most recent move, in February 1990, has been the acquisition of the profitable British regional Yorkshire Bank for 976.5 million pounds. With this, the National has 750 UK and Irish bank branches.

However, for Argus, US expansion is still some way in the future. He is uncomfortable with the shifting strategy of some of the US banks. Moreover, their exposure to the third world and leveraged buyout debt might cost the bank too much. He also thinks that the US banks 'are not good at cross-border banking. Moreover, once you go cross-border' you are looking at spending a lot on coordinating technology'.

For the National, for a while in 1989, the prospect of a merger with ANZ seemed a possibility. It would have resulted in a world class bank and rationalised costs. But in 1989 and again in 1990, the Treasurer vetoed the merger of two big banks. However, the logic behind the proposed merger remains valid.

Argus said in December 1989:

> There is no doubt it makes sense that banks such as the ANZ and ourselves start to look at some of the high costs we have and what benefits we can derive from sharing some of these high costs. Technology is the first area you look at. You look at how you do your networking . . . Five years down the track, the back-office branch work will be processed in some factory in Mulgrave or somewhere that provides a ready labour market. This will go in tandem with labour trends where people want to work near home. The branch itself will change and have two separate operations: the professional selling of financial products and the credit function. The manager will no longer be responsible for both. In this game plan, the more networking they can do and the more centralised the bank office work becomes, the greater the savings.

Looking into the future, and measuring up the bank's strengths and the challenges that lie ahead, Argus said, 'I think we are good people managers in this bank. It's a high productivity bank. Technology, and the way we deliver our products in the future, is also going to be a major challenge.' Argus wished he had started getting involved with technology earlier than he did. His interest in it developed after he went to Harvard and he said he was learning to use his PC. But he did not think his lack of extensive technical grounding, would be a minus for him.

> I believe I am developing a knowledge as well as any other decision maker around the place on technology. There are so many different views on technology that I think if you've got a strategy and stick to that strategy, you can't go wrong. I am not suggesting for one moment that we've got the right strategy for technology of the future. I don't think anyone would be game enough to put their hand up and say that.

He acknowledged that the bank has a fair way to go yet in technology, but said that it is on the right track with its customer information systems and that this strategy is already contributing to the profits of the bank. At the end of 1989, the bank completed its customer information files. And in early 1990, according to Trevor Bennett, principal account manager, retail system, at the bank, they were able to identify their profitable customers.

Once the bank can target customer needs, it will have a flow-on effect on service standards: 'The Australian banks haven't got it right yet; and though it's a glib statement, the first one to get it will be perceived as a very successful bank.'

Perhaps the most significant challenge for the bank in the 1990s, Argus said, is liability management. When the big slice of free money that the major banks still attract from their customers begins to dry up, you will 'have to trickle feed back to the shareholder base'. That is the only place where a bank can get large pools of relatively cheap funds for a period of time. However, Argus said, for this the banks have to 'present a quality balance sheet and quality earning potential. If the banks don't do that, they will have to raise funds in other geographical locations and find ways of hedging their exchange risks. That may not be palatable to the federal government.'

If the bank wants to raise money back in Australia, it will come up against the fact that only the over-50s in the community are saving. There is no incentive for people under 50 to save. 'So it is not only a banking problem but an economic problem Australia has to address.'

In the years ahead, Nobby Clark said, 'Very big entities will emerge at the top. At the bottom end there are going to be some niche players and not too much in the middle.' Globally too, he sees an opening up of financial markets and a rationalisation. These changes, he said, make it 'difficult to keep pace in terms of your control and checkpoints, your audit techniques and systems'. There are new prudential requirements for capital adequacy. All in all, he said, 'The last 3 or 4 years, the degree of complexity is probably enhanced by a factor of two, I think.'

Looking back over his more than 40 years with the National Australia Bank, from the days of alpaca coats and dress hats, high desks and blue ink, to the present world of the computer and deregulation, Clark said, 'Some of our people find the differences very offputting.'

However, both Clark and Argus reached their positions because they thrive on change. Argus said:

> I think banking is a terribly challenging game. You have to be watching what other banks are doing, and watching what's happening in the financial services industry generally, so that you are not missing out on an opportunity that you should be looking at. It is moving so quickly that you have to move with it. That's my whole thrust.

7 An identity crisis? The Commonwealth Bank of Australia

Don Sanders, 63, took over as chief executive of the Commonwealth Bank of Australia in March 1987 in a blaze of controversy. Though he had started his banking career with the Commonwealth Bank at 16, he was seen as an outsider. In 1960, when the Reserve Bank of Australia separated from the Commonwealth Bank of Australia, he had opted for the central bank. As he had been the deputy governor of the Reserve Bank before being appointed the head of the Commonwealth Bank, some saw him as the visible hand of the federal government interfering with its wholly owned commercial bank. This started a very public succession battle, unusual in recent banking history.

In moving back to the Commonwealth Bank, Sanders heads the only government-owned national bank in Australia. Even the atmosphere is different from that of the other major trading banks in the country. The bank's headquarters in Sydney in mid April 1990 are in an old building of polished granite, solid and elegant on the outside, reflecting a history that goes back to 1912. However, it is also a bank that is losing its pre-eminent place in Australian banking. Despite its external solidity, the building is slightly shabby on the inside. There is a friendly atmosphere, but there is no attempt to portray a corporate image. An inattention to the details of good housekeeping is apparent.

Though some of the starch is missing, this is the headquarters of the largest retail bank in Australia, with the biggest customer base. Possibly one in two Australians banks with it; but starved for capital, it has been steadily losing market share since deregulation. In 1989, it showed a dramatic improvement in profitability, compared with 1988. Its cost structure remains high, though the productivity of its staff has improved. Greater commercial freedom appears to have worked.

At the end of May 1990, with the focus on the bad debts of the major private banks, the heat is off the Commonwealth Bank. The victory of the Labor Party in the federal elections in March 1990, means that the bank will not be privatised in the near future. Though the bank remains wholly public, it will still have to face questions of identity. Is it a commercial bank that should be judged by its profits? Or is it an instrument of public policy that should be judged by its service to the Australian public? For the Commonwealth Bank, it is often a matter of damned if you do and damned if you don't. When it shows poor results, it is an indictment of the government ownership of the bank. When it moves aggressively to compete by following the private banks in charging fees, it is seen as reneging on its social responsibilities as a people's bank and going against its reason for being.

These questions of identity have been with the Commonwealth Bank of Australia since it started operations in 1912 and revolve round the very rationale of a government-owned bank. In a deregulated banking environment, these questions have become even more pertinent.

A government-owned national bank

The Commonwealth Bank of Australia occupies a special place in Australian banking history because of its position as the country's only government-owned national bank. It is interesting that this is such a distinctive feature of the bank, for in other countries of the Asia-Pacific region government-owned banks are not unusual, and in many countries they are the dominant, if not the only, banks. In 1988, ten of the top 20 non-Japanese and non-Australian banks in Asia, according to *The Banker*, were government-owned ('Asia Top 200,' September 1989). Added to this is the fact that government-owned banks are the biggest even in countries where banking has not been nationalised, such as Indonesia, Malaysia, Singapore and Taiwan. However, in Australia, the private banks are the norm; they dominate the banking system; the government-owned bank is the exception.

The Commonwealth Bank occupies a particularly special place in Australia. When it started operations in 1912, it was the culmination of a long-held desire for a publicly-owned bank. The concept of a people's bank has for close to a century been specially tied up with Labor ideology. It was part of the platform of the Labor Party in different states in 1891. It was felt that a people's bank would regulate the private banks along the Bank of England model. It would protect the interests of the ordinary depositor, putting this above the profit motive. The banking crash of 1893 only emphasised the need for such a bank. So when Labor came into power in 1910, with a clear majority in both houses of Parliament, it was able to establish the Commonwealth Bank, which had been high on its agenda.

From the outset the bank had four aims, which did not always converge: to be a bank for the people; to be a commercial bank run on business principles; to be the largest and in time the only savings bank in the country; and to be a central bank. The history of the bank is a history of how it dealt with these different strands. Prime Minister and Treasurer Andrew Fisher, moving the second reading of the Commonwealth Bank Bill into federal Parliament on 15 November 1911, touched on all four aims. He said, 'This will be a bank belonging to the people, and directly managed by the people's own agents. . . . (Commonwealth of Australia, 1911: 2644) This is a business concern pure and simple, and not a matter for idealism' (p. 2646). He hoped that the bank would 'ultimately become the bank of banks rather than a mere money-lending institution' (p. 2661). He also said that he believed that, in time, the Commonwealth Bank would become the only savings institution in the country. So, for the first time, an Australian bank was empowered to do both commercial and savings banking.

The bank grew by emphasising some of its aims during one period and changing tack in others. Much of the initial success of the Commonwealth Bank was due to its first governor, Denison Miller. In 1912, he had been with the Bank of New South Wales for 36 years and was the bank's inspector of metropolitan and suburban branches. As Ian Harper and Boris Schedvin note in their piece on Sir Denison Miller in Appleyard and Schedvin's book *Australian Financiers* (1988), there is some uncertainty as to how Miller was selected to be governor. However, he left the Bank of New South Wales with the blessing of its general manager, Russell French, to take up his new post as governor of the Commonwealth Bank of Australia. Noel Griffiths (1955), in an article in the *Bankers' Magazine of Australasia*, notes that, at a 20 minute meeting, Fisher and Miller read the Commonwealth Bank Act 1911 and agreed that the salary of the governor of the bank was worth 4000 pounds a year, higher than that of the Prime Minister himself.

Miller was formally offered the job in May 1912. A condition of his acceptance was that he would not be subject to any political interference in the running of the bank. So while he was governor, from 1912 to 1923, he was answerable to no board or member of the government.

Miller started with the bank on 1 June 1912 in a small upstairs room in Collins Street, Melbourne. There were just him and a messenger boy lent by the Treasury. He started recruiting choice staff from sixteen commercial banks and six savings banks. Miller's aim was to build 'a good sound bank on quiet safe lines', as he wrote to the Prime Minister. Having no capital, Miller started the savings bank first, as it was a business waiting to be picked up. The post offices, which had previously been agents of the state savings banks, now became agents of the Commonwealth Bank. Miller, like Fisher, also saw the Commonwealth Bank in time emerging as the main, if not the only, savings institution in the country. This approach also gave him time to prepare for the start of commercial banking.

So on 15 July 1912, 6 weeks after Miller's appointment, the bank started its savings bank operations from Collins Street and 489 post office agencies in Victoria. By mid January 1913, the savings bank had gone national. This is why initial opposition was greatest from the state savings banks, which saw the Commonwealth as a direct and unnecessary competitor. However, Miller went slowly and fixed the deposit rate at 3 per cent, which was half to 1 per cent lower than that being offered by some savings banks. He also fixed a 300 pounds maximum for deposits.

On 20 January 1913, the Commonwealth Bank started commercial banking simultaneously in Sydney, Canberra, Melbourne, Brisbane, Townsville, Adelaide, Perth, Hobart and London. Miller also at the time shifted the bank's headquarters to Sydney, the largest city. In 1913 too, the Tasmanian state savings bank merged with the Commonwealth Bank.

The private banks were wary of the new bank, as Commonwealth government accounts were transferred to it. It also did away with the 5 shillings half-yearly charge on a current account if there was more than 50 pounds in the account or if it was overdrawn. Accounts of local government bodies and charitable institutions were not charged at all. The private banks had to follow. However, much of their apprehension was diluted by governor Miller's policy of cooperating rather than competing with the private banks. There was an unwritten understanding that the Commonwealth Bank would not take another bank's overdraft account, unless the borrower's bank was not treating the borrower reasonably. This became so much a part of the way in which the bank did things that, in 1945, the bank was specially directed by legislation to compete in general banking business with the private banks. C. C. Faulkner (1923), writing of the early history of the Commonwealth Bank, notes that the governor frequently consulted with the chief executives of the private banks on important matters. He also maintained his close personal relations with his colleagues at the Bank of New South Wales. The thrust of the Commonwealth Bank during Miller's time, from 1912 to 1923, was towards establishing itself as a people's bank and a savings bank and developing as a central bank. He downplayed the other aim of competing with the private banks.

The bank expanded in its early years by going wherever Australians lived and worked. One of its more dramatic chapters was extending banking to the several hundred men who worked on the trans-Australian railway between Port Augusta in South Australia and Kalgoorlie in Western Australia. Without a savings bank, the men would spend their money on drink and gambling. In April 1914, a postal official acting as an agent of the savings bank started accompanying the paymaster every fortnight. Agencies were set up along the line. Faulkner (1923) writes that 'Every fortnight the Government paymaster drove out with his team of four mules and his boxes of money. Behind him, riding a horse or a camel, came the travelling agent of the Commonwealth Savings Bank' (p. 55). In 3 years, one bank officer travelled 60000 miles.

The men deposited their money through deposit slips. The passbooks were with their wives, who could operate the account through any post office branch or the Commonwealth Bank in Australia. Though the line had its share of wild and lawless men, there was a tacit understanding that nobody was to touch the 'bookmaker's bag' into which all the deposits went. The bank officer carried it round his neck, and it remained safe. By the time the railway was completed in October 1917, many men had enough savings to buy homes or war bonds and to provide for their retirement. Some had made so many deposits that they were on their second passbook. A typical request was that of a man who said, 'Give me back the old book; it's the first I've ever had. I'd like to keep it' (Faulkner, 1923: 60).

The First World War broke out soon after the bank started, and the Commonwealth Bank followed the Australian soldiers on the warships, in the field and even in prison camp. When an Australian soldier was a prisoner of war, he was provided with a book of cheque forms on the London office. Even if the soldier did not have an account with the bank, he could issue up to 10 pounds a month, and it would be borne by the army headquarters. When army prisoners of war were repatriated, a Commonwealth Bank officer met them immediately they arrived in England, to see that they did not want financially. While waiting for their transport back to Australia, soldiers could draw on the bank, the arrangement being that they would settle accounts in Australia. There wasn't a single case when this did not happen. Harper and Schedvin note that the military authorities did not share Miller's vision of being the banker to the Australian soldiers, for they thought of the bank as a 'socialistic enterprise' (Appleyard and Schedvin, 1988).

During the war, however, government banking business expanded and the bank grew with it. It became banker for the governments of Tasmania, Western Australia and South Australia. It also slowly started acquiring the functions of a central bank. It helped to manage the government's finances and was responsible for floating and managing 257 million pounds worth of war loans and the secret shipment of gold to Britain. It arranged the finance for the primary producers to provide the armies with food. It also arranged for finance at short notice to help to purchase fifteen ships to transport this food. However, the war ended without the bank being in charge of note issue; so in an important aspect, it had yet to develop as a central bank. It was only in 1920 that the Treasury ceded control of note issue to a separate note issue department of the bank, and in 1924 that note issue came directly under the control of the bank.

After the war ended in 1918, the commercial banking side of the bank again slowed down, because Miller did not choose to compete aggressively with the private banks. Its savings bank business received a boost by amalgamating with the state savings banks in Queensland in 1920.

Governor Miller died suddenly of a heart attack on 6 June 1923, leaving behind a commercial bank that did not compete with the private trading banks and a national state bank that was independent of government control. After Miller's death, the bank continued his non-aggressive policy towards the commercial banks. As a result, its trading bank business declined, but the savings bank continued to grow through amalgamations with other state savings banks. In 1931, after the Government Savings Bank of New South Wales had experienced difficulties because of the Depression, it amalgamated with the Commonwealth Savings Bank. L. F. Giblin (1951), writing in *The Growth of a Central Bank*, notes that there was a public perception that, instead of rescuing the bank, the Commonwealth Bank saw it as an opportunity to become the dominant savings bank of the country. Earlier in the year, in October 1931, it merged with the State Savings Bank of Western Australia. So by December 1931, the Commonwealth Bank had become the largest savings bank in Australia, as envisaged earlier by Miller. Its only competitors in the field were the state savings banks in Victoria and South Australia and the two small trustee banks in Tasmania. The savings bank business remains the core business of the bank. In 1989, it contributed more than half (59.4 per cent) of the net profit of the group.

Sir Denison Miller had achieved much with the Commonwealth Bank of Australia, but one aim continued to elude him: he was unable to establish the Commonwealth Bank as a central bank. Though a central banking role was critical to the concept of the Commonwealth Bank, the Commonwealth Bank Act 1911 did not give it too many specific powers. As Harper and Schedvin note (in Appleyard and Schedvin, 1988), the Act gave the bank no control of note issue nor regulatory powers over other banks. The only formal central-banking function it did have was management of the government account. So the formal coming of age of the Commonwealth Bank as a central bank was in 1924, when note issue was transferred from the special note issue department to the direct control of the board of the Commonwealth Bank.

The Second World War gave the bank additional regulatory powers over the banking system. These were incorporated in the Banking Act 1945. However, problems of identity remained, for the Commonwealth Bank Act 1945 also directed the bank to compete vigorously for general banking business. Private banks soon saw these two aims as incompatible.

A commercial bank

Within the Commonwealth Bank, the directive to compete openly came as a liberation, Don Sanders said in Sydney in February 1987:

> The Commonwealth Bank had been a very important savings bank but a less important trading bank, because it was subject to a bit of dispute as to how hard it could compete with the other banks. But liberation came with the 1945 legislation. It got the bank into the capacity for hire purchase, for instance. I happened to be in the Woonona branch on the south coast of New South Wales in 1945. The power to write hire purchase came, and the manager was alert and saw the business. He wrote what I believe is the first hire purchase written by an Australian bank. It was for transport equipment.
>
> It established the central bank side of the bank as an identifiable function. It introduced credit foncier housing loans. It also gave a lot of formality to staff arangements. It introduced a lot of regulation that paralysed, but at the same time it was the beginnings of raising the sights of the Commonwealth Bank and the new attitudes.

The private banks, however, opposed the fact that the Commonwealth was going to be an aggressive commercial bank as well as a central bank. The lines of battle were clearly drawn when Prime Minister Chifley announced in 1947 that the government was going to nationalise the banks. Because the Commonwealth Bank was supposed to take over the business of the private banks on nationalisation, it did not seek its commercial business as aggressively as it could.

Don Sanders told how, for some time after 1949:

> . . . there was suspicion of the Commonwealth Bank by the other banks that it could be used for nationalisation by stealth. Since the central bank and the commercial bank were in one organisation, there was the fear that the Commonwealth Bank as central bank would repress the other banks.

To provide reassurance that this would not happen, the commercial and central banking functions gradually separated within the bank. This inevitably led to their formal separation in 1960 into the Reserve Bank of Australia and the Commonwealth Banking Corporation. The latter includes the Commonwealth Bank of Australia and its subsidiaries plus the Commonwealth Development Bank (established in 1960). So it was only in 1960 that the Commonwealth Bank was free to go all out as a commercial bank.

Before this, however, the Commonwealth had to fight to retain its dominance of savings banking. In 1956, the private banks were allowed to open savings banks. This decision was greeted with dismay by the Commonwealth Savings Bank. It was as if the government had gone against its intention that there be one savings bank in the country: the Commonwealth Savings Bank. However, just as the state savings banks had responded in 1912 to the challenge of the Commonwealth Bank, by opening more branches, now the Commonwealth Bank started opening new branches.

Sir Bede Callaghan, managing director of the Commonwealth Banking Corporation from 1965 to 1976, said in Sydney in February 1988, that, in retrospect, the wholesale opening of branches right into the 1960s was a mistake. In defence of that he noted that, till the 1970s, the inflation rate was only 5 per cent: 'The staffing costs of a three-handed branch were probably no more than $10 000 a year. Moreover, it was felt that new branches were also providing service.' However, because of this increased branch network, the number of staff rose from 15 000 in 1965 to 25 000 in 1976. This contributed to the bank's becoming the largest retail bank in the country and outwardly the least efficient.

In 1960, banking was highly regulated, and the private banks had gone into finance companies and merchant banks for flexibility. The Commonwealth Bank was left out of this non-bank expansion. Callaghan said that the bank was not allowed to extend the hire purchase business, which was developed by the industrial finance department of the bank and later taken over by the Commonwealth Development Bank in 1960: 'The view from Canberra was that it should be forced into extinction. If it had been allowed, the Commonwealth Development Bank could have become a very big hire-purchase operation.'

In the 1970s, like the private banks, the Commonwealth set up its merchant bank with four other European banks. This was the Australian European Finance Corporation in 1970. Callaghan said that the bank was able to compete despite strong non-bank institutions, for the bank had a big branch structure and a retail base:

> The merchant banks did not pose a great problem to us. We did the biggest financing of the time in 1969 when Bougainville Copper was formed. We were responsible, with the Bank of America, for finding something of the order of $180 million, which was regarded as very big time 20 years ago.

For Vern Christie, managing director of the Commonwealth Banking Corporation from 1981 to 1987, this Bougainville Copper transaction made him feel that the Commonwealth bankers could compete with any in the world. In Sydney in December 1987, he said:

> When I went to San Francisco for the negotiations, I was appalled at the general lack of knowledge in international consortium arrangements. Sitting round the table, I felt that Australian banks had no reason to be modest about their performance. That gave me a thirst for international and commercial banking.

Corporate business grew during Christie's time:

> The part I enjoyed most about being managing director was getting out and talking to the corporate leaders and saying, 'Why don't you have a banking association with the Commonwealth Bank? We're bigger and brighter and better than anybody else.' They responded, and the results are on the board.

In 1986, the Commonwealth Bank beat all the big private trading banks in profitability, and its return on average shareholders' funds was in line with that of the private banks.

Don Sanders comes aboard

Just when the people at the Commonwealth Bank thought that they were at their most competitive, a public succession battle broke out. Vern Christie was to retire in early 1987, and the board of the bank recommended that Peter Wilson, the chief general manager, retail banking, take over as managing director. Very much in the style of the private banks, the Commonwealth Bank since 1960 had become used to having the chief executive come from within the bank. When it was announced in December 1986 that Don Sanders, deputy governor of the Reserve Bank of Australia, was to head the Commonwealth Bank, Vern Christie openly voiced his opposition. The Commonwealth Bank Officers' Association wrote to Treasurer Paul Keating that going against the board's recommendation and having an outsider as chief executive was an 'unjustified' vote of no confidence in the management, staff and the performance of the corporation.

Even 9 months after Don Sanders took over, the succession controversy was still alive. In December 1987, Christie said:

> It is public knowledge that when the question of succession arose in the bank, I very aggressively opposed what the Treasurer wanted to do, and that is to appoint someone from outside the bank. We've bred our own. We've bred tremendously good bankers for the system. You've only got to look at any significant financial institution in Australia and you'll find someone is Commonwealth Bank-trained there. So when they reach the senior positions, they not only have tremendous training in banking, but they have a great background of the Commonwealth Bank itself.

Not only was Don Sanders seen as an outsider, but also he was a central banker. This only added fuel to the fire. Vern Christie, pointing to Don Sanders' lack of commercial banking experience, said:

> If somebody out there had a reputation and the runs on the board to prove that he could do a better job than anyone in the bank could, then obviously he should get the job. I argued also that I saw difficulties for the business community and the staff in perceiving that someone coming from the Reserve Bank was putting a restraining hand on the aggressive corporate business. That may be a total misconception on my part, but nevertheless that was the perception of the staff. We always regarded ourselves as more commercial than the commercial banks.

Representatives of the staff went further, to say that, with Sanders' appointment, there was a distinct perception that the bank would now be an instrument of public policy, rather than a commercial bank. This was especially damaging, for, Vern Christie said, in his time he had no day-to-day problems with the government: 'None at all.' He said that any notion that the government was using the Commonwealth Bank as an instrument of government policy in housing or interest rates 'is completely incorrect. I swear it. The government does not interfere in any way with the policies of the bank.' So the only time that the Treasurer interfered with the running of the bank was when he overrode the board's recommendation on succession.

The problem with the succession was that nobody could find a reason why the government had to break with tradition and create such an uproar. The bank was outperforming the private banks and contributing handsomely to the government in both dividend and tax. So there was no commercial reason. The candidate recommended by the board, Peter Wilson, was seen as an able successor. There was some suspicion that the Treasurer might have blackballed Wilson because he once spoke out on interest rates for housing, but Vern Christie dismissed this, saying that the Treasurer could not have been as petty as that.

Tom Mockridge, press secretary of the Treasurer's Office in 1987, said in a telephone interview in Canberra in December 1987, 'It was a matter for the Treasurer's judgement. He was the best bloke for the job.'

Talking to Don Sanders in February 1988, it was easy to see why the Treasurer was impressed. He has a precise and incisive mind and is able to place facts in their global context. He comes through as a man who has thought long and hard about the country's banking system.

It is also easy to like Sanders. He has an old-worldly charm and a mix of formality, humour and grace that is found in the best central bankers. He talks easily of bankers in the region, for his work has placed him in close touch with them. He talks little of himself. Asked a pointed personal question, he answers politely, but then goes on to what he sees as the more important, broader picture. The first impression is that of a formal dignified man. Conservatively dressed in a grey suit, he was the only chief executive interviewed who did not have a tinge of red in his tie. People who have known him in the Commonwealth Bank or the Reserve Bank say that he is a person who has deep friendships and is an easy mixer and a good hand at the piano.

Sanders' curriculum vitae is impressive by any standards. He started with the Wollongong branch of the Commonwealth Bank of Australia in 1943, aged 16. Son of a teacher, he said that:

> I slipped into banking. I thought of some other occupations, but some of them were not feasible in terms of costs of tuition. And the suggestion was put to me by the local manager of the Commonwealth as to whether I would

Don Sanders, managing director, Commonwealth Australia Bank (courtesy BRW)

> like to be a banker. I thought about that, and it was something I could handle, and yes, I would give it a try.

He worked his way up. He studied part-time for a degree in economics at the University of Sydney. That changed direction for him in the early 1950s. Like many Commonwealth bankers, he moved from the retail side of the bank to its central banking functions. In 1960, when the Commonwealth Bank of Australia split into the Reserve Bank of Australia and the Commonwealth Banking Corporation, he opted for the Reserve Bank. In July 1975, he was appointed deputy governor of the Reserve Bank. He had implemented much of the bank regulation since the 1950s and in the process had become an avowed free-market man, knowing the futility of much of the regulation. In the 1980s, with more sympathy, he helped supervise a banking system that was shedding the controls of the last 40 years.

He knew that he would not be governor of the Reserve Bank, for in 1982 Bob Johnston, head of the secretary's department in the bank, had been appointed governor. Around 1985, when he was 58, Sanders said, he indicated that he wanted to retire. When asked the reason, he asked in turn, 'Don't you ever do anything for long enough?' After 42 years of banking, of which 33 had been devoted to central banking, he said, he decided to call it a day:

> I don't believe you should be in central banking and touting for a job at the same time. So I decided to technically retire and see what happens. Maybe

> somebody would have asked me, Would you like to do this? Or would you like to do that? Or again, nobody would have wanted me to do anything. I had no special anxiety about that. There is more to life than central banking.

Not very long after he indicated his desire to retire, he was asked by the Treasurer whether he would accept being considered for the job of chief executive of the Commonwealth Bank. He did not go into any details of what was said, saying, 'I don't bother to talk about it. I'm saying to you that the opportunity came, and I thought about it and said, yes, I was willing to be considered, I'd like that job and I could do it.' Was it a question of duty to accept, since he had been asked? 'No, no, no bounden duty,' he replied.

He had anticipated that there would be a public furore, particularly as governmental processes were involved: 'If I hadn't seen the possibility of that, I wouldn't have been very bright.' Talking of the shift he has had to make, from being a central banker to being a commercial banker, he said:

> I don't think it has been particularly hard. I've been watching commercial banking all my life. I was in the same industry, but it was like coming in through a different door each time. Sure, I don't have the background in corporate lending, but we have experts in corporate lending. You recognise your deficiencies. You can't do it all. I think you bring your own fund of experience.

Peter Wilson left the bank to be the number two man in Westpac's finance company, Australian Guarantee Corporation. A few senior people chose to retire. Sanders, though, did not take this particularly to heart:

> Retirement is a very personal decision. Everybody has to make it for themselves, but I don't believe there was a rash of retirements on my account. You certainly lose experience when good people go. That can be tough. On the other hand, it also opens up opportunities for younger people to come and make their mark. I don't think my coming has done anything to daunt ambition.

Reeling from a lack of capital

It would have been healing for Don Sanders to have a good financial year after he came in, but the 30 June 1987 results were 'a disappointment', as the bank itself put it. For the first time in 5 years, profits declined — by 32 per cent. The Commonwealth Bank did worse than any of the major trading banks.

This downturn cannot be attributed purely to poor morale or the succession battle. Some of it was because the bank was particularly stung by its high proportion of housing loans at the regulated interest rate of 13.5 per cent, when deregulated housing loans were going at

15.5 per cent. However, the major reasons for this poor performance were lack of capital and commercial flexibility.

Ian Payne, deputy managing director of the banking group, talked of the latter at great length in his Sydney office in December 1987. He said that the bank was hampered by legislation that 'spells out chapter and verse, how the bank can manage its staff':

> It was too rigid. We want to run a far less uniform organisation. In essence, that's what has happened to banking. Twenty years ago, a bank was an organisation; its key aspect was uniformity, from the pin-striped manager at the top of the heap to the customer service people at the front desk. Now banks have virtually split up into heterogeneous units. We are looking at how we can run ourselves as a close-knit aggregation of business units. The products are shaking down into discernible groups, and you want to put managers in charge of them in such a way that you can measure performance and hold people accountable for performance.

The rigidness of the legislation meant that the Commonwealth Bank was not able to restructure its administrative set-up like the major private banks. It was also not able to go into lucrative areas like insurance.

The main problem for the bank in 1987, however, was its lack of capital. The bank started in 1912 with a loan of 10 000 pounds sterling. This was repaid within a year. The only subsequent direct government contribution to the bank's capital was in 1984, when it injected $A15 million. Vern Christie said that, even in 1984, 'the Treasurer had promised me $50 million, but when it got through the Cabinet processes, it got down to $15 million'. Not only has the government not put in substantial equity, but it has extracted handsome amounts in tax and dividends of up to 50 per cent for many years. So the group's capital of $A4 billion in 1989 was made up mainly of retained earnings, bolstered by rising values of bank property and $US700 million in undated floating-rate notes. This perpetual debt was raised only in the 1988/89 financial year, to enable the bank to comply with the Reserve Bank's risk asset ratios. It has given the bank some breathing space, but it is a limited option under the current capital-adequacy guidelines.

In a regulated environment, when none of the banks could do very much, the Commonwealth's lack of capital was not so noticeable; but with impending deregulation, the private banks sought to shore up their market share by acquiring financial institutions at home and abroad. The Commonwealth Bank, without the needed capital, has by and large had to build up its assets by using its retained earnings. This has hurt it particularly in its international operations, specially in the Asia-Pacific region. The Commonwealth Bank group has little more than the basic branch network spanning Tokyo, Hong Kong and Singapore. The rest of the region is serviced through area offices. It was able to expand to New Zealand only in May 1989, by acquiring 75 per cent of ASB Bank Ltd, a retail bank in the Auckland and Northland regions.

The Commonwealth Bank has also not been able to invest in customer information systems to the same extent as the private banks. So instead of using its large customer base, with some 5.5 million customers and 11 million accounts, as a base for cross-selling services and increasing profits, its large savings network and retail operations only add to the costs. Towards the end of 1989, only half of its accounts were on a customer information file.

It was this problem of capital that pushed the Commonwealth Bank right into the centre of the privatisation debate in 1987 and 1988. Commercially, one can look at the Commonwealth Bank as a great investment, a veritable cash cow, which returned $1.1 billion in income tax and $659 million in dividends from 1978 to 1989 for a $15 million investment; or one can see it as an over $2 billion asset, which returned a dividend of only $110 million in 1989.

The bank's strengths became very evident when there was speculation in 1988 that the Commonwealth Bank could possibly be merged with a major private bank. Every major private bank got into position. This was the great opportunity for dominating the local market. Here was a well rounded bank, the largest retail bank in Australia with the biggest customer base, the number one lender to housing, the biggest savings bank, with a great treasury and a well trained staff. Who could afford to let go of such a plum? However, as the 1988 privatisation debate within the Labor Party showed, the Commonwealth Bank is too deeply rooted in history and political ideology for a purely commercial decision. The Liberal Party made it clear before the 1990 federal election that, if it were elected, the Commonwealth Bank would be privatised.

The senior management was cautious about expressing an opinion on the subject. Ian Payne in Sydney, in May 1988, at the height of the privatisation debate, said:

> The attitude within the bank is that we will keep an open mind and look at any of the options according to the degree to which they give us access to capital. I just keep saying, rank the options in accordance with access to capital. The one that gives us free and timely access to capital is the one that we'll favour.

Past chief executives have been more articulate. Nugget Coombs said in December 1987 in a telephone interview in Canberra:

> There are other possible forms of public enterprise for a publicly owned bank with responsibilities for financial and economic policy other than the government corporation. I think it well worth the bank's and the government's while to consider some of the other possibilities.

He still feels that:

> ... the existence of a publicly owned bank competing with privately owned banks is an important contribution to financial management. I would regret very much the disappearance of such a competition. My interest is the importance of the role of the Commonwealth Bank as an instrument of public policy.

Vern Christie said:

> I've come to the view that inevitably the bank will be privatised. I firmly believe the bank's not properly capitalised. The staff have already shown they are good commercial bankers and can hold their own with anybody. If the Commonwealth were given adequate capital, you wouldn't see which way the bank went for dust.

The Commonwealth Bank Officers Association, however, moved from considering the privatisation option to total opposition. The fear was that many of the Commonwealth staff would be retrenched if the bank were merged with another private bank. Some retrenchment will be inevitable as branches are closed, but some of the staff will be shed also because the Commonwealth Bank has a higher staff per branch ratio than the other private banks. Taking a more uncharitable view, it could also be noted that Commonwealth Bank employees are not as efficient as those of the major private banks. The Commonwealth Bank's nickname was the Elephant, to symbolise a solid, wise and weighty bank. This symbolism has turned against the bank, however, for the elephant is also being seen as slow and unwieldy. In 1989, its employees generated the least profit per employee among the major banks and looked after the least value of assets. Ian Payne countered this observation earlier in December 1987 by pointing to the high percentage of savings bank business in the Commonwealth Bank compared to the other major banks. Savings bank business is people-intensive business. The point made often in the Commonwealth Bank is that its retail costs have to be compared with the retail costs of the other banks. However, as such figures are not available, the question remains open.

Many of the bank's problems began to be solved in 1988 and 1989. The Treasurer announced in the May 1988 Economic Statement that government business enterprises would be freed from a range of government controls. In turn, they would be required to improve their efficiency and profitability and follow a corporate plan approved by the Treasurer. Reflecting this change, the Commonwealth Banks Act 1959 was amended to allow the bank more commercial flexibility. Remuneration for its senior executives has increased, and award restructuring is taking place at the lower levels. In July 1989, Don Sanders' post was advertised, and he was reappointed.

This greater flexibility has translated into increased productivity.

Don Sanders said in the group's 1989 annual report that this was achieved by making the administrative structure flatter and more regional. The 1261 branches in June 1989 were organised into 58 regions, with each regional manager responsible for between ten and 21 branches.

In 1988/89, the bank also was able to increase its capital through $927.6 million's worth of undated floating-rate notes. Its capital rose from $2.7 billion to $4 billion, an increase of 48 per cent. This allowed the bank to increase its assets more vigorously in 1989. The group's post-tax profit moved up, registering a massive increase of 81 per cent in 1988 and 33 per cent in 1989. The bank no longer languishes at the bottom of the scale vis-à-vis the other major trading banks. Taking pre-tax profit as a percentage of average assets, the Commonwealth Bank has moved up to second position in 1989, ahead of the Australia and New Zealand Banking Group (ANZ) and Westpac.

The bank in 1989 saw itself as a commercial entity, 'operating on a totally commercial basis in a very competitive industry', as its chairman, M. A. Besley, put it in the bank's 1989 annual report. For the public, this shift in orientation became very clear when the Commonwealth Bank followed the major private banks in November 1988 by introducing a $1.50 monthly fee on savings and cheque accounts with a balance of less than $250.

The bank's reasoning, like that of the major private banks, was that it costs the bank more to service these accounts, and so at least part of this cost should be retrieved from the customer. Len Spencer, the bank's chief general manager, retail, said in a press release in November 1988 that the introduction of the fee was 'a necessary business decision'. However, the Commonwealth Bank was surprised by the intense consumer protest that followed. The protest was strong enough to make the bank backtrack and grant further exemptions to the fee.

John Koch, general manager, retail, said in a telephone interview from Sydney in October 1989, 'We were surprised. Research had shown there was an element in the market that was virtually reconciled to the inevitability of fees, but the market really sees the Commonwealth Bank as a special animal with a special role.' He said that image surveys showed that the reaction was, 'Yes, all the other banks do it, but we didn't expect it of the Commonwealth Bank.'

Again the bank faces a dilemma. Does the bank go for profit, or does the bank go for social responsibility? There is growing consumer pressure that, in a competitive environment, banks should not forget their social responsibilities; and in the case of the Commonwealth Bank, any perceived departure from the concept of a 'people's bank' invites an even greater backlash.

Reacting to consumer concern over the fees issue, the bank has taken a few important steps. In 1989, it appointed a customer relations executive to look after customer complaints. Perhaps the more important long-term effect is that the bank is looking at ways in which this special image of the bank can become a marketing tool. Koch said, 'We feel we should capitalise on this market perception.' So the bank is finally trying to use its identity problems to its commercial advantage.

At the end of May 1990, the Commonwealth Bank looked in good commercial shape. Its future for the next three years at least will be as a government-owned bank. It has been able to raise some capital and has greater flexibility. But its position in the banking system will be determined by the changes taking place among the private banks.

8 A bank that grew too fast: the State Bank Victoria

For much of 1989, the State Bank Victoria was a bank under siege, reeling with losses of $1.3 billion dollars, the largest in Australian corporate history. The state government picked up the tab for $795 million of the losses to ensure the capital adequacy of the bank. Heads rolled in February 1990. Bill Moyle, the chief executive of State Bank Victoria went on leave pending his retirement in May 1990. All but one of the directors of the bank were forced to resign. The only director to remain, joined the bank after the losses. The Labor Party lost heavily in Victoria in the March 1990 federal election. Rob Jolly, the state Treasurer, was pressured to resign soon after. Meanwhile, Ian Johns, chief executive of Tricontinental Holdings Ltd (the State Bank's wholly owned subsidiary till mid-1989), is in court answering charges of insider trading.

The postmortem will no doubt show that one of the problems was bad management. The chief executive, Bill Moyle, by his public statements, showed that he did not know what was happening in his banking group. He also had, as members of his group team, top executives whose integrity is being questioned in the court. And with the benefit of hindsight, one can question the lending practices of the banking group, especially the group's merchant bank, Tricontinental Holdings Ltd, which made many bad loans while chasing margins and market share. This led the State Bank Victoria group to declare a loss of $196.6 million in June 1989. In December 1989, the loss rose to $1.3 billion. This massive loss has raised questions about the state government's responsibility towards its wholly-owned bank. And behind the specifics of the case looms the dark side of financial deregulation and the problem of adequate supervision of the non-bank subsidiaries of banks.

The 1989 loss was shocking not only because it was so huge, but because this was the first time in the state bank's 147 year history that it had declared a loss, for till 1988 the story of the State Bank Victoria was a tale of unsullied success.

Like the other state banks in Australia it started as a savings bank, tapping household savings. It coped with the deregulation of the banking industry by growing its assets and transforming itself from a savings bank to a full-service commercial bank. Between 1984 and 1989, the banking group grew faster than the major private banks; it nearly quadrupled its assets, while the major private banks increased their assets approximately two and a half times.

While doing this, it retained its position as the fifth-largest bank of Australia and the largest regional retail bank in the country. In June 1989, it had a third (34 per cent) of the retail and housing market in Victoria. At the same time, however, the bank extended its operations, so that in 1989 about 30 per cent of its business was corporate, with the bank having a relationship with almost all the top 100 corporations in Australia. In 1985, it acquired 100 per cent ownership of the merchant bank, Tricontinental Holdings Ltd. In 1988, Trico was the largest bank-owned merchant bank. The State Bank Victoria also had offices in Sydney, Brisbane, London, New York and Hong Kong. Added to this was a growing superannuation and unit trust business. In 1988, the State Bank Victoria was the most profitable established trading bank in the country in terms of its return on shareholders' funds; but in mid-April 1990, it looked more like a bank that grew too fast.

A savings bank

The State Bank Victoria belongs to a different genre of banking compared to the major trading banks. In early Australian banking history, there was a sharp difference between savings banks and trading banks. Savings banks were set up on the British model and accepted deposits, however small, from 'the man in the street', while trading banks depended on issuing notes and their own capital. All trading banks till 1912 were privately owned, but all savings banks from 1833 to 1956 were government-owned. Further, till 1988, the savings banks operated under different prudential regulations.

The State Bank Victoria started in 1842 as the Savings Bank of Port Phillip in the Port Phillip district (now Victoria) of NSW. Trevor Craddock and Maurice Cavanough (1967), in their history of the bank, write that the greatest need at the time was to provide some kind of banking for the shepherds who worked alone all year long and came in to Melbourne once a year with their annual cheque of about 40 pounds. Without a savings bank, the money went for drink and women, so the demand was for a savings bank like the ones already operating in NSW and Tasmania.

When the Savings Bank of Port Phillip opened, it did not encourage easy banking. It was located on the upper floor of the Melbourne Fire and Marine Insurance Company building on the corner of Collins and Queen Streets. It received deposits for only 2 hours a week: 1 p.m. to 2 p.m. on Wednesday and 7 p.m. to 8 p.m. on Saturday. People could withdraw money for only 1 hour a week: 1 p.m. to 2 p.m. on Wednesday. A week's notice was required for any withdrawal up to 5 pounds. For 500 pounds, for instance, 2 months' notice was required. And in the first fortnight of January, the bank was closed altogether.

Its depositors were salaried workers like shepherds, hut keepers, household servants, milkmen, carpenters, tailors, bullock drivers, shopmen, water carriers, clerks and other labourers. It grew as a conservative bank. While trading banks competed to set up agencies in canvas tents during the gold rush in Victoria in 1851, the Victorian savings bank stood aside. It was not a season for thrift with fortunes to be made in a week at the goldfields. Only on 1 December 1855 did the bank open a branch at Castlemaine. To save money, the bank operated part-time and opened on Mondays from 1 to 4 p.m. for deposits and on Fridays from 2 to 4 p.m. for withdrawals.

While the trading banks were expanding their branch network, the Savings Bank of Port Phillip was going through its own changes. In 1851, Victoria became a colony independent of NSW. In 1853, the structure of the savings bank changed. Instead of having one savings bank set up branches in different towns, separate savings banks were established in Melbourne and country towns in Victoria. Each savings bank was looked after by its own board of trustees, and these trustees were overseen by the Commissioners of Savings Banks in the colony of Victoria. This split management and control meant trouble, with the Commissioners having the upper hand. Nevertheless, this structure remained till 1912, when the various savings banks in the state again came together as the State Savings Bank of Victoria.

To go back to the goldfields, the Commissioners of the Victorian savings banks accepted a suggestion that, in the British tradition, the post offices supplement the work of the savings banks. So the first Post Office Savings Bank started in Victoria in 1865. Soon though it became a rival to the savings banks. Like a mini run-up to later nationalisation plans, the government proposed that the Post Office Savings Bank absorb the Commissioners' Savings Banks in Victoria. However, the idea of being taken over by a government department was not taken kindly. Instead, in 1897, over 378 post offices became agencies of the Commissioners' Savings Banks.

The next phase of Victoria's development — the opening of the wheatlands in the 1860s — also passed the savings banks by. Their strength was with the factory workers. However, the savings banks also stood aside from the hysterical rise in land speculation in the 1880s. So while some trading banks failed or temporarily closed in 1893, the Victorian savings banks, like the other state savings banks, remained open. The government boosted confidence by guaranteeing the savings banks' funds, and customers were paid in gold.

It was soon after the banking crisis, in 1894, that the Commissioners' Savings Banks started their most popular scheme: the 'credit foncier', that is, 'credit founded on land'. At the time, a Victorian farmer could mortgage his land for 3 to 7 years and had to pay 8 to 10 per cent in interest. After this, the mortgage had to be renewed, or there was a forced sale. Based on the system in Austria, Germany and France, the savings banks started giving mortgages for a term of more than 20 years at 5 per cent interest.

The credit foncier system worked so well for the farmer that, in 1910, the savings banks moved to lend for houses and shops on the same principle. This was the beginning of the saga of the bank that has housed Victoria. In time, the State Savings Bank of Victoria established its own building and design department to supervise the construction of low cost houses. The borrower had to put in 50 pounds, and he could borrow up to 1000 pounds on timber-framed houses or up to 1300 pounds on a brick building. Alex Cooch, the chief executive of the bank from 1929 to 1937, said in an address to the Constitutional Club in 1929 that if the borrower 'has more than three children up to 14 years of age, the deposit is reduced to 25 pounds, provided the site is within three-quarters of a mile from a railway station or tram line' ("The romance of the Savings Banks," *Bankers' Magazine of Australasia*, Feb 28, 1929, p. 107). Some of these houses from the 1920s can still be seen in Melbourne today.

The start of the Commonwealth Bank of Australia's savings bank operations came as a rude shock to the state savings banks. Alex Cooch was particularly upset: 'For one people to have two Savings Banks — one under State law, the other under Federal law — without any possible gain to the community, injuring each other by competition, and bewildering the public, is surely a violation of commonsense, a ridiculous state of things' (1929; p. 105). All the state opposition was in vain, however, and 5 weeks before the Commonwealth Bank was to start, the State Savings Bank of Victoria handed over the post office agencies. However, this only spurred the savings bank to open more branches, and it did better than before. The savings bank philosophy of encouraging thrift also led it to the schools and factories. More than any other bank, the State Savings Bank of Victoria reached to the household.

Alex Cooch said that in 1929 the deposits of the savings bank were more than the deposits in Victoria of the Bank of Australasia, Union Bank, Bank of New South Wales, Commercial Banking Company of Sydney and English, Scottish and Australian Bank (ES&A) added together.

There was yet another shock to come: the entry of the private banks into savings banking in 1956. This time the Commonwealth Bank joined in the protest, for savings banking had from the beginning been nearly wholly confined to the public sector. Nevertheless, as before, protest had no effect. Again the savings banks set up more branches.

In all these moves, the strength of the State Savings Bank of Victoria rested in that it was fiercely Victorian. Harry Torrens, chief executive of the bank from 1977 to 1983, said in February 1988 in Melbourne that this was one of the drawing points of the bank. It even found it easier to recruit staff, for 'if you joined the State Savings Bank of Victoria, you knew that you wouldn't have to shift all over Australia'.

The entry of the private banks into the savings bank market in 1956 led the state savings banks to introduce some features of the trading banks. In 1957, the State Savings Bank of Victoria started providing cheque account facilities. By a series of small steps, it expanded its operations to give overdrafts and business loans. In 1980, following changes to state banking legislation, it became a trading bank, renamed the State Bank of Victoria. With deregulation in 1984, it was clear that, if the bank was to compete, it had to keep the strength of its savings banking background but at the same time to offer commercial banking and get into wholesale banking and global treasury operations. Hence arose the need to look outside the bank for experienced commercial bankers.

A successful succession

Bill Moyle was the first outside chief executive in the state bank's history. Looking at the uproar that took place in the Commonwealth Bank when it appointed Don Sanders, it is remarkable that the succession was so smooth in what was an insular bank.

Harry Torrens, who was chief executive before Moyle, had to retire because of health reasons. Though he retired on 31 January 1984, he was away from the bank from October 1983. Jack Ryan, his deputy, held the fort. When it became known that the state government was inviting applications from outside, Torrens said, he did not speak out, for 'I don't think that sort of thing is going to make any difference in the long run if the government is really determined.' The board also did not take a view on it, Torrens said, for:

> I believe there was no point taking a stand on it. I was cut up about it for it took away incentive. But the government wanted a new outlook as far as the bank was concerned. They decided things had to be done more quickly. They couldn't change the Board. In 1984, they saw an opportunity to change the chief executive.

Bill Moyle, 54 at the time, must have seemed tailormade to head the State Bank of Victoria. He was sympathetic to the philosophy of a public sector bank, yet he had had experience in competitive commercial and merchant banking.

Moyle's father was one of the early recruits to the Commonwealth

Bill Moyle, managing director, State Bank Victoria, 1984–1990 (courtesy BRW)

Bank of Australia, joining its Ballarat branch in 1916. He rose to become a branch manager in country towns in Tasmania, Queensland and NSW. Bill Moyle also joined the Commonwealth Bank in 1947, after completing school. Like a few bankers his age, he completed his accountancy degree part-time while doing banking.

What makes Bill Moyle's career unusual is that after 31 years he left the Commonwealth Bank to go to a private finance company. He was not the first banker to leave his bank, but in 1978 it was unusual enough for it to be talked about. He moved to become chief executive of United Dominions Corporation, a troubled finance company. In 1981, he moved on to become managing director of the merchant bank Chase NBA (now known as National Australia Ltd). Then it was back again to retail banking and the public sector in August 1984, to become the first outside chief executive of the State Bank of Victoria. So his career bridged the public and the private sector, merchant and retail banking.

In February 1988, in his office on the second floor of the State Bank headquarters in Melbourne, with the city as a backdrop, Bill Moyle talked slowly, each sentence rounded, as if standing alone. To an outsider, he seems an amiable, informal person. Officially christened Lindsay Gordon Crossley Moyle, he is known as Bill Moyle in the banking world, because his father used to call him Bill. He says he is not given to introspection. A keen rugby player, a competition swimmer in his school days, he enjoys the roar of a football crowd. For relaxation, he drives the tractor on his farm and gets right away from banking.

Bill Moyle eased into the job with little difficulty. He gave much of the credit to Jack Ryan, who stayed on to see him launched in the new job. Ryan and Moyle had known each other for many years, and that helped. Bill Moyle acknowledged this assistance:

> Jack did everything possible to make the transition as smooth as possible and did a great deal to introduce me to people in the State Bank and to introduce me to the culture of the bank and to educate me to the people, problems, opportunities, strengths and weaknesses of the bank. I recognise the debt I owe him and was very appreciative of him.

Jack Ryan left the bank after 9 months to act briefly as chief executive of the State Bank of Victoria's wholly owned merchant bank, Tricontinental Holdings Ltd, becoming its non-executive deputy chairman in 1986.

The other thing that was different in the case of the State Bank of Victoria was that there was a clear reason why someone from the outside was brought in. Moyle said, 'The bank staff knew that a big job had to be done to equip the State Bank to compete in a deregulated environment.' The bank needed to change from being a savings bank to being a full-service commercial bank. A new range of specialised skills were needed; and because of the imminent entry of the foreign banks, this change had to be made quickly. 'So bringing in new folk to handle those new jobs was seen as a very necessary part of that preparation for deregulation, and I believe that was perceived and accepted by the majority in the bank.'

The corollary of that acceptance was the realisation that the staff needed to be retrained. Moyle said:

> It was something I was very conscious of. At the time we were recruiting from outside, we were also upgrading our training and development programmes within the bank. We now have a formal executive succession programme. We've reviewed our approach to executive remuneration. Profit sharing was introduced as a bank initiative rather than a union request. We were the first bank to enter into a health and safety agreement. We were among the first banks to adopt affirmative action. The bank wouldn't make the progress I hoped it would make, unless we got our industrial and staff management practices right. So the bank has devoted a lot of effort to this.

For those who could not cope with the savings bank becoming a full-service commercial bank, early retirement options were made available at 55, instead of 60.

Changes came fast. The bank was reorganised in September 1985, according to its functions: retail, corporate and international and treasury. It was in September 1985, too, that the bank upped its 25.8 per cent stake to 100 per cent in the merchant bank Tricontinental Holdings Ltd. There was also a total overhaul of image. In 1986/87 the bank changed its marketing name to the crisper State Bank Victoria, though its legal name remained the State Bank of Victoria. A new corporate logo and uniforms were introduced. Behind these cosmetic changes was a significant change of style. This bank used to attract staff who were possibly a shade more conservative and provincial than staff in the trading banks. Now the state bank had become international, not only because it had offices in different parts of the world but also because its business was global. Until the early 1980s, the passbook account was the largest part of all savings banks. Its business used to be to bring in the small deposits of the household sector and lend this money for housing and to purchase government and state securities. However, in January 1988, when Moyle talked of a great move by the bank, he talked of placing a $US300 million issue in London in competition with Bankers Trust Australia.

A state bank stumbles

Everything was going well for Bill Moyle and the bank. The changeover had been smooth. Unlike the Commonwealth Bank of Australia, State Bank Victoria had no trouble increasing its capital via perpetual debt in 1986. In 1988, it was more profitable than the major trading banks. Its retail market share was increasing.

Enjoying a record first half in 1988/89, the bank sprung a takeover bid for Australian Bank Ltd in December 1988. This bid was contested by the major shareholder, Lend Lease Corporation Ltd, but State Bank Victoria increased its price and gained 100 per cent of the Australian Bank for $106 million in January 1989. The idea behind taking over the Australian Bank was that the Australian Bank would then, subject to Reserve Bank go-ahead, buy State Bank Victoria's merchant bank, Tricontinental Holdings Ltd, for up to $180 million. This would be financed by the Australian Bank raising $400 million through a series of private placements. This would in turn dilute State Bank Victoria's stake in the Australian Bank to under 10 per cent, as required by the Reserve Bank.

If the deal had worked out, it would have had two desirable effects. Firstly, it would have reduced the assets of State Bank Victoria and so reduced the need for capital to comply with the Reserve Bank's increased risk-assets ratio. Secondly, it would have given State Bank Victoria a capital gain from the sale of Trico. In the market there were rumblings that perhaps the bank wanted to get rid of Trico, because it was uncomfortable with the high risk business of its merchant bank. However, in March 1989, Bill Moyle denied that State Bank Victoria was unhappy with Trico's business. He told Beth Quinlivan of *Triple A*, 'They have a different risk profile, but they have managed it well' ("State banks hit by growth pains", *Triple A*, March 1989, p. 19). At that time, the point that Moyle was making was that the sale of Trico would depress the profits of the group. He said:

> For the bank figures, the only change would be that we no longer get the dividend — last year it was $10 million — but on the other hand, we will have the capital gain to reinvest. The group position is that we will be divested of $3 billion in assets and lose profit in excess of dividend of $12 million (1989: p. 19).

State Bank Victoria had, however, been trying to float off Tricontinental Holdings Ltd in 1987, but the stockmarket crash prevented that. The 1989 Australian Bank deal was the bank's second move to divest itself of its merchant bank. The stated reasons were that, with deregulation and the new capital-adequacy guidelines, it was no longer profitable for a merchant bank to engage in lending operations. Moreover, there was a fair degree of overlap between State Bank Victoria's and Trico's corporate and treasury operations.

When State Bank Victoria bought 100 per cent of Tricontinental Holdings Ltd in 1985, Trico was a merchant bank owned by a conglomerate of banks. Its operations had invited the poorest possible rating from the credit-ratings agency Australian Ratings. From Trico's point of view, state bank ownership added to its creditworthiness. The State Bank Victoria for its part saw it as a strategic move. It said in its press release on 29 March 1985 entitled 'State Bank acquires control of Tricontinental' that 'it will be controlling a profitable merchant bank, with extensive corporate business in Australia and Southeast Asia. This development is fully in keeping with its strategic objectives' (p. 2).

Indeed, Trico was profitable, and for 1987 it contributed a net profit of $26.1 million, which was 27 per cent of the group's profit. In 1988, Trico's net profit was $23.3 million, 23 per cent of the group's profit. Then, between February and June 1989, Trico was struck with liquidity problems. Moyle told the *Financial Review* in May 1989 that the State Bank Victoria had pumped 'some hundreds of million of dollars' into Tricontinental Holdings since banks and institutions began cutting its credit facilities in February ('SBV poured "millions" into Trico,' *Financial Review*, 23 May 1989). Just to give the final dollop of bad news, three former employees of the merchant bank were charged with insider trading, and there were rumours that the chief executive and the executive director of Trico were being investigated too. In July 1989, Trico's chief executive, Ian Johns, was arrested to face five charges, including one of blackmail with unwarranted demand with menaces and one of insider trading.

The independent directors of the Australian Bank, now wholly owned by the State Bank Victoria, sought an indemnity against assets being acquired. This meant that the state bank would have to guarantee Trico's loans, before the Australian Bank could buy it. That would have meant the State Bank Victoria bearing 100 per cent of the losses for only 10 per cent of the equity. So towards the end of May 1989, the State Bank Victoria decided to integrate Trico's merchant banking operations into the bank itself. This left the bank with Trico's disastrous loanbook, the need for more capital and having to dispose of 90 per cent of the Australian Bank. It was the worst possible ending to what had looked like an astute move in January 1989.

There was more to come. Trico, in gaining market share, had run great risks by going in for entrepreneurial lending to the higher risk companies. Ian Johns, its young chief executive, had publicly been dismissive of a merchant bank going in for fee income alone, saying that the real profit came from lending — and that too from lending to private companies that were growing fast, instead of the top 100 companies. 'We get our hands dirty,' Ian Johns had said in 1987 (*Financial Review*, 23 May 1989). However, after the October 1987 stockmarket crash, some of these companies began unravelling in a high risk environment.

The disturbing feature of this situation was that the parent bank was apparently unaware of the full extent of the losses. Though Bill Moyle was on the board, subsequent events showed that he had little hands-on knowledge of what was happening in the merchant bank. It was left independent of the group's controls.

Towards the end of May 1989, Bill Moyle was quoted in the *Financial Review* as saying that Trico would write off $52 million from loan losses in the 1989 financial year. He was, however, expecting that Trico would still yield a net post-tax profit of between $4 million and $5 million (Ibid).

In early July, there were reports that Tricontinental's debts could total $100 million. The Victorian state Treasurer, Rob Jolly, was reported in *The Australian* on 2 July 1989 as saying that he knew very little about the way in which Trico had been run. He added, 'It is only in recent weeks that the chief executive [of the State Bank, Bill Moyle] has been aware of the extent of the problems at Tricontinental' ('Bank's loss sparks call for Jolly to quit,' *The Australian*, 2 July 1989).

Even this was a hopeful statement, for the State Bank Victoria's annual report for the year ending 30 June 1989 reported a $667.8 million specific and general provision for possible loan losses in 1989. Trico's losses had been massive enough to convert the bank's $78.8 million net profit into a group loss of $194.6 million!

The 1989 annual report, however, stated that, despite these losses, 'The Bank expects normal Group profitability to be achieved in 1989–90.' Then came fresh revelations in February 1990 that the group had lost $1.3 billion up until the end of December 1989. There is the threat of more to come. The moral of the story is that the board of a company should not delegate its authority. It has to provide the checks and balances to direct the company's operations. The unanswered question is why a banker of Moyle's experience allowed the situation to develop in the first place.

The troubles for the bank group were not confined to the losses of its merchant bank. In the 1988/89 financial year, it also suffered a loss of $104 million from the failure of the National Safety Council of Australia (Victorian division). State Bank Victoria was its major banker. It was, as Bill Moyle said in the annual report, a 'unique and bizarre failure'. Revelations in court showed that the chief executive of the National Safety Council of Australia (Victorian division) submitted false accounts to bankers keen to lend. He said he pointed to empty containers, passing them off as container-loads of sophisticated equipment. Though the State Bank Victoria was not the only bank to be taken in, it was one of the most enthusiastic lenders. The State Bank Victoria looked at its loan approval procedures and found that they were in order. However, to have been caught in such a large scam there must have been serious deficiencies in the loan-monitoring processes.

All in all, as Bill Moyle told the *Financial Review* of 23 May 1989, '1988–89 has not been a good year for me personally or [for] the bank'.

Not only do the losses raise questions of management and control within the State Bank Victoria group; they also raise questions about the relationship of the state government and its wholly owned bank. The two questions of corporate flexibility and independence that arose with the Commonwealth Bank are just as relevant for State Bank Victoria. Asked how the state influences the way in which he does his banking, Moyle said in January 1988:

> In my time with the bank, there has been no political pressure for us to do or not to do a particular class of business. The government has the right to be consulted by us before we form a new venture. They have no right of veto, but say before we invested in Tricontinental, before we launched our equity investment trust, the Act required us and we did consult with the state Treasurer. That process of consultation is all that the Act requires and is all that the state Treasurer requires.... We have no exclusive right over the Victorian government's banking.

The bank is required to pay tax to the state government in lieu of the federal government, as if it were a public company engaged in the business of banking. In addition to this, Moyle said:

> We pay the state government a dividend which is determined by the Treasurer after consultation with us. And the moral obligation is to report annually to the Parliament in Victoria on our results and activities for the year. Apart from this, there is no other obligation to seek the approval or consent of government to our normal banking activities, and the government doesn't seek to provide such advice to us.

The state government, however, has the right to determine the nature of the bank by appointing the board and the chief executive. The common denominator of the board in 1989 was that all the members had worked in an administrative or consultative capacity with the state or federal government. As Moyle pointed out in some detail, they have behind them a wealth of business experience as well. But the board did not include a single head of the first ten private corporations of the country. The 1988 legislation provides for the state Treasurer to appoint a person to the board. Moreover, the Treasurer is specifically given the power to overrule the board in case there is a difference of opinion.

Behind this formal relationship, however, was a network of social relationships with people in the government and business. What is also interesting is that, despite protestations of commercial freedom for the bank, which come from the state government and the bank itself, the State Bank Victoria has been exposed to the major state projects that have gone sour. Not only did it lend nearly $104 million to the failed Victorian division of the National Safety Council of Australia, but it also faces a loss with the Victorian Economic Development Corporation. Unless it is assumed that state public servants and state bankers share a common culture and so go together into disaster, there is the distinct possibility that there is pressure on the state bank to support state ventures.

When the bank was doing well, it was easier to grant it commercial independence; but when things went wrong the state government had to pick up the tab. The state government has instituted more frequent and detailed reporting procedures. It has instructed the bank to stop 'entrepreneurial lending'. And in an unusual move, the Reserve Bank of Australia has agreed to formally supervise the state bank's prudential standards. Other state banks still have only voluntary agreements with the Reserve Bank. They keep to the central bank's prudential guidelines, but are not formally supervised by it. These prudential guidelines alone did not prevent Trico's losses. At this stage it can only be a matter for speculation as to whether the central bank's informal supervision would have helped contain the losses.

Despite the bank's current problems, it is perhaps important to note that the State Bank Victoria has been a very profitable proposition for the state government. Between 1985 and 1989, the bank returned $332.4 million in taxes and dividends for $45 million subscribed in capital.

When the light is shining harshly on the bank, it is perhaps appropriate to remember that, in the 1980s, the State Bank Victoria moved from being an insular savings bank to being a financial services group. It expanded vigorously in the face of competition from the major Australian banks as well as from the sophisticated niche operations of the foreign banks. It was successful in tapping the markets to raise perpetual debt for its capital base. Its retail performance improved, with a growing customer base and a larger market share. It is still improving its customer information systems. In its traditional activities, its assets remain good, dominated by well secured mortgages. It still remains the premier example of regional banking in the country, keeping its position as the fifth-largest bank in Australia. Paul Rizzo, the new chief executive, will be hoping to exploit these strengths.

9 'Good idea but faulty execution': Mark Johnson and the Australian Bank

'Good idea but faulty execution. That's got to be the verdict,' Mark Johnson said, summing up his failure with the Australian Bank. At 50, he is stocky in build, of medium height and slightly balding. Talking of the experience in January 1988, 17 months after he left the Australian Bank, he laughed often and seemed to be at ease with himself. Sitting in the conference room at the Macquarie Bank in Melbourne, looking out at a great view of the Yarra River, there was a clinical detachment in the way in which he spoke of his 6 years with the Australian Bank.

When the Australian Bank opened in August 1981, euphoria ran high. It was the first new national bank since 1923, when the Primary Producers' Bank of Australia Ltd was promoted in Queensland. It was path-breaking in that it was the very first bank ever to open under the Banking Act 1959. It was to be the bank that would shake the Australian banking world out of its complacency and stupor. It was headed by the bright young sparks of the merchant banking world, who were going to show the older bankers how a bank should be run.

Instead, within 4 years, the bank was caught up in bad loans that ate up more than a third of its original capital. It was just about set up, when Australian banking deregulated at an unexpected speed and sixteen of the strongest banks in the world entered the scene. Mark Johnson's merchant bankers left one by one. Johnson, who for 6 years had been identified with the bank, left in mid-August 1986. He went back to the Macquarie Bank, the merchant bank he had left in 1981. At the end of May 1990, the Australian Bank still survives, but as a banking licence in search of an owner.

Looking back at his time at the Australian Bank, Johnson said that, soon after he left, he gave himself a 'C minus' on his report card:

> But now when I look at all the banks that had started all around the world and what has happened to them, I think I probably deserve a B. We tried very, very hard. We made some mistakes, but you've got to remember that now there is a bank that wasn't there before. It is now a different shape to that which I would have preferred, but the organism has survived, and I think we changed attitudes quite remarkably for our size.

When asked how he felt about the ending of his dream, it seemed as if he was asking himself that question for the first time. It was as if he did not want to probe too deeply himself and so slipped from under the question. Asked whether he cried when it fell apart, he laughed, saying, 'I cry when I hear brass bands, but they didn't have one out for me.' He unravelled in spurts. The actual day he left the bank was not traumatic, he remembered, 'for I had told them I was going more than 12 months earlier. It is like a bad loan. It sort of goes up and down. I knew when I was going, so I cleared stuff out 2 weeks before. You don't cry for 2 weeks. It is not a single dramatic exit.' He said that he felt relieved more than anything else. 'I sometimes feel sad,' he said. Then, as if thinking it out, he qualified this, saying, 'I didn't feel sad. I felt regret. I felt responsible that I'd damaged or hindered the careers of a number of people who had come in with aspirations, who would have liked to have seen the bank succeed. I suppose that's what I felt worst about.' His regret was also for the shareholders 'who had put up the money for a brave endeavour that didn't make them any return'. However, 'I am not remorseful,' he said, 'because being remorseful is not productive. It can make you feel rotten. It's not going to change history.' He added, 'I think there is a streak of the Polynesian in me,' referring to Fiji, where he was born and where he went to school. 'The Polynesian attitude is, you can't look back too much. You can't live with tragedy too long. Tomorrow is another day.'

After the Australian Bank, Mark Johnson took 6 months off. No, he said, he wasn't licking his wounds:

> I needed a rest. Very few people have the luxury of taking 6 months off in the middle of their careers. I was very lucky in the sense that enough people had been nice to me and said that, if I'd decided to come back, please talk to us. So I had a safety net. I didn't feel insecure. I'd decided I wasn't going to make up my mind till the New Year.

So he and his wife spent 6 weeks in Italy, where they have friends and he has a sister who lives in Turin. Then he did an acquisition in London for some good friends of his. After that, they went to Boston, his wife's home town. A major mission there was to see the Red Sox win the 1986 World Series, but they unfortunately lost in the last innings of the seventh game, and that *was* a great tragedy, Johnson said. 'It was a good time to wander around and do nothing. I read a lot. I drank a lot of red wine, and I had a lot of pasta, and ran a little to keep the weight under control.' No, he said, he was not running away, 'because I always intended to come back'.

There had been speculation that Johnson would join Wardleys. Instead, he went back to the Macquarie Bank, his old merchant bank that he had coheaded with David Clarke in 1981. He came back in 1987 to work in the corporate department under Tony Berg, who used to be his junior. He said that going back did not faze him at all and that his changed position in the hierarchy did not strain old friendships.

Speaking as if articulating this for the first time, he said that he went back:

> Partly because I knew the cast of characters and its culture. I guess I know these people very, very well. David Clarke [the present chief executive] and I shared an office for 10 years or something. That's probably harder than being married, I'm sure.
>
> And I got the most wonderful charter from Tony Berg. I only have to work on the things I enjoy. I can work on the deals side of the business without getting deeply involved in the administrative side. Tony is a superb manager. He manages this whole operation very well, which is a task that would be beyond me. I do not envy him in the slightest. I think he has the worst job in Macquarie Bank. I've got about the best.
>
> Macquarie Bank is the biggest corporate finance operation, I think, so there is plenty to do. What I like about it is that I'm not meant to be here full-time. There are a couple of private things in the United States that I'm interested in doing in my spare time, so I regard myself as having the best of all possible worlds. That's probably a rationalisation — I don't know — but I certainly didn't feel a compulsion to take a job with another bank, simply because I didn't want to go back to the bank that I knew well.

A brave new world

The beginnings of the Australian Bank have already become legend. The story starts with Garrick Agnew, a mining millionaire and an Australian Olympic swimmer and marlin fisherman from Perth. He died in August 1987, at 56, of a heart attack after one of his regular swimming sessions. One version of the story says that Agnew and John Stone, then the Secretary to the Treasury, were flying together and Agnew told Stone how fed up he was with the lousy banking service. So Stone replied, 'Why don't you start a bank yourself?' Another version of the story has them having lunch with the same conversation.

John Stone in mid-1988 in a telephone interview said that it was over lunch that the conversation did indeed take place, 'a year or so before Australian Bank made an application to start'. That would place it around 1979. 'He was not a close personal friend,' John Stone said, 'but a well-known West Australian.' Both of them had studied at the elite Perth Modern School, where Stone was a year senior to Agnew.

Mark Johnson said that Agnew returned to Perth and thought about it for a few days. Then Agnew asked Stone, 'Do you seriously think it could be done?' and Stone said, 'I don't know. But there's only one way to find out.' So the ball was set rolling for what would be the first new national bank in 58 years.

Garrick Agnew mentioned it to Mark Johnson one night when he was having dinner at Johnson's place in Sydney. Johnson and Agnew had become friends through their involvement in the Robe River iron-ore float in 1969–70. Johnson said:

> When Garrick first talked about setting up a new bank, I thought it was a wild idea. I had accepted the conventional wisdom that it couldn't be done, that the Banking Act was a sieve designed to exclude everybody, and I hadn't seen that you could actually find your way through and comply.

What was special, though, about Garrick Agnew, Johnson said, was that he was a visionary, who could make some of his visions come true. 'He was a very skilled negotiator, and he was also very ethical and a rather honourable man. He had a vision of Australia of how it should be. He was one of those people who genuinely wanted to make it a better place for his kids.'

About 1979, when Johnson had moved to London to head Hill Samuel Australia's international division, 'Garrick said to me, "If I can get a good indication from the authorities that I can get a bank authorised, will you come back and help me put it together?"' Though it meant coming in from the freer merchant-banking set-up to a highly regulated and strictured banking environment, Johnson accepted. 'Well, it was the best deal of 1980, you know,' he said laughing. 'Provided I do not sound too pompous or pretentious about it, I thought it was a very interesting challenge to see if it could be done.'

Johnson said that, to understand the significance of the Australian Bank, it is necessary to understand the banking environment of the time. 'Bankers did a conscientious job, but some of the people in the big banks were a bit stuffy and self-satisfied. They didn't think competitively, and so their attitudes were a little high-handed. They were not particularly receptive to new techniques.' It was these attitudes that riled entrepreneurs like Garrick Agnew, but Johnson said, 'The basic reason for that attitude was the strictures placed on the Australian banking system by the authorities.' However, the environment was changing, and the Campbell Committee report was coming out. The interim report was tabled in Parliament in August 1980. It made for a change of attitude. 'When we came to negotiate with the authorities in 1979 and 1980,' Johnson said, 'I think they wanted to make it happen, so they were constructive about their interpretation of the laws.'

Speaking of the application in 1980 to start the Australian Bank, in his empty new offices in Melbourne in January 1988, Richard Beetham, then head of the financial institutions division of the Treasury, but now Commissioner for Superannuation, said:

> When the Australian Bank first started its exercise of seeking a banking authority, it was something that was quite new for both the Treasury and the

> Reserve Bank. While we had a number of general enquiries, which had not gone very far, most of them were for organisations which were more merchant-bank-oriented. Then along came Garrick Agnew. The difficult part was that we'd never really developed all the various processes that were associated with the granting of a banking authority. It was really path-breaking. . . .
>
> For me it was an exciting venture. It raised an extraordinary number of new issues. To what extent should a new bank have different potential requirements to the established banks? Australian Bank was so significant because the policy of the new bank entry was largely developed as a result of its application.

The decision to apply a higher capital-adequacy ratio of 6.5 per cent to the Australian Bank, compared with 5 per cent for the established banks was later followed with the new banks in 1985.

Beetham said:

> When Australian Bank developed its proposal, the Campbell Committee reports were being considered. I didn't know at the time what changes might occur, but the general presumption was that it would ease up the requirements for entry into banking. I said to Garrick informally, 'Look, I have to ask you the question as to how sensible you think it is, to be going forward when Campbell may produce some changes.' I frankly suggested to him that maybe they could be setting up under arrangements that could be more restrictive than those down the track; but he thought the balance of advantage lay with going early, getting an established presence and risk the changes that might occur thereafter. He was clearly eyes-open.

So the die was cast in 1980 that they would go ahead.

One of the stumbling blocks to the setting up of any new bank at the time was the restriction that a single shareholder could own no more than 10 per cent of a bank. That made it unattractive to many investors, but Agnew nevertheless was able to line up shareholders for the bank. Johnson too put in his savings of $250 000.

In another way, though, the 10 per cent rule proved to be one of the most difficult technical problems to cope with. Johnson explained:

> When we were close to incorporating, somebody who had been going to invest a million dollars only wanted to put in half a million. That threw everybody else. If he only wanted to put in half a million, it put all the other 10 per cent shareholders up to 11 per cent and put it all into breach. So you had to start and go right round and back. So some of the rules, like the 10 per cent, which looked very simple on the surface, were in fact very difficult to comply with.

Johnson says, 'I spent a lot of my spare time for about 18 months putting together a couple of feasibility studies for the Treasury and the Reserve Bank and as a basis for getting investors.' Nobody had really ever done a feasibility study for a new bank. 'It was very difficult. None of the banks at that time, for example, disclosed any of their bad debt experience. If I had known about it, it would have stood us in very good stead.' He laughed heartily. Asked how long it took him to laugh about the bad debts that wiped out two-thirds of the bank's capital, he replied, 'You only do these things if you have a sense of humour':

> The important thing about Australian Bank is that it never got a single exemption or variance. It complied with all the legislation and ended up getting an unconditional banking authority. We played completely by the rules. So it could be done, but nobody had put in the perseverance.

Seven years later, in Jaunary 1988, Johnson could not really remember what it was like on the first day that the Australian Bank opened to the public. What he did remember was how they received a telephone call in Melbourne from the Treasury in September 1980: 'They gave us permission to use the word "bank", so that we could incorporate the company. I remember we had a meeting in North Broken Hill, and I think Lawrence Baillieu [managing director of North Broken Hill] produced some champagne and we all had a glass.'

The Australian Bank opens

The Australian Bank opened in Melbourne on 14 August 1981 in a blaze of publicity. The Australian Bank was the 'little Aussie battler' against the uncaring banking giants. Journalistic copy flowed every day. Their first day. How they had to get the pencil sharpeners, their strategy, their people — all got due mention. 'It was a double-edged sword,' said Mark Johnson, 'but when you have no advertising budget and represent only one-half of 1 per cent of the banking assets, any publicity is free advertisement.'

A lot of the attention was focused on Mark Johnson himself. He had an unusual background. His father was an Australian born in Fiji and was managing director of a major trading group in the islands, W. R. Carpenter. Johnson too was born in Fiji. Instead of being shipped away to boarding school at age 8, he stayed on in Fiji to go to school. He did not talk much of school, except to say that the sailing in Fiji was good. His brother had built him a 7 foot (2.1 metre) sailboat, so after school he would get on his bicycle and in 10 minutes reach the yacht club, and then it was sailing for the remainder of the day.

He went on to study law at Melbourne University at the select Trinity College in 1958. The Trinity College connection did not last, for in his last year he was thrown out. 'Maybe I did not go to chapel enough,' he quipped. He completed his law degree, which he saw as a good basis for getting into the advisory side of business; then it was on to the Harvard Business School to do his Master of Business Administration (MBA).

A chain of Harvard connections led him then to investment banking:

Mark Johnson, managing director, Australian Bank, 1981–1986 (courtesy BRW)

> There were only three investment banks in Australia in 1966. They were Australian United Corporation — that's one of the pieces that has been absorbed into Morgan Guaranty — there was Development Finance Corporation, now part of the ANZ, and Darling and Co., which is now Schroder Darling.

He was promised a job at Australian United Corporation at 3000 pounds sterling a year:

> But Sir Ian Potter who was the chairman of AUC said, 'That's too much. Pay him 2500 pounds per year.' This was before I started work, so I decided I couldn't really come back, take a job and have my salary reduced before I'd actually started work. So that reduced my potential employers to only two.

Through Jim Wolfensohn, who had been at Harvard and was then with Darling and Co., Mark Johnson came to Darling and Co. in 1966. David Clarke, who was a year behind Johnson at Harvard, joined Darling and Co. in the same year. Johnson said:

> What was interesting was that you couldn't describe yourself as a banker, since you couldn't use the word 'bank'. So one of the great social struggles of the late 1960s was to get acceptance of the name merchant banker as an occupation. Sometimes, we didn't call ourselves anything.

Mark Johnson and David Clarke both left Darling and Co. in 1971 to join Hill Samuel Australia (now the Macquarie Bank), the new British merchant bank, and soon they became joint managing directors. In 1977, Johnson moved to London, as joint head of the corporate services division. Then in 1980, he started with the Australian Bank.

By this time, Mark Johnson himself had become a role model for younger merchant bankers. He was able to attract some of the cream of the merchant banking world to join him in his new bank. Bill Gurry, a director with Hill Samuel Australia, joined as executive director, corporate services division. Leigh Scott-Kemmis, who was executive director, money market at CitiNational, became the new bank's treasurer. David Saunders, also from Hill Samuel Australia, looked after corporate finance in Sydney.

The essence of the Australian Bank was that it set itself up to be different from the big banks. Leigh Scott-Kemmis said in Sydney in October 1987:

> The relationship with the other banks was very difficult. They would cut our throats as soon as look at us. At the time, though, you wouldn't get anybody at Australian Bank saying the other banks weren't cooperative. It just wasn't in our interests to cause any aggro. We kept going around saying how nice they all were.

Mark Johnson, though, said that some of the major banks were 'very supportive' at the chief executive level. He singled out Vern Christie of the Commonwealth Bank and Bob White of Westpac as being particularly helpful. John Milne of the Australia and New Zealand Banking Group (ANZ) was very straightforward. Johnson said that it was the National Bank people who were not nearly as friendly. They called on Jack Booth at the National Bank. 'He was offhand and a real sourpuss. I think we got a cup of coffee. That's it, pretty much. They were never friends of ours.' His experience varied with middle management: 'One time you got people who were on side, and another time you got people who were very much against us.'

The Australian Bank and the big banks had their share of battles. Recruiting staff from the majors did not endear the bank too much to the others. The biggest hurdle was getting into the clearing system so that the bank could clear cheques. The major banks weren't keen to have a newcomer use a system they had set up. Moreover, there had never been a case quite like this, so the price had to be set. Eventually, prodded by the Reserve Bank, they let the Australian Bank in and charged it a joining fee of $250 000.

Another confrontation centred on the Visa card. At the time, because the major banks supported Bankcard, that was the card used within Australia. Visa card was issued to Australians when they travelled overseas. Visa, of course, wanted to get into the domestic market. The Australian Bank said that it would take Visa on. That started something of a mess, but the Australian Bank became the first bank in the country to offer the Visa card domestically and to link it up to their automated teller machines (ATMs).

All this gave the Australian Bank a high profile. The bank soon grew into a four-branch operation in Sydney, Melbourne, Perth and Brisbane. It started to accumulate deposits through its cash management trust, which in effect meant giving interest on the current account. The bank became profitable from the third quarter of the first year. However, within 2 years, the loans started to go bad. By 31 January 1985, the bank had lost one-third of its capital. Within the bank, there was dissension as to how the bank should be managed. Slowly, Mark Johnson's merchant bankers left. Bill Gurry left in 1983, David Saunders in 1984 and Leigh Scott-Kemmis in 1985. New shareholders came in with additional capital and a new philosophy for the bank. Garrick Agnew stepped down as chairman in 1985, and Mark Johnson left in August 1986. The bank continued, but it was not the same bank that Agnew and Johnson had wanted to build.

What went wrong

What had gone wrong? The short answer is: strategy and management. The bank was aimed at the middle-sized corporate market and at personal banking for high-net-worth individuals, but it found itself sucked into providing the whole gamut of retail banking services: deposits, cheques, ATMs, plastic cards. It opened four branches, some of them in opulent buildings complete with state-of-the-art pneumatic tube systems for transmitting money from a central security point to tellers. It invested in the latest computer software. By 1986, it had more than 500 people working at the bank. Though Johnson and Agnew had really wanted to have a bank that was doing merchant-banking operations, they found that they had underestimated the costs of being a bank. As Bill Gurry said in Melbourne in December 1987, 'There wasn't a vision of where we would be in 5 years. It was basically a mishmash right from the start.'

The people hired by the bank were first rate in their own specialities and went on to head important banks of their own. However, as David Saunders pointed out in Melbourne in March 1988, they were square pegs in round holes. The expertise they brought to the bank was in mergers and acquisitions, treasury and the money market. There were no senior experienced people for lending and personal banking, and these were the very areas on which the bank was focusing. It was not for lack of trying. Johnson said, 'People with hands-on lending experience with the big banks were more sceptical as to whether we would succeed, and partly [their reluctance to leave] was because they were often tied in with superannuation packages.'

This lack was all the more serious because the middle market is a hard market even for experienced bankers. What did happen was that Mark Johnson, who had had no lending experience, headed the credit committee. He himself (Melbourne, January 1988) acknowledged that the right systems for granting and reviewing credit were not in place:

> We should have had a system in place that would have ventilated the bad loans earlier. A couple of the big loans that got into trouble, in retrospect, we should have canned earlier. I kept in place too long people who shouldn't have been there. In that sense it was a management problem.

This, though, was not evident in the beginning. As Johnson said:

> A loan doesn't go wrong overnight. It emerges. You live with it. Sometimes you think it's turned the corner. Sometimes you think it's gone wrong. It's how I imagine living with a bleeding ulcer would be like. It's awful, particularly when you've got to put a relatively bold face on it because you don't want everyone worrying about it.

Bill Gurry said:

> The real story was the board of directors lacked a vision. The board of directors did not know what it was doing. Since I was a member of the board, this is also a self-criticism. Nobody was in charge. Strength on the board was not displayed, with the one exception of John Dunlop, for whom I have nothing but the highest admiration. Unfortunately, he died. I can remember sitting in on a meeting where we had a $2 million to $3 million exposure to a company. It was in very bad shape. I was strongly in favour of pulling the rug, but I was outvoted, as the managing director wouldn't vote with me and the directors supported the managing director.

Though the board was not 'calling Mark', David Saunders said, Johnson was receiving the same kind of critical feedback from his staff, but he vetoed that. Personal relations worsened. The excitement of the first 18 months faded. It came to the point, Bill Gurry said, that he 'had an open conflict with the chairman about the direction of the bank and the board not playing a proper role'. So Gurry left in 1983, and slowly other bright people followed, when they found that they could not influence what was happening.

Mark Johnson glossed over these personality problems in the bank, but Bill Gurry talked of them at length 'I've worked with Mark for 10 years. Nine and a half years were exceptionally good times.' The rift hurt, Gurry said, for Johnson was under the impression:

> . . . that I was trying to shaft him. At the time I was there, it was inconceivable that Australian Bank could have ever lost Mark Johnson. What I was trying to do was to help fix the situation. I think I had some skills to offer and I think he misinterpreted what I was trying to do. There were times when I sat down and said, I think this is going wrong, but he would not address the problem.

> When I left I gave him a copy of Ken Williams and I wrote that we had had some absolutely marvellous times, and that we had some differences of opinion in the last 6 months which had not been good, but I trusted they would disappear and time would heal them.

He said that, a year after he left, Johnson and he again developed a very warm relationship.

The overall problem was one of management. Johnson was a good investment banker but not a good manager. Running the bank was proving harder than he had anticipated. Looking back at the Australian Bank experience, he admitted that the major problem was that he was not suited to managing a commercial banking operation:

> I guess one of the reasons I am probably a better investment banker than I am a commercial banker is that investment bankers have much shorter time horizons. If I could see the rest of my life plotted ahead before me, I wouldn't really want to do it. I had an opportunity to work for Morgan Guaranty when I was 23 or 24, while doing my MBA, but the thought of knowing that you were going to be in a great big structure and provided you didn't screw up your life, you would progress till you were 60 — even today I find that an appalling thought. If I knew where I was going to be in 5 years' time, I don't think I'd want to go there.

This need for a variety of experience, he said, serves him well in investment banking.

> But in commercial banking, or indeed in any major commercial enterprise, you've got to run a bureaucracy. It's a living organism and requires control and discipline and all the techniques of management that I think are the hardest work of all. I'm not sufficiently disciplined to go through all of that.

This bit of self-knowledge, though, was learnt the hard way.

When the problems started mounting, the existing shareholders did not come up with more capital. Instead, two new shareholders bought into the bank in May 1985: property giant, Lend Lease Corporation Ltd, and its 49.45 per cent-owned subsidiary, Mutual Life and Citizens' Assurance Company Ltd (MLC). Together they took 25 per cent of its enlarged capital: 10 per cent non-voting shares for Lend Lease and 15 per cent voting shares for MLC. By then, the Banks (Shareholdings) Act 1972 had been amended to allow a shareholder up to 15 per cent of a bank's capital. Banque Paribas sold its share in the Australian Bank's merchant bank and took 15 per cent of the bank. This increased the paid-up capital of the bank from $35.4 million to $56.6 million. This enabled the bank to continue business, but the new shareholders had a different vision for the bank. Vic Martin, chairman of MLC and previously managing director of the Commercial Banking Company of Sydney, took over as chairman in 1985.

Though Mark Johnson accepts the managerial responsibility for the bad loans, he thinks that the problems became worse because they were operating from a very small capital base of $30 million:

> If we'd had more capital, we would have had more capital to support us getting going. We would have had slightly greater profits. We wouldn't have had to push for profits as quickly. We'd have had a bigger cushion to absorb our mistakes. The small capital base was inadequate, really. We realised this as we started to get the business in.

With no one loan to exceed 10 per cent of the bank's capital, it meant that their biggest loan could only be $3 million. This was prescribed. 'What we hadn't realised', Johnson said, 'was the growth in entrepreneurial activity and the private company market.' There were private company groups that individually had requirements more than $2 million or $3 million. Johnson said that he was not implying that a lack of capital pushed the bank into a lot of small and terrible loans:

> No, it's my responsibility. But there were some commercial pressures. Clearly we were operating at the end of the market that was high risk, yet we couldn't get big enough to get any sort of economies. When the lending system went wrong, it was a double whammy because of our smaller capital base.

Johnson said dispassionately, 'Probably one of the key structural mistakes we made was not arguing much more strongly with the Reserve Bank for a larger capital base. We wanted to raise an initial $50 million.' The Reserve Bank wanted the bank to have only $30 million. Johnson said that the bank's shareholders were willing in principle to put up the capital:

> There was an exchange of correspondence with the governor about that in the latter half of 1980. The Reserve Bank finally said no, $30 million was enough. They never gave us chapter and verse of why they'd come to that conclusion. $30 million capital translated roughly to 5 per cent of the new lending, and I think that's about as much of the market share they thought we could have, which would be tolerable to the other banks.
>
> In retrospect, that was a big mistake on our part. I guess we should have argued more persuasively, thumped the table or said we wouldn't go ahead. I don't know what we should have done. But we didn't appreciate at that stage how great our need would be for that capital. In retrospect, that was one of the key mistakes.
>
> After discussion with the Reserve Bank and debating it backwards and forwards, when the Reserve Bank indicated they thought $30 million was adequate for us, it was a bit like somebody putting the seal of good housekeeping on it. I'm not suggesting for one moment that it should have been their responsibility. It was our responsibility. We got it wrong by not persuading them otherwise.

A senior spokesman from the Reserve Bank in Sydney gave a different perspective in February 1988. He said that the concern of the

Reserve Bank was not so much with market share as with prudential issues. The Reserve Bank was worried that a larger capital would have encouraged the Australian Bank 'to grow more quickly than its management procedures and systems'. The Reserve Bank's point of view was that it was better to start small, to allow the management systems to cope with the lending. What happened to the Australian Bank was the very scenario they feared. When this argument was put back to the people who worked in the Australian Bank, they said that the Reserve Bank by its actions brought about the very thing it feared. Since the management systems were not developed, it was more difficult for the bank to deal in the high risk end of the market.

While the bank was struggling with its bad loans, the whole banking environment was changing much faster than anyone had anticipated. The Campbell Committee Report was tabled in Parliament in November 1981. This was followed by the Martin Report in December 1983; and by February 1985, sixteen new banks had been allowed entry to Australia. Garrick Agnew and Mark Johnson's gamble of getting the bank established before the deregulation had failed. Johnson said:

> It was the luck of the draw. Among the biggest mistakes we made is that we hadn't anticipated the addition to the system would be as big and as powerful and come as quickly. We had assumed when we set up Australian Bank that things would change, but that it would be rather more gradual and would take longer, before there was free entry to the big system.

It was little consolation that they were not alone in being surprised at the pace of the change. Richard Beetham (Melbourne, January 1988) said, 'I would never have believed that in 1985 we would get sixteen new banks of which a significant number would be 100 per cent-owned. I didn't think it would happen even several months before it happened.'

The Australian Bank applied to the Reserve Bank to be considered a 'new bank'. They would then come under the more relaxed shareholding regulations that had been applied to the new banks. These allowed a shareholder to own more than 15 per cent of a bank, if it was in the national interest. Citibank, for instance, was allowed 100 per cent ownership of its Australian bank. Others, like Chase Manhattan and the Royal Bank of Canada, were allowed 50 per cent ownership in Chase AMP and the National Mutual Royal Bank. Johnson said:

> It was very clear that we were far too small. We hadn't had time to build a business face. We had some real problems in our loan portfolio. The competition for staff was grotesque, for all the new banks were staffing up, plus all the big building societies were changing their status. So we were in a very, very difficult position. So we said, we think we ought to be treated as a new bank, so that we could do a deal with somebody to increase our size and standard.

Here the picture becomes muddied. With foreign banks seeking out the Australian market in the early 1980s, the Australian Bank should have been the first point of call for many of them. Why had the bank not struck a deal with a strong foreign partner? David Saunders (Melbourne, March 1988) partly raised this question and said that there was discussion of this in 1983 and 1984. Partly it was felt that Australian Bank was under an obligation to go with Banque Paribas, as it had been associated with the Paribas group from the beginning through its merchant bank associate. Partly it was Johnson's pride in not letting go the identity and control of the bank.

Johnson did not talk of this, but the request of going with a foreign partner, presumably Banque Paribas, was denied. Asked about it, Johnson played down his feelings at the time, admitting to feeling 'irritated'. Leigh Scott-Kemmis, however, was more forthcoming, (Sydney, February 1988) saying, 'The Reserve Bank has much to answer for.'

Richard Beetham (Melbourne, January 1988) said, 'Essentially, the Reserve Bank did not have a concern with foreign investment policy. Treasury had this responsibility.' And in the Treasury, the feeling was that the Australian Bank had to play by the rules of the game. It knew the score when it came in. Beetham said, 'It wasn't a new bank. It was an established bank.' If it had been allowed to change status, and a foreign bank allowed to take over the bank, 'basically it would have been a backdoor entry into Australian banking. It would not have been fair to the unsuccessful applicants for a banking authority.'

The Australian Bank was also a different case from Chase AMP and the National Mutual Royal Bank, where two well-known foreign banks had teamed up with indisputably strong Australian financial institutions. The Australian Bank had no domestic shareholder of that quality, so it would have meant the foreign bank being in control. Beetham said, 'It would not have been good politics, if nothing else, to allow an Australian bank to be taken over by a foreign interest, particularly one who might not have made application for a banking authority. Australian Bank had made a very great play on the fact that it was Australian.'

Was the Australian Bank's lack of success due to the inflexibility of official regulations? Was its lack of success due to commercial decisions and bad management? Beetham said:

> I was very enthusiastic about it being successful, but I thought it would have a tough time. It had a lot of talent and was a very good team. Mark's a pretty good guy, and I've got a lot of time for him, but I think they underestimated the extent to which being a bank carried its responsibilities.

Beetham suggested:

> There might not have been problems with Australian Bank if the owners had been willing to put in more capital. You had to be naive to think you could set up as a bank this year and expect to get a dividend for a long time. There was an assumption that a banking authority was some kind of a licence to print money. There is no comprehension for the quid pro quo for the status of having a banking authority.

Basically, he said, they were passive investors. 'I'm not saying that Garrick could have done any better with the Shareholdings Act saying none could hold more than 9.99 per cent, but none of Australian Bank's shareholders had the connections and the wherewithal to make that a commercial success.'

Against this litany of problems, there was much that Australian Bank got right. Johnson said:

> I think we had a much greater effect on banking than our financial resources. In financial terms, we were miniscule. We were the flea on the elephant. But first of all, the fact that somebody could come in at all, shook the conventional wisdom. Then the fact that we did things like treasury management well, demonstrated to the big banks that there must be some other approaches.

The most important difference was their orientation towards the customer. 'Banks provided services because they suited the bank, and the customer had to conform. We, however, designed a few things that fit what the customer wanted,' Johnson said.

Special account officers offered to help customers. Bankers went around to businesses to develop relationships. All of this was pretty novel in its time:

> The big banks were running factories. The tellers were no longer going into the big banks as a lifetime career. They were going in there to fill in a few years when they would rather be surfing. The quality of the service had been deteriorating. The big banks had become bigger and hadn't realised that they were neglecting their interface with the public. The deposits would come in anyway.

Because the Australian Bank recruited people who were better educated and were enthusiastic about changing this attitude, and wanted to succeed, the service was better. Johnson illustrated:

> Some nice things happened. 'Once a customer called me up and said, 'It is 10 past 5 and I am outside the Supreme Court in Sydney. We've just got a judgement and we have to pay $100 000 today to get back some shares over which there had been a dispute. Can you fix it for me?' We got him a cheque in 20 or 25 minutes. He really appreciated that and sent flowers to the girl who had worked on his cheque. After that we had ten new accounts, because people would come in and say he had told them this was the only bank to deal with.

Some of the good things still continue to flow:

> The nicest thing 3 months ago was at Palm Beach in Sydney. A man I had never met said to me, 'I'd really like to shake your hand, for I wouldn't be in business for myself today if it wasn't for Australian Bank.' What we had done was to help him buy back a small division of an American company. We'd actually done a leveraged buyout [borrowing to buy] before leveraged buyouts were fashionable. This set him up in his business, which is now prospering. That's the kind of thing that makes you feel good about it.

The single product that made the Australian Bank receive a lot of attention was the tie-up of its cash management trust to its cheque system:

> Effectively, what we did was to pay interest on the current account, when nobody was allowed to do that. It was partly based on the Hill Samuel cash-management trust, except that, since they weren't a bank, they couldn't hook it with a cheque at that stage. I think that that really was what got the big banks scared. It got the building societies thinking they had to get cheques. That product probably caused more talk and ferment in the industry than anything else.
>
> We had it in our first feasibility study. Really, what I had envisaged was more of a facility for smaller companies to manage their cash, because the bigger companies could use the bill market and unofficial market. As it turned out, a lot of individuals wanted it as well. That's just how I misjudged the market, if you like.

The cash management trust meant that the Australian Bank did not enjoy the interest-free current accounts of the other banks. To make up for this lack of free money, the treasury department was especially important as a profit centre for the bank. It had to make the most of the bank's narrow margins.

Because the bank was new and small, it was able to to have a fully integrated computer system and could tell what a customer's balance and account history were straight away. 'We tried a number of things in our systems and probably got people to think more about their computer systems and delivery systems in relation to the customers,' said Johnson. 'Before that, computer systems were something in the back office that helped the banks process their paperwork.'

The attempt to make a go of the Australian Bank, as Garrick Agnew and Mark Johnson had conceived it, was given up in 1985, when MLC and Lend Lease came in as the dominant shareholders.

Market talk had it that Johnson was told to leave, but Johnson said:

> I told the Board in the middle of 1985 that I didn't want to stay on, because I didn't want to be an administrator. I'm not a very good administrator. I didn't enjoy it. I wasn't doing it well. I don't know what the circularity is, but I'd worked pretty hard for 5 or 6 years. And this business of executive

committee meeting on Monday morning, budget committee on Tuesday morning, credit committee on Tuesday afternoon, another committee on Wednesday morning and start the whole cycle off the next week — stretching ahead of me, was something that I didn't really relish. So I told them in June 1985 that I wanted to quit when the right replacement was found.

It was quite clear that the bank was going into a different environment, with different shareholders, and it required different people. I was not sympathetic with the retail route, because I had reservations about its likely success. So it was time for me to go, and it was time for them to get someone else. In May 1986, they got Dick Morath in, and I stayed 2 and a half to 3 months to allow him to get settled in, and then I left.

After Mark Johnson

After Mark Johnson, Dick Morath steered the Australian Bank in the direction of a niche bank. His first priority was to stop the losses. He had come most recently from the State Bank of New South Wales, but he had worked with Vic Martin before that at the Commercial Banking Company of Sydney. The Australian Bank delayed its plans for listing. It withdrew from issuing Visa cards. In mid February 1987, it sold its retail branch banking network in Melbourne, Perth and Brisbane to the Bank of New Zealand. The successful cash-management trust was sold to MLC but continued to be managed by the bank. The strategy was to keep the strength of the treasury operations and move into specialised retail-banking products.

So the Australian Bank stopped being a retail bank in the traditional sense of the word. It even became difficult to locate in 1988. The sign was there in its old premises, but the bank itself was now located up a short flight of stairs. There was a small counter and half a dozen people working in the office area behind it. The bank offered deposit and chequebook facilities mainly to corporate customers, like insurance companies, that were likely to have $500 000 in their current accounts. Other than that, the bank made it plain, it was not going to be involved in transactional banking.

What the Australian Bank was interested in providing, Morath said in Sydney in February 1988, was 'specialised retail products that are very low in transactional requirements'. The bank launched Equity Credit, its first such product, in November 1987. Morath described it as a flexible home loan that can be used as an overdraft for any purpose. The bank markets it through direct mail and advertising, and people respond by telephone. So essentially, the Australian Bank replaced its branches by five telephone operators in North Sydney. These can be backed up by a total of 35 telephone operators looking after Lend Lease and MLC products. Australian Bank products, Morath said, 'piggyback off your transactional banking account'. Since the bank does not have to maintain 25 000 people and 1000 branches, he said, it can offer better service and competitive prices.

Though the Australian Bank was no longer the bank Mark Johnson and Garrick Agnew had dreamt of, it was also no longer a bank that was losing money. In the financial year ending 31 June 1987, the bank paid its first ever dividend and made a small operating profit of $1.7 million on shareholders' funds of $72 million. Its return on shareholders' funds was 1 per cent, which in 1988 rose to 1.4 per cent.

This, however, was not enough for the bank's shareholders. In January 1989, State Bank Victoria successfully bid for majority control of the Australian Bank. The treasury operations of the bank had already been sold to State Bank Victoria the year before. One objective of the bid was to inject Tricontinental Holdings Ltd, the wholly owned merchant-bank subsidiary of State Bank Victoria, into Australian Bank. This would have reduced the asset base of State Bank Victoria and so reduced its need to gear up to meet the new 8 per cent risk–asset guidelines. However, in May 1989, that game plan came unstuck. Trico was plagued by bad loans, allegations of insider trading and liquidity problems. So instead of a reverse takeover of the Australian Bank happening, Trico's operations were integrated with those of State Bank Victoria. The Australian Bank's retail products, like Equity Credit, had already been sold to MLC Life. So at the end of May 1990, the Australian Bank still has a banking licence but no banking networks or banking products. It is unclear whether it will survive even as a separate name.

The questions that arise from the Australian Bank story are: Is it possible to start a medium-sized retail bank from nothing in a deregulated environment — a bank that restricts itself to the middle corporate level and personal banking for professionals in the cities? Mark Johnson and Garrick Agnew were not doing quite that, for they had started in a regulated environment and then found themselves hurtled into the wide free world. However, from what Johnson says — if he had been a better manager; if he had put into place a better system of credit controls; if he had been able to employ experienced retail people with hands-on experience in lending; if the bank had had more capital in the beginning to absorb the start-up costs and its later mistakes — then the bank still would be viable. The Australian Bank had merchant bankers of high calibre. It scored on service, on innovation, on retail products, on its treasury operations. So if anybody could have done it, they had a better-than-average chance.

Dick Morath's answer in February 1988 was that it is not possible to start a medium-sized retail bank from scratch in Australia today, 'not if you want to do all of it. But if you want to do a few things with low transactional costs, then yes, it is possible.' He said that the Australian Bank under Mark Johnson 'tried to do everything. It was certainly a dead duck strategy once fifteen new banks came in. It was just never on, from that point of time. You had to specialise.' Morath was also convinced that branch networks are not the way to go for the new banks:

> To try and do what the existing majors have done already with their branch networks — it's got to be like bashing your head up against a wall. The four big guys have sufficient economies of scale, so that the little-sized player who tries to go their way with the branch network, I don't think he is going to win.

In the event, Morath also failed, as the shareholders were not getting an adequate return for their investment. The general new-bank experience supports Morath's assertion that building a branch retail network for a new bank is not possible.

Not everyone agreed, however. Bill Gurry, head of the National Mutual Royal Bank, built up a 180 branch network to reach 750 000 customers. But at the end of May 1990, even his bank has been swallowed up by ANZ. However, his story is worth telling in its own right, and much of what he tried to do had its beginnings in the Australian Bank.

Mark Johnson, after a 6 month rest, went back with the Macquarie Bank as a director and as chairman of its corporate service division. He said that one thing the Australian Bank experience made clear to him personally is that he has 'no desire to be an administrator, no desire to head an organisation...I'm certainly better at the deals business than I am at running a business,' he said. Trying to explain the enjoyment he gets from the deals side, he said:

> By and large, our business is on the conservative side of merchant bank business; but when you look at many of the deals that we have done, there is something there that wasn't there before. And in economic terms often there are efficiencies and there are advances, and that's quite nice. The cleanest kind of deal I've ever done was 15 years ago when we started to put together what is now the Bundaberg Sugar Co. It was a tiny little thing, Fairymeade Sugar Co. It took over Gibson and Howes, and it got a bit bigger. And then it took over the Millaquin Sugar Co., which made an efficient industry from something that was little fractions. If left like that, it would have got broken into pieces. It's a good operation, and one hopes that many mergers and acquisitions lead to similar efficiencies.

He is now making deals, which he said is 'good fun. Shouldn't have left, probably.' He laughed again. He looked out of the window and said that no, he had nothing more to say. He hadn't talked this much about the Australian Bank in a long, long time.

10 End of the new retailing: the National Mutual Royal Bank

The National Mutual Royal Bank was one of the few new banks to attempt retail branch banking. It was seen as the one most likely to succeed in the 1980s. However, at the end of May 1990, after a few twists and turns, the bank was sold to ANZ. Soon, the name of National Mutual Royal will disappear.

For Bill Gurry, 43, the chief executive of the National Mutual Royal Bank, the story is more of a 'dream turning into a reality and then turning into a nightmare'. Still feeling 'fragile' about the situation, Gurry talked of it a week after ANZ first took over the bank in April 1990 in the Melbourne headquarters of the National Mutual Royal saying:

> A number of us had a dream in the 1970s of starting a significant retail operation in Australia. I had three years in Australian Bank and it wasn't successful. So I was motivated to prove that I could do it. Seven years later I have established that it can be done. So it makes it even sadder.

The National Mutual Royal Bank opened in February 1986 and was equally owned by National Mutual, the second-largest insurance company in Australia, and the Royal Bank of Canada, the largest bank in Canada and one of the largest retail banks in the world. Within 13 months, in a dramatic coup, it had merged with the United Permanent Building Society, the third-largest building society in the country, acquiring an instant branch network and customer base.

In April 1990, Gurry said, the bank has '750 000 customers, 180 branches and 1100 people working directly in the branch network'. The push was to have innovative products and better service to distinguish the National Mutual Royal from the major banks. 'You weren't getting perfect service at the National Mutual Royal,' Gurry said, 'but you were getting better service than at the major trading banks'.

According to Gurry the bank was on target, despite the fact that the National Mutual Royal had not grown as fast as the major banks. In 1989 it returned only 7.2 per cent on its shareholders' funds — approximately half that of the major banks. However it has also avoided the bad loans experience of big and small banks in a difficult environment. Gurry maintained the bank's assets would have grown from $5 billion to $8 billion over five years returning 17 to 19 per cent on equity. 'We were half way there,' he said.

There were plans to expand via a number of small acquisitions worth less than $100 million. Gurry explained:

> One was a building society in Queensland, one was a building society in Victoria and the third leg was a small bank in Tasmania. They would have given us the sort of breadth we wanted in branch infrastructure right through the eastern coast of Australia.

There are many questions that emerge from this story. If the bank was 'on track', why did it get sold? Did the shareholders change objectives mid-stream? Or did conflict between the two equal shareholders spell the end of the joint venture? Does the sale of the National Mutual Royal mark the end of medium-sized retail banks in Australia? Or does it mean that branch banking is not viable for a medium-sized bank?

The National Mutual Royal is sold

Bill Gurry and Eric Mayer, managing director of National Mutual, agree on two things. The National Mutual Royal Bank was successful. And its success was, in part, responsible for its takeover by ANZ. But the rest of the story changes perceptibly depending on whether Gurry or Mayer is doing the talking.

Gurry said in April 1990 that the bank got sold because National Mutual changed its objectives mid-stream in 1988 and 1989. In 1986 it had wanted a medium-sized bank. But in 1989, it wanted a $25 billion bank that could provide the distribution network for its financial services. Merger with a major trading bank was the only feasible way to make this happen. In this sequence of events, Gurry said, both the Royal Bank of Canada and the National Mutual Royal Bank were 'innocent bystanders. We've sat back whilst they've [National Mutual and ANZ] negotiated their positions. We were subsidiary to the main play.' He says he was not involved in the merger discussions, except with the Canadian shareholders and in some talks concerning the price that ANZ would pay for the National Mutual Royal. 'From a personal point of view, one of my great disappointments is that I really have been on the outer.'

The first hint of National Mutual's desire to move into banking in a big way came in mid-1988, when it considered buying the Bank of New Zealand with Credit Suisse as a partner. According to Gurry that initiative came unstuck in November 1988 because the Bank of New Zealand had greater problems than had been anticipated. In April 1990, Gurry said:

> At that point Eric Mayer asked the Royal Bank whether they would support more offshore branches of the National Mutual Royal Bank and grow aggressively in Australia. The Canadians said, 'We have been very supportive of National Mutual Royal. We are very happy with the development. But we never had any intention of owning 50 per cent of a $25 billion bank in Australia. We will continue to support you in reasonable expansion, what we previously talked about — an $8 billion bank in the first five years.' They said they wouldn't stand in the way of National Mutual, providing they could exit with profit and honour.

Eric Mayer of National Mutual countered this interpretation, saying it 'is probably overdramatising the change' in strategy to say that National Mutual had moved from wanting an $8 billion bank to a $25 billion bank. He said in an interview in his office in April 1990, 'I think National Mutual always did want a retail bank in Australia that was large enough to be able to service all of its Australian policy holders properly and indeed it wanted a similar size bank in New Zealand.' He said that in 1986 National Mutual was not expecting 'to build a bank as large as the majors.' But at the time, they thought it would be possible for National Mutual Royal to grow to a much larger bank much more quickly.' According to Mayer, National Mutual did not contemplate a merger with a major bank when they set up National Mutual Royal in 1986. The proposed merger with ANZ was 'a change in strategy in a very significant manner'.

The change resulted from National Mutual's desire to become a 'significant, international, profitable, broad financial services organisation'. Such a change would require sizeable capital, and according to Mayer, National Mutual have been working on options to raise this capital for a couple of years.

In April 1990, he said that the option of going to the market direct was considered and rejected.

> In the current depressed state of the market . . . you would not get a proper price for your capital and you could give a windfall gain to a predator company. We didn't think that was in the best interest of policy holders . . . We were very well advanced with a strategic study early in 1989 that showed that our best method of proceeding could well be to have a merger with a major bank.

This would not only gain National Mutual the capital it desired, but the synergies of the merger would make National Mutual more profitable than before.

At about the same time, the ANZ Bank had realised the need to align with a large superannuation organisation as it is expected that throughout the 1990s savings will flow more than ever before into superannuation to the detriment of the savings banks. In May 1989, Will Bailey of ANZ approached Eric Mayer asking whether National Mutual would be interested in getting together. Mayer recalled, 'We said yes. Very. To give them the credit, they approached us. We were very ready to be approached because we were within a cooee of approaching them.'

The Royal Bank of Canada was asked for its comments about this version, but chose not to reply. This was unfortunate, for the National Mutual Royal story questions the inherent stability of joint ventures. Bill Gurry's attitude toward this particular joint venture has changed over the years from one of unqualified enthusiasm to one of restraint. In December 1987 in Melbourne, he said that the structural similarities of the banks in Australia and Canada had helped to make the joint venture successful. Moreover, both partners brought different strengths to the deal. He said:

> On the one hand, you have National Mutual very strongly involved with the retail market place, but without an understanding of how you do that on the banking side. On the other hand, you have the largest retail bank in the world on a similar population and geographical basis. Royal have been really terrific. This joint venture has been very successful. I can't promise that this is always going to be the case.

In December 1989, he was more cautious, saying his hesitancy sprang from 'the passage of time. The shareholders fall further out of love and the honeymoon period is over. It is difficult to get the parties to have a single view.' In April 1990, after the National Mutual Royal was sold, he said 'the ending of a joint venture is not ipso facto proof of the failure of joint ventures. In fact, joint ventures succeed by ending by allowing one or other of the partners to achieve some other goal. I think we are an illustration of that.' He pointed out that both partners had profited from the deal. 'The shareholders' funds stand at $310 million,' he said, 'but some of that includes bonus shares. So actually, each put in about $130 million.' With the National Mutual Royal being sold for $400 million, each partner made a profit of $70 million. 'Not a bad return for four years from start up,' Gurry noted.

He said that his experience with the National Mutual Royal has taught him 'the importance of getting the shareholder structure right and making sure that everybody is absolutely clear about objectives. If there are changed players in the joint venture, you've got to make sure there is a continuation of the same objectives and beliefs.' In this case he said, at the start there was a recognition by both shareholders that 'patient capital was required.' His verdict is that the Royal Bank stayed with the initial objective, whereas National Mutual moved to wanting something else.

The end result was that on 2 April 1990, National Mutual Royal was sold to ANZ for close to $400 million. The Treasurer approved this on principle on the basis that if the merger did not go ahead, ANZ would hand National Mutual Royal back to National Mutual. In any event, the Royal Bank of Canada bowed out. Soon after, Bill Gurry announced his intention to leave at the end of June 1990, having declined ANZ's offer of a senior position.

The merger was vetoed by the Treasurer on 23 May 1990. This made for a ticklish situation, for at the same time, the guidelines that were announced made it impossible for a mutual life association to own a bank. This however did not overly deter National Mutual as on 25 May it announced it would take back National Mutual Royal, making it the centre of its banking strategy. However, on 30 May 1990, it back-tracked and declared that due to the 'onerous' conditions that had been placed on the mutual life office owning a bank at this stage, it was going to re-sell National Mutual Royal to ANZ. The National Mutual Royal Bank had been used as 'an aerial ping-pong' for so long that even Bill Gurry welcomed the final decision to go to ANZ instead of being a bank in limbo.

The dream

Much of what Bill Gurry did and did not do with the National Mutual Royal had its roots in the Australian Bank experience. He said in December 1987, in Melbourne, that one lesson learnt is that it is crucial to have a 'critical mass' of customers: 'That's why we went the United Permanent way'. He, of course, had the luxury of strong shareholders who were willing to put in the capital to make the acquisition.

He also learnt that it was important to spend money on the fundamentals like growing sufficient volume of business, getting the customers, and having the infrastructure in place. Gurry said that the Australian Bank experience showed him the importance of having a clearly defined strategy of where the bank wanted to be in 5 years:

> I think it influenced me very strongly in believing that indecision is the worst thing the staff can deal with. Actually, staff are prepared to live with a bad decision rather than no decision.

In an important way, as with the Australian Bank, Bill Gurry pitted himself against the established banks. The launch of the National Mutual Royal in February 1986 gave the message: If you are fed up with the dullness and lack of innovation of the big banks, here is a bank that will do the same things better.

In award-winning commercials launching the bank, a man doing a party act is imitating a steam engine. After the puny efforts of the previous competitors, the National Mutual Royal man announces that he too is going to imitate the steam engine. The crowd boos, expecting more of the dull fare, when the new man blows the whole party away. The message is clear: Here's *our* act, and there is theirs.

Gurry said:

> Traditionally, the major trading banks have treated customers very, very badly. I can remember when I was a director of Hill Samuel, and probably earning three or four times as much as my bank manager — I approached the bank manager for a $10 000 loan and was knocked back. I think it was basically because the bank manager at the Commercial Bank of Australia looked at my application and said, 'That young whipper snapper is earning three or four times as much as I, and he is half my age, and I resent that'. And the tellers were never taught to provide a service. They were taught to stand there, look supposedly efficient and not be friendly.

Bill Gurry thinks that his bank's building society culture leads to a more friendly and less impersonal bank.

Gurry is passionate on the subject of the major banks, for in some ways the identity of his bank depends on being different from the majors. The National Mutual Royal Bank came up once in conversations with the chief executives of the major banks; but for Gurry, the major banks are a constant backdrop. He sees the senior executive echelons of the four big banks as still being traditional and hidebound, despite deregulation. He sees this reflected in their traditional boards of directors: 'Look at the two boards in Melbourne. Traditionally, the chief executive of X company has been appointed to the board of Y bank. And traditionally, such and such a family has been represented on a bank board, and it remains.'

He saw the National Mutual Royal Bank as strong because of its differences from the older banks. 'Though we are only a mosquito' compared to them, he said, the National Mutual Royal was more flexible and innovative. The majors, because of their free deposits, would have 'withdrawal symptoms' if they had to match the bank's policy of paying interest on the daily balance in a current account.

Gurry's dealings with the major trading banks were formal. He said, 'I would be more reluctant to give them a call than my other colleagues. There are some barriers which still exist.' Then he became temporarily diplomatic and said, 'The major banks have been very nice to us.' Reverting back to form, he added, 'Though they may be quite rude behind our backs.' The clash has been most particularly with the Australia and New Zealand Banking Group (ANZ) in the fight for the United Permanent Building Society. Gurry said, 'ANZ has been very, very nice to me at a senior level. On the other hand, they have done everything in their power to rip us apart. I guess I find it slightly flattering.' Reflecting on this particular relationship, he commented, 'I am not sure why we clashed with the ANZ. It certainly hasn't been intentional on our part.'

Though Bill Gurry hoped that his bank would be different in significant ways from the big banks, the National Mutual Royal Bank was the only new bank that, like the majors, based its retail operations on a sizeable branch network. This proved more difficult than he earlier anticipated. Though the National Mutual Royal had representation in all the state capitals, at the end of May 1990, it was far from being a national bank of that order.

The bank's branch network is supplemented by electronic banking services, but Gurry saw the future of retail banking tied up with a branch network. 'People do prefer to deal with people rather than with machines,' he said, provided that the service is personal. 'Customer acceptance of the new technology is not particularly high. We will obviously be involved in the technological side, but we will also want to have the human side.' In December 1989, he acknowledged that branch banking had proved more expensive than earlier anticipated, but he said that he remains 'absolutely convinced' that the retail branch network is the way to go. 'This is real banking. The other stuff [niche banking and investment banking] is not real banking.'

It was the National Mutual Royal's branch strategy that made it different from the other new banks. Of the fifteen foreign banks that entered Australia in 1985 and 1986, few chose to clash head on with the established banks by going the retail route. Some of the most successful, like the Macquarie Bank and Bankers Trust Australia, have consciously tried to do as little retail banking as possible, while building up their investment banking products. The value of a banking licence for them has not been in tapping the household sector; rather, it enabled them to get a better credit rating and cheaper money. The strengths of the new banks have largely been in the wholesale area, corporate lending, the money market and foreign exchange. They have done especially well on their off-balance-sheet business.

The new foreign banks have found it harder than they thought to crack the retail market in Australia. The start-up costs have been high, especially when the banks were starting from scratch. The established banks have fought back with greater innovation than anyone expected from their stilted image. Customer loyalty too has been hard to shake, even though many of the new banks have only wanted to be the 'second bank'. The Bank of America was the first dropout from the retail scene, despite its link-up with the retail giant, Coles Myer.

Chase AMP, nicknamed the Champ in its early days, also has had a faltering record. It started in February 1985 with a view that it could service its customers through a national automated teller machine (ATM) network and a 24 hour telephone banking service. It believed that the profits were in the retail business and hoped to gain 2 to 3 per cent of the top half of the Australian consumer market by 1990. It went to the market with a cheap Visa card and quickly added 70 000 customers, thinking that it could piggyback another four to five services off the card. It also had agency arrangements with the biggest building society, the St George Building Society.

In November 1987, though, Chase AMP was admitting that its early research had been 'overly optimistic', as in 2 years the bank had lost $7.9 million. Its retail thrust moved away from the electronics network to the traditional 'brick and mortar' set-up of the AMP sales offices. Its future again became clouded in December 1989, as it found itself significantly exposed to companies caught in the downturn.

Other than the National Mutual Royal Bank, the only other new bank significantly in retail is Citibank Ltd. It has its eyes set on being a major lender with select deposit and lending products through extensive advertising, direct mail and the telephone link-up. It is, however, more up-market, in that its cash management account, housing mortgage and leasing products are aimed at high-net-asset-worth individuals and its corporate lending at the top 250 companies in Australia. Citibank's retail operations were built on the business of its existing finance company. It also concluded agency arrangements with retailers. Added to this, it has fifteen branches and access to the more than 1500 ATMs of ANZ, the National Australia Bank, the building societies and the credit unions.

Citibank's strategy has put it ahead in terms of overall performance. This still did not make Gurry question his strategy. He pointed out that part of Citibank's success is because it has access to greater capital.

The Catholic boy who made good

Young, self-assured, Bill Gurry was dressed in a dark blue suit with a red tie and gold cufflinks. He has blue eyes and platinum hair. He pointed to the leather chair, himself taking a straight chair, because he needs it for his back. Not only did he want his bank to be different from the major trading banks, but he could not see himself living the lives of the chief executives of the big banks, where some of them received their first managerial appointment at 40 plus. He could not imagine how somebody would be content to spend their whole life in banking, let alone in a single bank. He said in December 1987, 'Life wouldn't be worth living under those circumstances. I don't wish to be a Bob White or a Nobby Clark and be 60 years old in a bank. I'll be doing much more interesting things.'

Bill Gurry also sees his private life as separate from his banking career. 'I don't get into the social activities of banking. No, it does not hurt me. I have really strong views that that is a thing of the past.'

Meg, his wife, too has very strong views about that. Talking to her illustrates the chasm in world view separating the older style of banker and one of Gurry's generation. Asked what it is like to be a banker's wife, she reacted sharply. Sitting in their house in Malvern in the lounge with a dark brown comfortable sofa, scatter rugs, Indian embroidery and pots, and the netting of the front door undone, she said in December 1987:

> I was never aware of being a banker's wife till Bill went as managing director of Capel Court. A few weeks after that there was a Christmas party. I remember this senior guy came up to me and said, 'Well, I suppose you're going to be very busy from now on.' I said, 'No, I'm not.' He said, 'Now that your husband is managing director, you'll be busy.' I said, 'Sure as hell, it is going to make Bill busy, but why should I be busy?'
>
> It is the first time I articulated it. Bill has no expectations of me, that I am going to be part of his banking life. I am supportive in that we are very close and we talk about Bill's work and mine. I don't want to sound patronising; but if women want to support their husbands that way, it is their choice. For a lot of women, it is a full time career. Some of the wives of the bankers at the Royal Bank of Canada have lived in sixteen different places. They have gone wherever their husbands have gone.

Bill Gurry's background and networks also set him apart from the older bankers. He grew up in Coburg, a Melbourne suburb, in a large old rambling house. His father was a general practitioner and a respected citizen of Coburg. 'Being the son of a GP in Coburg was not quite Toorak,' he said, 'but I consider myself as coming from a very privileged background in the sense of having a very happy family life, going to a good school.' He had the lot: books, music, tennis court, a holiday house where they swam and rowed. 'We had what we needed,' he said.

Gurry belongs to a large Irish Catholic family with six boys and a girl. The history of the Irish in Australia has been of a community against the establishment, so the financial world of Melbourne, reputedly the most conservative of establishments, was a new frontier for an Irish boy from Coburg. Interestingly enough, he said, 'I don't think being Irish or Catholic has ever interfered with my progress. I've never felt it as an obstacle. I've never had anybody ask me about it. I think, possibly, Catholics may make their own barriers.' However, it hasn't helped him either, he said, because Irish Catholics do not network to make for success: 'An Irish Catholic will look after a fellow he has found outside his front door, drunk and derelict,' but Irish Catholics will not say, 'I will help my fellow Catholic to become successful in this area.' This is what distinguishes them from Jews, he said, who try to help each other in business and politics; and it is also different from, say, people from the establishment Melbourne Grammar School:

> Nine and three-fourths time out of ten, a Melbourne Grammar man will pick a Melbournian for a job rather than the other guy, regardless of merit. If a person came with a Xavier [Melbourne's leading Catholic school] tie, I would treat that person as I would treat the next person. Maybe that is why Irish Catholics haven't succeeded. Maybe I should look after my fellow Xaverian, but I have no wish to live my life that way.

The Irish in Australia have also been linked specially to the Labor Party, and Gurry's family were Labor sympathisers. Bill Gurry himself is a Labor enthusiast and active behind the scenes on the advisory council of the Labor Premier of Victoria. Meg made the point that it is not particularly radical to support present day Labor, but even that places him apart from the traditional image of the Australian banker, who is more Liberal than Labor.

Being Catholic permeated all aspects of Gurry's life. Meg who comes from an Anglican family in Melbourne said, 'I think it was a motivating factor for him to succeed and to achieve, to break into a very conservative white Anglo-Saxon Protestant establishment.' She mentioned that it was important for him some 10 years ago to become a member of the establishment Melbourne Club:

> Now it doesn't matter at all; but 10 years ago, I think it would be a motivating factor.
>
> His mother was an important influence. She's very Catholic and goes to Mass every Sunday. She is a very strong woman, with a strong sense of self. She instilled in him that it is okay to compete, gave him confidence that he could do what he set out to do.

In more physical ways, being Catholic dictated that he go to Xavier College, because it was the leading Catholic school in Melbourne, even if it meant travelling an hour and a half each way to Kew. It meant that ethics were seen as basic to life, and Bill Gurry even now chaffes at the lack of ethics and morality in the community. Being Catholic also meant that nothing in his family and school life led him to the world of finance:

> Catholics are very service-oriented. You became a doctor, lawyer, joined the civil service or the priesthood. You were not encouraged at school to go into politics, business or the media, to go into the more powerful positions in the community.

As with many traditional Catholic families, the second son in the family became a priest. Bill Gurry also thought of becoming a priest, but decided against it. After that, it was more or less understood that he would go to university. All six boys in his family went to university, and his sister became a nurse. Gurry said, 'In large Catholic families, it was nice to be seen to be achieving. And if all the children were going to university, you were seen to be achieving.'

Having given up the idea of being a priest, he felt that he now had to choose between being a doctor or a lawyer. Since he hated physics and chemistry, he opted for law at Monash University. Talking of Monash, he related how he became captain of the rowing club, his first leadership role at university. The club had being going for only a couple of years, he said, and 'I took it over. We went from being a maiden performer in 3 years to winning the Oxford and Cambridge cup, which is the highest you can do at university level.' He continued his captaincy for 6 years, even though in his third year he transferred to the University of Melbourne.

Bill Gurry, managing director, National Mutual Royal Bank (courtesy BRW)

In 1968, when he was in his fourth year of law, he found that he was not particularly keen to attend university. He had worked part-time for Geoff Webb, a stockbroker, and that was his introduction to the world of business. 'I found it very exciting,' Bill Gurry said. 'I did invest my $200 a week and I lost my $200 as a result of investing in that boom. It was a wonderful lesson. It was marvellous that I learnt so quickly how treacherous the whole investment process is. All markets come to an end.'

Geoff Webb introduced him to Bob Dalziel, a former lawyer who had retired as a stockbroker. Working for Dalziel part-time, to manage a portfolio for the trust that he ran, was what made the pieces come together for Gurry, for Dalziel would tell him the history of the companies and how the different people interacted with each other in the different companies. 'He told me all about the world of commerce,' Bill Gurry said. 'He knew the ins and outs of each company. He just whetted my appetite enormously.'

While working for Dalziel, Gurry completed his law degree, though he attended no classes during his fourth year. By now, he was intrigued by merchant banking:

> I did not know much about it. It was even difficult to find articles about it, but every one that I found, I devoured. Merchant banking just sounded so interesting. It was involved in corporate finance. It was involved in analysing companies, in mergers and acquisitions. The reason that mergers and acquisitions appealed to me is that it requires a great deal of critical analytical skills; it requires some numeracy skills; and it requires very

> strong planning and structural skills — and they are all things that I enjoy immensely. I enjoy particularly thinking through the politics of a situation.

To illustrate, he talked of how Dunlop acquired Olympic and rationalised the tyre industry in Australia. This also allowed it to build the cable industry. 'Pacific Dunlop is now one of the healthiest companies in Australia,' Gurry said. 'I am strongly in favour of that type of acquisition. The kind of acquisition I am opposed to is the entrepreneurial paper chase.'

Merchant banking in the early 1970s was very new. Once when Bill Gurry and Meg went to a party, a woman asked Meg what her husband did. When she said that he was a merchant banker, the woman replied, 'I'm so sorry. He must be spending a lot of time overseas,' thinking that Bill worked in the merchant navy. 'Nobody had ever heard of merchant banking,' Gurry said.

His entry into merchant banking came through a rowing contact, Paul Espie, who later became managing director of the Bank of America in Australia. Espie at the time was a merchant banker, and through him Gurry started work in Sydney in 1973, at International Pacific Corporation Ltd, now Rothschild Australia Ltd.

After two years, he said:

> Basically, we made a family decision to live in Melbourne; and at that particular moment, Hill Samuel approached me. Mark Johnson asked me to have a cup of coffee with him, and I had a cup of coffee with David Clarke, and I walked out with an offer under my arm to come back to Melbourne with them.
>
> Hill Samuel was marvellous. It was 6 absolutely superb years. I learnt so much. Both David Clarke and Mark Johnson were older brother figures for me. They were my heroes. They were both terrific. I had a great ambition to be a director before I was 30. I got to be a director before I was 27 or 28. All of my expectations at Hill Samuel were met.

From 1977 to 1980, he was the director in charge of the Melbourne office:

> There was the traditional Melbourne versus Sydney situation at Hill Samuel. I'd like to think I succeeded in establishing the Melbourne office as a viable operation. In the Melbourne office, we were financial advisors to Telecom, the largest company in Australia. We had worked on the largest industrial takeover ever in Australia and the largest mining takeover ever in Australia.

These were Dunlop's acquisition of Olympic in 1979 and CRA's acquisition of the mining assets of Broken Hill South in 1978.

The problem that did crop up was about equality, he said. He thought that all the directors should have an equal stake, as the six of them made the decisions together, but this was a minority opinion. At that time, the Australian Bank offer came up. Mark Johnson had come down from London and went to talk things over at Gurry's house. Since Meg was going out, they ordered some takeaways from Maxims. Though the money was better at Hill Samuel, Bill Gurry decided to move. 'It was unknown, it had not happened before,' he said. 'That was part of the excitement.'

After 3 years, when he was frustrated with the Australian Bank, he again had the luck of the Irish. He and his colleague David Saunders, who is now with Byvest Advisors Ltd, sat down and worked out their priorities and options. Saunders opted to start an investment company in his own right, buying and selling companies as a principal. Gurry said:

> The alternative that appealed most to me was to go to an institution which had said it wanted to go into retail banking. At the same time, just out of the blue, I received a phone call from Geoff Dewar of National Mutual, who said, 'If the managing director post of Capel Court [National Mutual's merchant bank] came up, would you be interested?' I said yes, I would be interested. He said, 'Leave it with me.' I was actually going for a holiday for a week, driving through the Flinders Ranges, so I went away. The day after I came back, it was announced that the previous managing director had resigned, and the headhunter rang up and asked if I was interested in that job. National Mutual also said, 'We'd like you to be interested in that job.' And that was that.

Gurry had come to know Dewar and Ian Ferres (then National Mutual's general manager, investments; now managing director, Meridian Global Funds Management) when he was at Hill Samuel Australia and was advising CRA on its acquisition of the mining assets of Broken Hill South in 1978. 'So within 2 months of sitting down and doing that exercise with David Saunders, the one that was top of my list came up,' Gurry said. 'Extraordinary luck.'

Setting up the National Mutual Royal Bank

When Gurry joined Capel Court Corporation in 1983, it was really with two aims: 'I was employed as managing director of Capel Court, but I was also employed to help National Mutual get into retail banking. But there was nothing specific. The initial thing was to think through how we were going to do that.' The National Mutual at the time was already becoming a financial conglomerate. It had a controlling interest in Mercantile Credit, the biggest non-bank-owned finance company. It owned the National Mutual Permanent Building Society and a trust company, National Mutual Nominees. It had the merchant bank Capel Court and an internal cash-management trust. It also had National Assets Management, which dealt with listed and unlisted property and equity trusts. With deregulation, the banks were moving into insurance; so as a defensive move, the National Mutual saw that it had to move into banking, to defend its client base.

In 1985, Ian Ferres and Bill Gurry drew up a list of eight or nine overseas banks that could be possible partners for the National Mutual's bank. The Royal Bank of Canada was not on the list, even though there are striking similarities between the Australian and Canadian banks. In both countries, there are a few large banks with widespread banking networks to cover a huge country with a similar population. Gurry said, 'Unfortunately, in the past, nobody thought of Canadian banks. They were sort of part of North American banks. They've become stronger in profile only in the last few years.'

While looking at the other banks, Bill Gurry said:

> I had seen Orion [the Royal Bank's operation in London] when in London. I had been very impressed and suggested to Ian that he should also go to Orion. When he was at Orion, they said to him, 'Have you ever thought of having a Canadian as a partner?' We got a submission from the Royal Bank, and we found it was interesting. When Ian came back, we sat down and worked it out. We shortlisted three banks: National Westminster, Sumitomo and Royal. We spent 3 weeks away, talking to the Canadian and English banks. We had decided it was highly unlikely the Japanese would be a player. Basically, we found it very frustrating to deal with them. They changed the people we were dealing with so many times. We had to go back to square one every time. We thought if it didn't work out with the Canadian and the British, we would stop off in Japan.

However, there was a hitch at the Canadian end:

> There was some dissension within their ranks about whether they should go ahead with it. They were having their own difficulties. At the time, to make a substantial investment in a country where they had very minor operations did not make a lot of sense to some. We were disappointed.

Against this rather troubling scenario, Gurry said, 'We got to Britain and we were feted by Natwest, and we were influenced strongly in their direction. Then we came back and corresponded with both of them.' In the meantime, the Canadians had decided that going with the National Mutual was a good deal after all, and so the National Mutual ended up signing with the Canadians.

The joint venture between the National Mutual and the Royal Bank of Canada was in place, and the National Mutual Royal Bank opened on 26 February 1986. The National Mutual Permanent Building Society was converted to a savings bank, and that gave the new bank a retail base of 80 000 customers and 46 branches.

Gurry said:

> It is fair to say we always thought we would have a presence in the corporate, investment and retail markets. It was easy to see how you can build up investment and corporate banking. It was far less easy to see how you could build up retail banking. We hadn't actually opened by the time discussion started with the United Permanent Building Society. A member of our board had a board membership in common with the chairman of

United Permanent. The chairman of UP mentioned that they were thinking about their position in a deregulated environment.

It took off from there.

Building societies, in a sense, were very much like savings banks. They drew their deposits from the household and lent for owner-occupied housing. The difference was that they were state-based, with state and territory authorities regulating their activities. When the savings banks were heavily regulated by the Reserve Bank of Australia, the building societies grew, because they could offer better terms to their customers. However, since the early 1980s, the building societies had faced increasing competition from the cash management trusts, superannuation funds and friendly societies, all trying for a piece of household savings. So when the banks were deregulated, the building societies found it hard to compete. They extended their product range and linked up with the electronic services provided by banks; but essentially, building societies were undercapitalised. In 1985/86, the capital of building societies was 3 and a half per cent of their total assets, compared to a 5 per cent capital-adequacy ratio for the established banks at the time. Moreover, the building societies had historically been less profitable than savings banks, because building societies were structured like cooperatives, to provide their members with better deposit rates, and so they operated with narrower margins.

Building societies had a few choices open to them, in order to compete: they could merge with other building societies; they could try to attract more capital, diversify their operations and make a go of it as they were; or they could transform themselves into savings banks. The last option, though, would require more capital, to meet with the necessary capital-adequacy ratio for banks at the time.

A bank looking at taking over a building society needed to put in more capital. The National Mutual Royal had the capital. The building society could in return offer a large number of outlets and a retail customer base. This was exactly what a new bank like the National Mutual Royal needed to build up its 'critical mass', to compete with the major banks.

The United Permanent had started thinking of the impending deregulation and had come to the conclusion that it was not large enough to succeed on its own. It was too stretched by its branch network and high cost of funds to be able to offer competitive products. In May 1982, it tried to merge with the giant New South Wales Building Society Ltd. However, virtually at the last moment, the United Permanent withdrew, saying that the management styles of the two organisations were different. It saw itself as a takeover target. In 1983, the United Permanent tried again, this time with the largest building society: St George Building Society. At the same time, the United Permanent was being assiduously wooed by the State Building Society. United Permanent members rejected the proposal to merge with the St

George, mainly because United Permanent staff were concerned about amalgamating with a building society twice its size.

So in 1986, it was the United Permanent's third attempt to restructure itself. This time, it looked at transforming itself to a savings bank and merging with the National Mutual Royal Bank. Neville Wran, then Premier of NSW, gave his approval, for the building society would move outside the jurisdiction of the state when it became a savings bank. The National Mutual Royal proposal to merge with the United Permanent was announced on 12 June 1986. At the time, the United Permanent had assets of $1.6 billion and was Australia's third-largest building society. It had 129 branches, 1014 employees and more than 700 000 accounts. The National Mutual Royal offered, in the main, better credit terms to the existing account holders, most of whom, according to the building society regulations, would have to vote on the merger proposal. The bank would reduce the interest on existing home loans by 0.5 per cent a year for the next 2 years and would guarantee the continuation of the loans. Members would receive an additional 0.75 per cent interest on their deposits for the next 3 years. To sweeten the deal for the state, the new bank offered at least $150 million in low interest loans to first-home buyers in NSW, with at least $40 million to be provided in the first year. The board of directors of the United Permanent figured that the minimum benefits to its members and future home-loan borrowers would be $60.125 million.

Soon, though, there were rival bids from the ANZ and the Advance Bank Australia. The Advance Bank had been the New South Wales Building Society Ltd, which in June 1985 had transformed itself into a savings bank. The St George Building Society also had some 'generalised correspondence' with the United Permanent.

Each side touted its offer and, depending on its perspective and interest scenario, proclaimed its offer as the most favourable. The National Mutual Royal increased its bid by another $39 million. Instead of offering depositors a flat increase of 0.75 per cent in interest for 3 years, it offered an extra 1.25 per cent in the first year, 1 per cent in the second and 0.8 per cent in the third. However, the crucial winning point for the bank was that the United Permanent staff wanted to go with the National Mutual Royal rather than with the other banks. ANZ and the Advance had over 80 per cent of their branches in the same suburbs as the United Permanent, so the staff saw possible retrenchments in accepting their offers. The National Mutual Royal, on the other hand, was a new bank with a building society base in Victoria. Gurry said, 'When it was announced that the ANZ had the intention of proceeding with the takeover, over 90 per cent of the staff signed a petition to say they favoured the National Mutual Royal and would not want to work with the ANZ. I think they viewed the ANZ as swallowing them up.' The staff, because they saw their jobs at stake, canvassed the members of the building society to go the National Mutual Royal way.

The board of the United Permanent rejected rival offers and unanimously decided to recommend the National Mutual Royal offer. United Permanent members were asked to vote on the proposed merger at an extraordinary general meeting on 8 July 1986, but this was postponed three times to allow members to consider the other offers and to meet with some objections from the Registrar of Permanent Building Societies. The final postponement, from 5 August to 12 August, was providential, for on 5 August Sydney had the worst rainstorm in a century.

There were many grey areas as to whether a person had to have a minimum of $1 or $500 on deposit to qualify to vote, so it could be that 175 000 were eligible, or 500 000. It was also uncertain whether the proxies that had come in a week before the meeting would be valid or not. What was clearly spelt out was that proxies had to be hand-carried to the meeting; a member could carry four, including his own. A non-member was only allowed three proxies. So the bank aimed to get the maximum number it could, so that the necessary two-thirds majority could not be questioned.

A major feat was to organise an army of proxy carriers. The bank contacted some 190 groups, ranging from the Rotary to lifesaving clubs, to carry the proxies. Each proxy carrier was promised $30 plus expenses for his or her club. In addition, two large planeloads of staff from the National Mutual Royal Bank in Melbourne were brought in.

The meeting was held at Sydney's Parramatta football stadium on a cold wintery night on 12 August 1986. There were 10 500 people present, representing 21 300 votes, and it was said to be the world's largest shareholders' meeting. Twelve giant screens showed the floodlit faces of the United Permanent officials. Free cheese, ham and pickle sandwiches were distributed. Questions remained as to why the United Permanent board had put only one proposal — the merger with the National Mutual Royal — to vote. Why were the other two proposals also not presented directly? However, with the voting scrutinised by Deloitte Haskins & Sells, it was learnt that over 90 per cent of members favoured the merger with the National Mutual Royal Bank.

Before the United Permanent and the National Mutual Royal could savour their victory, in mid-August, Ron Baker, the NSW Registrar of Permanent Building Societies, vetoed the proposed merger. Baker interpreted the Permanent Building Societies Act to mean that NSW building societies could not be taken over.

Reconciliation talks failed, and a legal battle started through the Supreme Court of NSW. On 22 October, the Supreme Court overturned the Registrar's veto. It upheld the National Mutual Royal and the United Permanent contention that the Registrar was just a 'letterbox', with no discretion to refuse to register resolutions put before him. Gurry said, 'The Registrar's action was purely political. When Neville Wran was the Premier, he welcomed the proposal. He was wholly in favour of it. Then unfortunately, 10 days later, he decided to resign.' Though the new Premier, Barrie Unsworth, had said that he had no objection to the merger, Gurry said:

> He didn't like it. The new Minister for Finance was totally opposed to it. I've met with him, and he makes no bones about it that he wishes it had never been allowed. He was entirely interested in the fact that United Permanent was going to move from a state-controlled function to a federally controlled function. I don't think he was at all interested in providing the customers with better opportunities, and my admiration for him is zilch.

The United Permanent Building Society first transformed itself into a company and then received a banking authority from the Reserve Bank. On 2 March 1987, the United Permanent branches opened as National Mutual Royal Bank branches. Staff and contractors had replaced the signs, posters, brochures and stationery with National Mutual Royal material over the weekend.

After the United Permanent deal, the NSW government made it more difficult for other building societies to convert to savings banks; but for the National Mutual Royal Bank, the United Permanent merger had been a great step forward. It emerged as a 175 branch network with $3.7 billion in assets within the first year of its operation. In 1986/87, its first full financial year, it declared a profit of $8.2 million. The bank had grown so fast that the two shareholders were putting in another $40 million to its $240 million in capital. This whole building-society episode earned Bill Gurry at the time the label of being 'Australia's most aggressive banker'. The rest is history.

The historical ironies of the story do not escape Gurry. For ten years he had a dream that he would be able to manage retail banking better than the major banks. This had as much to do with his own background as with the state of banking in a regulated environment. It led him to join the Australian Bank and it also hastened his departure. In his efforts to establish the National Mutual Royal, he often saw ANZ as the prime antagonist. His bank stressed its building society base and culture, but in the end was instrumental in delivering the building society to the ANZ. With Gurry leaving, it is interesting that all the major characters in Australian Bank will have bowed out of retail banking.

Gurry thought he was making history by establishing the first successful national retail bank in more than 70 years. He did show that it was possible to set up a medium-sized retail bank with a branch network. It was not inevitable that the bank be caught in the risky middle ground of small corporate loans. It was also possible to provide innovative service, which could be an alternative to the mass product. The one thing it did show was that a moderately profitable medium-sized retail bank becomes an attractive takeover target. It is also at the mercy of its shareholders, whose interests may not be best served by a medium-sized bank.

The fate of the National Mutual Royal also emphasises that the major banks have won the field in a deregulated environment. And other than the state banks, there are few players in retail banking that occupy the middle ground. And in the post ANZ–NM merger environment where the big banks cannot take over other big banks or life offices, the heat will increase for the small and middling players.

So in the final analysis, it is academic to judge the success or failure of the National Mutual Royal Bank. Gurry may well have succeeded, but this is a case of 'The operation was successful, but the patient is dead'.

11 Coping with deregulation

The stories of the banks show how they have increased their power with deregulation. Banks are now more important in the financial system than they were before deregulation. According to KPMG Peat Marwick's 1990 Financial Institutions Performance Survey, they increased their market share vis-à-vis other financial institutions from 58 per cent in December 1984 to 67.8 per cent in December 1989.

The major banks in particular have continued to dominate the system. They more than doubled their assets between 1984 and 1989, extending their reach into insurance, stockbroking and financial management, to become large international financial groups. At the end of September 1989, they have just over two-thirds of the banks' total assets. They are also the four largest companies in Australia according to assets. The trend is for even bigger financial institutions. The new foreign banks and their subsidiaries, instead of posing a threat, were confined to 9.4 per cent of the total financial assets at the end of September 1989, having risen a mere 2.6 per cent since 1986 (RBA Bulletin, January 1990).

This increase in the assets of the major banks has not been without pain. The quality of their assets has been declining as their bad debts increase. In 1989 and 1990 this was partly caused by the environment of rising interest rates. Much of the blame, however, must be accepted by bankers chasing market share by cutting margins and relaxing the guidelines for prudent lending. But as Ian Macfarlane, head of research, Reserve Bank of Australia says, one has to keep in mind that banks 'were just one group of players in a much bigger game. And the bigger game seemed to be saying wealth can be generated by gearing up to capitalise on increasing asset values' (Macfarlane, 1990: 33).

Add to this the changed mechanism by which credit is allocated in a deregulated system. For most of the post-war period, credit was rationed to the banks. In 1980, with banks free to set their own interest rate ceilings, this rationing by the central bank was replaced by the slower price mechanism (Macfarlane, 1990: 32).

The major banks were not alone in their bad debt experience, and according to KPMG Peat Marwick's 1990 survey, performed better than the state banks and the other banks. Though deregulation has meant some pain, the major banks have performed better than their competitors anticipated.

Bankers and deregulation

Before deregulation, nobody anticipated that bankers who had spent all their careers in a highly regulated environment could compete so successfully with some of the best banks in the world. However, as the stories of the chief executives show, they were men who could handle change; and when competition was allowed, they thrived. Nevertheless, the seeming ease with which they made the transition should not understate the immensity of the change.

When they joined their banks, as 16 or 17-year-olds fresh from school, banking was a womb-to-tomb career. A junior was required to add figures up and down and sideways and be careful about his handwriting. As long as a banker knew that there were a few definite things he could do and many he could not, he was assured of a secure job, social position and a gradual promotion.

Since deregulation, banks have transformed themselves into financial conglomerates. Work has become more complex with having to manage interest rates, exchange rates and risk asset ratios continually. The rules of the game have changed midstream for the 40 to 50-year-old banker. Middle range managers have now to see themselves as profit centres, constantly under pressure to compete, cut costs and increase productivity. Tertiary qualifications and an understanding of technology now give a person the extra edge needed to compete.

Wilfred Jarvis, a corporate psychologist in Sydney, said in February 1988:

> The majority of the men who would have felt they were candidates for promotion are now professionally unsuited. They don't have the skills and training to handle this complexity. It used to be a steady-as-she-goes philosophy. Now, with deregulation, the qualities required are innovation, flexibility, entrepreneurship and an ability to predict problems. I have observed through my work that this has generated a great deal of resentment and a loss of self-esteem. A number of them have retired early, either voluntarily or involuntarily. It is a period of disenchantment.

Bankers moved from being rationers of credit to becoming marketers of credit. There was little in their early experience to guide them. However as bad debts rose in 1989 and 1990, small business especially felt that the clamps had come down in an unreasonable way. So some bankers must experience the 'damned if you do, and damned if you don't' syndrome.

The difference at the teller level is even more pronounced. It is hard to find tellers today who join a bank thinking that this is going to be their career. They join to mark time, before moving on to something else. Many of them are part-time. The full time tellers who do stay do not easily see themselves going further than accountant level. There is a sharper line differentiating the counter staff from the management. Graduate enrolment and recruitment from outside are already changing the kind of social mobility that is possible in banks today. Will Bailey, Stuart Fowler, Nobby Clark and Don Sanders made it from tellers to chief executives. For the tellers of today, this will not be possible without tertiary and technological education.

Though the bankers have gone through some pain in adjusting to deregulation, banks today are perceived as more powerful. In a deregulated world, the banks have become important players in the implementation of the government's economic strategy. Banks have increased their market share in the financial system. In a system where interest rates have become the major instrument to transmit monetary policy, banks are free to set the price they charge for the money and services they buy and sell. The interest rates they charge affect the finances of every household and influence the way in which the electorate judges the government in power. The Labor government in 1989 was well aware of the political cost of high mortgage rates, when it timed a higher rate on the non-callable deposits of the major banks to coincide with a temporary cap of 17 per cent on mortgage rates. If the major banks had moved up to 18 per cent, as they were threatening, the homeowner and the Labor government both would have been in trouble.

Despite this increase in power, the heads of banks now talk of banking services as retail services rather than in terms of social responsibility. Stuart Fowler of the Westpac Banking Corporation, talking of his attempts to upgrade branch service, said in February 1988 in Melbourne, 'If they can do it in McDonald's, we can do it in Westpac.' Nobby Clark of the National Australia Bank said in much the same vein that a lot of the issues that confront retail banks are issues that confront Myer.

Like any retail organisation, the main aim of banks now is to increase profits. Social responsibility is no longer a key concept for the major Australian banks in a deregulated financial system. Dr Nugget Coombs referred to this change of attitude in Sydney in April 1988. This is not to say that the major banks are not involved with the community. Each year, in their annual reports, in a separate section on community involvement, they detail the donations they have made to community, art and sporting projects, to scientific research and education. Some of these donations reflect the interests of the bank's directors. This philanthropic activity is also good for the bank's image, as the 1988 report of the Australia and New Zealand Banking Group (ANZ) candidly notes.

However, no major trading bank details how it conducts its banking activities with a view to future economic growth, or how it helps the credit needs of the communities that deposit with it. Bank annual reports do not tell how the organisations's policy of social responsibility informs decisions of branch location and closure, the provision of affordable housing or help to small business, or how it has increased market penetration by providing consumer credit advice. In a deregulated environment, bankers see themselves as responding purely to economic demand.

Bank profits

Like any retail organisation, the banks' prime aim is to maximise profits. Yet because high interest rates in 1989 and 1990 are hurting households, small business and corporates alike, banks do not want to be seen as profit-hungry. So we have the interesting scenario of banks wanting to be seen to be up in the profit stakes when presenting results to their shareholders, but at the same time engaging in a massive public-relations exercise directed at consumers and the government to show that their profitability levels and margins have declined since deregulation.

It is true that the major banks in 1989 had a lower pre-tax profit as a percentage of average shareholders' funds compared to 1984, but shareholders' funds rose faster than assets during this period because of more stringent international capital-adequacy guidelines. However, as their operating expenses also fell during this period, their pre-tax profits as a percentage of average assets remained at the same level in 1989 and 1984.

This is one of the important successes of the major banks in the deregulated period. As the stories of the major banks have shown, they have concentrated on improving productivity. They have done this by streamlining branches and putting in place a flatter management structure with responsibility delegated further down the line. Technology has been harnessed to cut the cost of operations. Automatated teller machines (ATMs), have been one of the main initiatives in this field. Though the costing of electronic services remains a horrendous mine-field, electronic transactions per se are seen to be cheaper than paper transactions. However, each institution produces its own figures as to the cost of counter and electronic transactions, depending on its methods and assumptions. These measures though, have led to a decrease in the operating expenses of the major trading banks as a percentage of average assets in 1989, compared to 1984.

At the same time as banks have tried to cut costs, they have sought to increase their revenue by two major moves. Given the retail idiom, it was only a matter of time before banks started charging fees for transaction services. In 1987, when ANZ set the ball rolling, the other banks gratefully followed. The other major initiative in increasing profits has been the customer information system. Banking has always been seen as a people's business. The senior bankers say that one reason they took up banking was because they like people. Hear them talk, and one is left in no doubt that bankers in the 1960s personally knew their customers better than they do today. When bankers wrote out the transactions by hand, in a more leisurely fashion, there was more time to ask about the family and the business than there is today, when one is tapping information into a computer. Also, branches were more generously staffed.

At another level, however, the bank's systems knew little about the customers. When bank computer systems were introduced in the 1950s and 1960s, their main role was to replace the general ledger and tell how much money came in and how much money was spent. In a regulated system, with guaranteed margins, it was not necessary to know which customer was profitable. However, this information has become very important in a competitive environment. Unless a bank knows its customers, it cannot improve its performance nor design products to serve their needs.

The master plan is to be able to net all the financial dealings of the customer from youth to old age, so that the bank becomes a one-stop financial centre. Teamed with a marketing culture, the banks aim to cross-sell their products and services.

This strategy has been used to good effect by Citibank Ltd in Australia, using off-the-shelf software to provide a customer information file. Citibank sells prestige car leases to its investment account customers who have an average of $20 000 in their accounts. Those with a commercial property mortgage with the bank are seen as good prospects for an overdraft. Deferred annuities are marketed to cash-management-account customers. However, the real kill is when the bank sells these customers a cheque account. David Hollott, director of marketing, Citicorp Australia Ltd, in October 1987 in his Sydney office, said that with such cross-selling he could add another 20 000 accounts to the 15 000 accounts he already had. Most often, this is done by slipping additional material with the monthly statement. 'Your existing customers are the cheapest customers you can get,' he said.

So, partly because of these strategies, and partly because of their historically high interest and non-interest margins, the large Australian banks are very profitable. This emerges very clearly when they are compared with large banks in the major countries of the OECD (Organisation for Economic Co-operation and Development).

Any international comparison is, of course, fraught with difficulty. It is especially difficult to compare bank profitability across countries, for banking systems are structurally different. Banks vary in their delivery systems, the extent of their off-balance-sheet activities and their accounting standards. Also, it makes a significant difference if a bank is dealing more with the household or with corporate banking. Nevertheless, keeping these caveats in mind, independent comparisons place the Australian banks high up in the profit stakes.

Salomon Bros, in a June 1989 analysis, found that in 1987 (the latest year in their analysis) the major Australian banks had the highest operating profit as a percentage of average equity of large banks in the UK, France, Germany, Japan and the USA. They also had the highest net income as a percentage of average earning assets. They were second to the USA on operating profit as a percentage of average earning assets and second to Japan on net income as a percentage of average equity (Salomon Bros, June 1989).

The ratios differ in OECD studies. The only consistently worked figures are for the period 1978 to 1982, for after that Australia opted out of the comparative profitability series. Average figures for 1978–82 showed that the four large Australian banks had the highest pre-tax profit as a percentage of average total assets and as a percentage of average capital and reserves (Revell, 1985). Using Australian Bankers' Association figures for 1986, to compare with OECD data, again the large Australian banks come out on top, with a higher pre-tax profit as a percentage of average total assets (1.19) compared to large banks in France (0.24), Germany (0.98), Japan (0.50), the UK (0.85) and the USA (0.85) (ABA Research, 1989 and OECD, 1988).

In Australia there has been little focus on what makes for this high profitability of Australian banks. Though there are undoubtedly many factors that influence profitability, Australian banks have historically had the highest gross earnings margins (net interest plus non-interest income as a percentage of average assets) in the major OECD countries. What is even more interesting is that, in 1989, Westpac and the National Australia Bank charged Australians a much wider interest spread than they charged overseas. Data for the ANZ and the Commonwealth Bank were not available, as these two do not list in the USA and so do not have to present the additional information. However, all four banks in 1989 were more profitable at home than they were abroad. In 1990 ANZ broke this pattern when its foreign operations became more profitable than the beleaguered Australian sector.

Australian bankers and the Australian Bankers' Association have maintained that deregulation has seen a narrowing of interest margins and that the small saver has been better off since deregulation. Margins were indeed narrower in 1989 compared to 1984; but if we look at margins from the point of view of the individual consumer, the situation is more complicated.

It is particularly hard to compare margins for the community as a whole for the period before and after deregulation. In the regulated environment, when banks had to offer more interest to attract deposits, they raised their rates till they hit the interest rate ceiling. Then, instead of narrowing margins, the banks stopped lending. So a customer wanting to borrow for a house, for example, would have to take a personal loan and borrow at a much higher interest rate.

Margins are also a matter of individual perspective; the same person is not always a borrower and a lender. Moreover, both borrowers and lenders can use different products, so achieving different margins. Given these caveats, however, the best available figures show that the consumer — and especially the small saver — has been facing larger interest spreads since deregulation. Taking bank charges into account, the difference between deposit and lending rates is even greater. The margin for the small saver with an investment account and a home loan rose from 2 per cent in June 1980 to 4.75 per cent in June 1989. For the saver with less than $50 000 in fixed deposit and with an overdraft of less than $100 000, the margin has risen also, from 2.25 per cent in 1980 to 4.63 per cent in 1989. The saver with more than $50 000 in fixed deposits and with an overdraft of more than $100 000 has had to pay more also, but the increase has been less, rising from 2.72 per cent in 1980 to 3.00 per cent in 1989 (Singh, 1989a).

In the year to April 1990, the pattern changed as the banks tried to cope with some $3 billion in bad debts in 1988/89, and a potential $8 billion in non-performing loans in 1989/90. The large saver/large borrower faces the largest rise in the interest spread. This could be the beginning of factoring the risk in commercial lending, something that was overlooked in the chase for market share.

The banks' interest margins (that is, the net interest income as a percentage of average assets) have decreased in the last year, reflecting the large burden of bad debts and non-performing loans. Even the larger interest spreads for the consumer have not compensated for lost income. What is particularly interesting about the strategy of the major private banks, in the face of these losses, is that they have chosen to make the consumer pay, while keeping the dividend pay-out at the same level in March 1990 as in March 1989. National Australia Bank even increased it by 4 per cent. Available data shows that Australian banks still have the highest interest margins among the major OECD countries (Salomon Bros 1990: 151).

There are many reasons why banks have high margins. Jack Revell (1980), in his work on costs and margins, states as a general observation that inflation is the prime cause for the pressure to widen the margin. This is because inflation, among other things, increases both staff and non-staff costs. He also points to the volume and mix of business as being important factors. These relationships need to be studied in greater depth in Australia, for there is no simple causal relationship between these factors and the high margins.

One reason why Australian banks have higher margins and profitability, especially at home, is because they get a very large percentage of their money free or at very low interest rates. In March 1990, the major banks received $13.2 billion in free deposits. This sum accounted for 7.6 per cent of their total $A liabilities in March 1990, but for 11.4 per cent of their total deposits in Australia. International comparison of the structure of deposits is particularly tricky. What is important is that if the major Australian banks had had to pay 11.75 per cent on this free money (that is, the average interest on the investment account in the savings banks), it would have cost the major trading banks $1.6 billion.

Add to this subsidy the money the savings banks attract in low interest accounts. In March 1990, there was $8.9 billion in passbook savings accounts, which attracted 3.75 per cent for amounts up to $4000 and 6 per cent for amounts over $4000. This rate has remained constant for at least the last 11 years. There was another $8.1 billion in statement savings accounts, which attracted 9 per cent. These statement and passbook savings accounts meant another subsidy of at least another $735.1 million a year, compared to the 11.75 per cent interest on investment savings accounts. So if consumers had placed their money in better-yielding accounts, the $2.3 billion would have wiped out 82 per cent of the major banks' post-tax profit for 1989, which came to $2.8 billion.

Judy Taylor (1989), in her study *Bank Deregulation*, also points out how some of these retail banking products actually yield far less than the nominal rate of interest. The effective rate of interest — when the method of calculating interest, the fees and other transaction charges are counted in — often means that consumers are paying to use their money in the bank, rather than the bank paying consumers for the money. So the effective consumer subsidy to the major trading banks is even larger.

Though the trend is slowly downwards, the major banks continue to attract a significant amount of cheap deposits. The other banks attract very little of the free money, because they lack the branch networks. Together they had only $2.3 billion in non-interest-bearing deposits in March 1990, compared to the major banks with $13.2 billion. These non-interest-bearing and low interest deposits have yet another advantage for the major banks: they do not vary with market rates, hence gear up the profits of the banks when interest rates rise.

Australian consumer behaviour and bank profits

The unanswered question in any discussion of bank profits is: Why do Australians continue to keep such a large proportion of their money in non-interest-bearing and low interest deposits? No studies have focused on this important question, but some statistical and anecdotal evidence points to five reasons: pensioners' reaction to the income and assets testing of age and service pensions; the behaviour of the lower income groups; the possible workings of the cash economy; the behaviour of different ethnic groups; and the behaviour lag of the Australian consumer in adjusting to a changed banking environment

Pensioners are a profitable group for banks, for they place much of their money in non-interest-bearing or low interest accounts. No figures are publicly available as to the average deposits that a pensioner has in such accounts. However, AGB McNair's 1988 consumer market profiles show that pensioners make up approximately one-third of those who have more than $500 in their cheque accounts and passbook savings accounts and more than one-fourth (27 per cent) of those with more than $2000 in statement savings accounts (Singh, 1989a). John Koch, general manager, retail at the Commonwealth Bank of Australia, said that pensioners are 'a win win situation. If one were to categorise this segment, one would say they were less interest-sensitive' (Ibid).

Social security and veterans' affairs professionals say that the reason for this preference is that pensioners do not want to fill out tax returns. Moreover, the threat of not qualifying for the concessional fringe benefits that go with a pension is potent enough for pensioners to minimise their income.

Anecdotal evidence also has it that pensioners often think only of the nominal value of their assets instead of their real value. If they have deposited, say, $10 000 in the bank, they are content to still have the $10 000 after a few years. They are not accustomed to taking inflation into account, so do not often realise that the real value of their $10 000 has declined over the years.

The elderly do not always have information as to how they can increase their returns on bank deposits while keeping within their tax and benefits thresholds. Lack of information is also a problem for low and moderate income consumers, who place much of their savings in these non-interest-bearing and low interest accounts. There is a considerable overlap between the low income consumer and the over 55 year age group. According to AGB McNair's data, 53 per cent of the over 55 year group have a gross household income of less than $20 000. The lower income groups are also associated with a poorer educational background.

Possibly, some of the money in non-interest-bearing current accounts comes from the cash economy. It is commonly held that the tax department does not bother with money in such accounts, for it does not generate income. In countries that have a withholding tax on interest earned, the impetus to park money in non-interest-bearing accounts is not so important. However, the importance of this factor will remain hypothetical till the tax file number system comes fully into operation.

Others point to the behaviour of recent ethnic groups, such as the Vietnamese. Like Australians who went through the Depression, these groups have seen great upheaval and like to know what they have. Also, faced with large complex banking institutions, they are more comfortable with the traditional passbook type of banking. Again, there are no hard facts on this aspect, as Australian banks have avoided doing any research or collecting statistics on the ethnic dimension of financial behaviour in the country.

Overriding all these factors is the behaviour lag of the Australian consumer. Bankers are comfortable speaking of their organisations and McDonalds in the same breath, but a customer does not see a loan and a hamburger as a similar commodity. People will shop around for the best value in a washing machine, but they are unlikely to call for three quotes for a loan. Moreover, under present disclosure standards, they may not be able to compare the full costs of the loan.

Market studies show that adult customers still resist changing their finance institution, for it is seen in terms of a relationship. A customer continues to feel vulnerable when applying for a loan. Rejection of a loan is the most frequently cited reason for changing a bank. Rudeness from a teller is another, and the biggest draw for a bank branch is a friendly bank manager who will greet customers by name. The major trading banks have benefited from this conservatism of the Australian consumer. Against all predictions that customers would desert the major banks in favour of the flash new banks with better service, customers kept their cheque accounts at their old banks. It was this conservatism of customers, more than any other single factor, that did the new banks in. And it is this attitude lag that is responsible for consumers' keeping to the traditional instruments of saving: the non-interest-bearing cheque accounts and low interest savings accounts.

'Banks are bastards'

In the euphoria following deregulation, the common notion was that customers were the winners. Indeed, some very evident benefits have flowed from deregulation to the consumers: greater access to credit, more flexibility of banking with the ATMs, and a larger diversity of products. Sophisticated consumers have been able to turn this to their advantage, so much so that 'yuppies' have become the banks' most unprofitable customers.

However, the more vulnerable consumers have had difficulty adjusting to a fast-changing banking environment. Psychologist Hugh Mackay (1985), in his study of broad middle-class Australian attitudes, *Marketscan: The Banking Market*, notes that 'The rapid-fire changes to the personal finance industry have had a destabilising effect on consumer attitudes and behaviour' (p. 23). Consumers are happy to have control over their money 'in a more imaginative and flexible way than ever before' (p. 23). The launching of Bankcard in 1974, he says, was 'the single most revolutionary event to have occurred in Australian banking history' (p. 79). It is this feeling of being in control that accounts for the great success of the ATMs, especially for withdrawing money. However, Mackay also notes, 'There is some anxiety and insecurity about the feeling that the customer must now "take charge"' (p. 23).

The consumer's complaint has changed. In a regulated banking environment, the main complaint was lack of access to credit. The customer had to go cap in hand to a bank manager, and a loan was something for which the customer had to be grateful. The customer had to show not only an ability to repay but also evidence of loyalty to the bank. The other side of the coin was the feeling that the banker was a trusted financial adviser who knew customers personally and made sure that they did not get in over their heads. Now, in a deregulated world, the complaint is that bankers no longer play this role: when times are good they become distant marketeers, selling and promoting credit like any other retail outfit. When the economic environment sours, bankers withdraw credit just as easily, without reference to the viability of the project. This is a change that sits uneasily with many consumers.

Much of this discontent with banks came to a head in May 1989, when mortgage rates hit 17 per cent. Farmers and small business people had suffered from high interest rates in 1986 and 1987; but when these hit the new homebuyer, they struck an emotional nerve in a country where close to three-fourths of the people purchase their homes. This rise in interest rates came at the same time as banks announced that their half-yearly profits had risen by over 50 per cent. Though polls and letters to the editor in the major papers showed that customers were aware that the government's monetary policies were behind the interest rate hike, the anger was still directed at the banks. The central accusation against the banks was that they did not have a sense of social responsibility. Households were hurting, but banks were adding to their 'indecent' profits by high margins and additional bank charges.

Grass roots movements sprang up, and again there arose the cry that banks should be regulated, that banks, especially the Commonwealth Bank, should go back to being a 'people's bank'. *The Bulletin*'s headline for its 2 May 1989 edition screamed 'Why the banks are bastards' and effectively caught the mood of the day. In 1990, the focus has shifted to the bank squeeze on credit especially for small business. The complaint is that the banks have swung to the other end of the pendulum, hurting the ordinary battler to pay for the indiscretions of the banks.

This turnaround in sentiment against banks has a familiar ring to it. In the nineteenth century, Australian banks operated in a competitive banking environment. When the 1893 banking crash froze the savings of ordinary people, there was a backlash against the banks, which paved the way for the setting up of the Commonwealth Bank in 1912. The recession of 1930 further entrenched the image of the big bad banks; and after the Second World War, the banks found themselves regulated for another 40 years.

However, as Boris Schedvin, Professor of Economic History at the University of Melbourne, pointed out in Melbourne in June 1989, in a telephone interview, customer unrest with banks at the turn of the century 'was a much stronger force than it is now. The Labor Party took it up and banks were seen as an embodiment of capitalist evil.' He says that at the time people 'most particularly believed the banks were a cause for cyclical unemployment through their pro-cyclical lending'.

In a deregulated financial system, in an ideal world, the market is supposed to look after consumer interests. Consumers in Australia, like consumers in the major OECD countries, however, have not found it such a perfect world. The concerns have been of the same pattern: access to financial services, especially for low and moderate income consumers: increasing bank charges and a decrease in basic banking facilities; lack of clear and available information on interest rates and associated costs of a banking product; poor information about product diversity, suitability and quality; declining levels of service; inadequate dispute-resolution procedures; overcommitment; and unfair credit contracts.

Consumer euphoria with deregulation was further punctured in Australia as service standards fell. Complaints about bank service mounted as banks decreased their counter staff in an attempt to prune costs. One-third of the 516 complaints received by the Banks Complaint Hotline over a 12 hour period in September 1989 related to service, and service was by far the single largest category of complaints. The most common complaints received related to long queues, insufficient staff, inadequately trained staff and lack of staff at the enquiries counter. There is also a growing perception that counter staff are rude. Moreover, when there is a problem, customers find it difficult to see the relevant person, and even less likely that they will get to see the manager. Even the popularity of the ATMs is seen as an indictment of bank service.

The fear in Australia, as in other OECD countries, is that, with deregulation, some consumer protections may also have weakened. Consumer groups are asking for more consumer protection to be built into national credit legislation. Protection for consumers is also uppermost in the push for more equitable dispute-resolution procedures relating to the ATMs. When there is a dispute, customers often find that it is their word against the bank's, with the bank acting as the prosecutor, judge and jury. Consumer concern has been vociferous enough to spark action. Though the Australian Bankers' Association at first dismissed the suggestion that there should be an ombudsman to help to resolve the issues, Westpac jumped the gun by announcing the setting up of an ombudsman. Soon the industry itself decided that an ombudsman, funded by the banking industry but independent of it, would be the answer. The banking ombudsman was appointed in May 1990.

In Australia, the official response to consumer concern has been to encourage the industry to work out voluntary codes and to self-regulate. This is especially true in electronic funds transfer (EFT). Having so recently unwound 40 years of regulation, the central bank and the Treasury avoid anything that may be interpreted as returning to the days of old-fashioned regulation. If this self-regulation does not work, however, ultimately there is the threat of legislative regulation. John Phillips, deputy governor of the Reserve Bank of Australia, said in August 1989 (Phillips, 1989c), 'If banks aren't behaving as the community thinks they should behave, whether or not the feeling is rationally based, pressure comes on politicians to legislate or on the authorities to regulate' (p. 22). However, he hastened to say that 'I don't proceed from a belief that markets always know best or that the authorities should never interfere with free markets; but equally, by conviction and through experience, I don't believe the authorities always know best' (p. 21).

Institutional forums for dialogue between consumer groups and the financial industry still have to be forged. The central bank also is currently feeling its way as to how best it can play the role of the balanced adjudicator between the two groups. The challenge for the future must be to combine social responsibility with a pursuit of profit in a competitive banking environment.

The distinctiveness of Australian banking

This book started with two major aims: to go behind the distinctiveness of Australian banking, and to study the unprecedented pace of change since deregulation. To achieve both, the focus has been on bankers, past and present. Through them, the history of their banks and the banking system has been told.

Three major aspects stand out when looking at Australian banking from the outside: the nature and extent of Australia's national banking network; the role of the central bank; and the deregulation of the banking system, accompanied by technological change.

The banking network expanded in three great bursts in the nineteenth century. When gold was discovered in 1851, bankers went to the goldfields. The second wave came in the 1860s, with the opening of wheatlands; then competition between the banks was so intense that a sure way of winning business was for a bank to be physically present. The third spurt came with the suburban expansion in the 1870s, when banks and building societies rushed to lend for land in the cities and suburbs. By this time, the banking network was national in scope and continental in spread.

Because of the way in which the banking network spread, the Australian banking system has an unusual rural penetration. This can be appreciated by looking at countries like Malaysia, where banking, even till the 1950s, was mainly urban and rural savings bypassed the banking system. In Australia, even a township with a population of less than 1000 is likely to have at least two banks competing with each other. Though the rural areas are most likely overbanked now, the network effectively closes the door on any other bank getting in.

In Australia, banking has largely been Australian in character. This may seem tautological; but in many countries of Southeast Asia, banking till recently has had a distinctly foreign flavour.

Another key difference from banking in the Asia-Pacific region is that Australia has had no family banks. The absence of family-owned banks has gone a long way to ensure that there has been no banking caste in Australia. By the 1870s, as banks expanded, a banking career was an exceptional avenue for social mobility. Bankers were drawn largely from the Anglo-Saxon Protestant majority, and banking was a middle class phenomenon. It was seen as a secure way up the social ladder for sons of farmers, traders and teachers. It became ingrained in Australian banking culture that a person started as a junior at age 16 or 17 after leaving school. It is a tradition that is changing today, but even the present chief executives of the major trading banks followed this pattern.

Many other countries in Southeast Asia also do not have a banking caste, but bankers for the most part share an educational network. However, in Australia, tertiary education, though it may help, has not been essential for making it to the top.

The second major distinctive factor of Australian banking is the role of the central bank. Unlike many countries in the Asia-Pacific region, where the central bank has been an institution created from scratch, in Australia the central bank emerged from the banking system itself. For the most part, the governors of the Reserve Bank of Australia have come from the same banking tradition as those who head the trading banks. They share the same networks and career patterns. Together with the Australian distaste for excessive formality, this has given the central bank a more informal style than in many other countries in the region.

Bankers in Australia, because of their history, have had more of a public face than in other countries in Southeast Asia. This goes back to the battles fought over the attempted nationalisation of banks in 1947 and to the dominance of four banks in the banking system. It also is a reflection of the strength of private banks. This has to be noted, for one only has to look to China, India, Pakistan, Malaysia, Singapore, Taiwan and South Korea to see the dominance of government banks.

Thirdly, the most startling aspect about the Australian banking system is the pace and extent of deregulation, accompanied by technological change. The stories of the major private banks show how each of them saw deregulation as an opportunity and, contrary to all predictions, emerged stronger. Each moved in a slightly different direction: Westpac became a bank for the Pacific while keeping its lead status; the ANZ became Australia's international bank; and the National

Australia Bank emerged as the top retail bank and used that strategy in its international acquisitions. The Commonwealth Bank of Australia also grew, but its pace slackened as it was restricted by its lack of capital and direction. The state banks, especially State Bank Victoria, were transformed — perhaps too fast — from regional savings banks to commercial banks with feelers in the different states and even abroad. The Australian Bank, set up to change the way in which banking was done in a regulated environment, soon found itself overtaken by the pace of deregulation. The new banks have had to work out different strategies to survive. Most have taken to the niche strategy after some experimentation with retail banking. The National Mutual Royal Bank went with the concept that a new national retail bank can work. But it too has been sold to ANZ.

Overall, for the major banks, deregulation has proved a boon. They have emerged as more powerful and highly profitable institutions, but it has meant that bankers have had to cope with the rules changing halfway through their careers.

For customers, deregulation has meant more flexibility and at boom times, increased access to credit. However, the initial euphoria of deregulation is increasingly giving way to consumer concern over high interest rates, poor service, overcommitment, inadequate information and dispute-resolution procedures for electronic banking. The banking system still has to come up with effective strategies for more vulnerable consumers. How does banking remain competitive, deregulated and yet provide an essential service at an equitable price? This is going to be the central question for bankers in the next few years.

Postscript

The State Bank Victoria will be sold to the Commonwealth Bank of Australia. To fund the purchase, the Commonwealth Bank will be partially privatised. This was announced by the Victorian Premier Joan Kirner and the Federal Treasurer Paul Keating in Melbourne on Sunday, 26 August 1990.

This is a momentous decision. It not only marks the end of a savings bank which has been part of Victorian history for 148 years, but of state banks in general. It is also the end of the Labor dream that created the Commonwealth Bank in 1911. Whether it means that the Commonwealth Bank will no longer be a 'people's bank' remains to be seen. The decision to partially privatise the Commonwealth Bank was only the first step in Labor's move towards privatisation and competition. Nearly a month later on 24 September, Labor overturned its history by deciding to privatise airlines and end the monopoly of Telecom Australia.

At the end of September 1990, the deal still had to be approved by the state and federal parliaments. The final price was to be determined after the Commonwealth Bank completed its due diligence process. However, it is one of the ironies of history that the State Bank survived the banking crash of 1893 as a solid though dull savings bank, but in the deregulated world of 1990, nearly a century later, was brought down by the excesses of its merchant bank. Its losses of $2.0 billion are without parallel in Australian corporate history. For the Commonwealth Bank, the misfortunes of State Bank Victoria have created a great opportunity. The acquisition gives the Commonwealth Bank the largest share of the domestic market. And for the first time in its history, the bank may have access to the capital it needs.

Trico sinks the State Bank of Victoria

State Bank Victoria lost $2.0 billion by the end of June 1990, most of it through bad loans made by its wholly owned merchant bank, Tricontinental Holdings Ltd. The loss wiped out the bank's capital of $1.7 billion making necessary a total support package of $2.7 billion. The Victorian state government, facing an economic downturn, a loss of confidence in its non-bank financial sector, and a cut in federal government funding, couldn't handle such a loss. Going further into debt to finance the State Bank Victoria would have meant a charge of $400 million a year, every year, till such time as there was a budget surplus. So the bank had to be sold.

The preferred political option for the ruling Labor Left in Victoria — the most vociferous opponent of privatisation — was a sale to the Commonwealth Bank which would mean that the state bank would still be publicly owned. The price was the Labor Left's agreement to the Commonwealth Bank raising the preliminary purchase price of $1.6 billion from private sources. This would result in about 30 per cent of the Commonwealth Bank being privately owned.

Soon after the announcement of the sale, a Royal Commission was set up to look into the Tricontinental mess and provide answers about what happened and why. Ralph Ward-Ambler who became chairman of the State Bank Victoria on 23 February 1990, admits to not having all the answers. Sitting in his office on the second floor of the State Bank's headquarters in Melbourne, in September 1990, with his jacket slung over a chair and a John Brack painting dominating the room, Ward-Ambler spoke about lost hopes and unanswered questions.

In February 1990, he had no doubt that he and his new board could refocus the State Bank. 'There was a very valuable role for a large community bank aimed mainly at a retail market,' he said. He not only was impressed by the bank's $23.8 billion in assets, but like many other Victorians, Ward-Ambler's association with the bank went back to his childhood when he was given the bank's money box with two shillings in it as a birthday gift.

For Ward-Ambler and the new board of directors, the first hint of trouble to come was a routine report on problem loans in mid-March. The figures were disturbing, so the directors asked the management to look again at the $1.3 billion that had been specifically provided against the group's losses at the end of December 1989. Ward-Ambler received the first draft of the next quarterly revision of the problem loans report on 4 May. Reading it on a flight to London, he realised the problem was far worse than the board had thought. But it was not until about 20 May, when figures showed that the bank would need several hundreds of millions in additional provisions, that the enormity of the situation struck Ward-Ambler. The situation was so catastrophic, that only four people knew the full story — Ward-Ambler; Paul Rizzo, the new chief executive of the bank; Jim McAnany, acting chief executive from February to May 1990; and his assistant. By late May, the directors had also been informed. As it took time for the ramifications of the numbers to be fully realised, it was not until 5 June that Ward-Ambler discovered that the bank needed extra provisions of $700 million to $800 million over and above the $1.3 billion that had already been provided in December 1989. At this point, the need to inject up to $1.1 or $1.2 billion into the bank became obvious.

Twenty minutes after the damning figures became available, Ward-Ambler, Rizzo, and McAnany kept an appointment set earlier to see their shareholder, Victorian State Treasurer Tom Roper. They told him they had another disaster on their hands. Roper has not spoken about this meeting, but is said to have terminated it abruptly after a shocked silence. Only three months earlier everybody had been assured that all the bank's problems had been identified and handled.

Ward-Ambler's first feelings upon realising the enormity of the losses were anger and frustration. 'You just get a sick feeling.' Then he experienced 'a feeling of disbelief that this can't be true.' Despite the extent of the damage, and the huge mopping-up process required, Ward-Ambler did not feel as if he had failed:

> A failure is when you can't do the possible . . . To solve that kind of problem required not just being able to walk on water, you had to jog on it.

The biggest shock was for Paul Rizzo, 45, who joined the bank on 7 May 1990. He knew he was joining a troubled institution when he accepted the job, but, as the *Australian* reported on 9 May, Rizzo saw the appointment as perhaps 'the bigest challenge in the country'. At the time he promised that 'the important thing is that I'm not carrying the baggage of history with me into the position. I will start fresh.' Within two weeks he found that the baggage of history had followed him. And within days of becoming chief executive on 1 June 1990, he had to face up to the fact that his bank was technically insolvent.

Rizzo had headed ANZ's New Zealand operations, and was seen as one of the three contenders for the top job when Will Bailey retired. At the time, ANZ was planning to merge with National Mutual. Speculation within ANZ has it that Rizzo could not see himself heading the larger conglomerate, and decided to take the State Bank job. Rizzo has chosen not to comment.

The directors met on 7 June amid more shock and horror. Ward-Ambler and Rizzo left the board meeting for Ward-Ambler's room to telephone Bernie Fraser, the Governor of the Reserve Bank of Australia. Ward-Ambler said:

> At that stage, I think one of the sick feelings that came to us was that if indeed the provisions that we thought were necessary were necessary, and the money was really not recoverable, then we probably were a bank operating without capital.

It was already the first week of June. The bank needed an assurance of state government support by the end of its financial year on 30 June. Otherwise, the bank not only could be breaching the Reserve Bank capital adequacy guidelines, but could be breaking covenants of its loan agreements in Luxembourg, London and New York. Ward-Ambler said:

> I think the most onerous conditions were in New York, where it was obligatory to advise the market if you thought there may be adverse material change in the bank's circumstances. And since [this would be] . . . like advertising the bank had failed, it really would have been a disaster.

The assurance was never in doubt, and it arrived in the appropriate form at 6 p.m. on Friday, 29 June. It capped a particularly bad month for the state government. On 24 June, the largest building society group in Victoria — Pyramid, Countrywide and Geelong of Farrow Corporation -- closed its doors. The loss of confidence in the non-bank financial sector over the next month spilt over to property trusts and friendly societies and precipitated a run on the Bank of Melbourne, which until recently had been a building society. For good measure, at the end of June, Victoria suffered cuts in federal funding.

As Premier Joan Kirner said at her press conference on 26 August 1990, Tricontinental was the 'albatross' around Victorian taxpayers' necks. Of its total assets of $3.4 billion at the end of June 1990, it had lost $1.6 billion, that is, nearly half its loan book. Ward-Ambler said at the same press conference on 26 August 1990 that 'Tricontinental had a special facility for lending to people who like to go bankrupt'. Much of the loan book was high risk, backed by relatively poor quality security in shares in unlisted companies and developmental or tourism real estate. Ward-Ambler said, 'Some of their documentation was very poor. So even when you have assets you could try and reclaim, you end up in court arguing about it'.

The present board and management must feel that some of the responsibility rests with their predecessors. The customary expression of thanks to past directors and the chief executive was conspicuously absent from the bank's annual 1990 accounts. At an early stage of its tenure, the new board had considered entertaining its predecessor. But as events unfolded the idea was shelved. Bill Moyle, contacted on his farm outside Melbourne, declined to comment, saying it was 'inappropriate for me to say anything at this stage'.

Replaying the sequence

The one thing that is clear in this story is that the State Bank Victoria had huge losses. With the state Budget due on 28 August, it was evident that the State Bank would have to be sold. And selling State

Bank Victoria to the Commonwealth Bank suited the Victorian Government, the federal Treasurer and the Commonwealth Bank. What tangles the plot are the different versions given by the parties as to how the events unfolded.

It is hard to say definitively how the deal with the Commonwealth Bank was hammered out. Was it a 'done' deal that was dressed up to look open? Treasurer Paul Keating told his version of the story at a press conference in Canberra on 28 August 1990, saying the Victorian Treasurer, Tom Roper and the Victorian Minister for Industry and Economic Planning, David White came to see him in Canberra, 'about the 19th of June' and told him that State Bank Victoria had lost its capital. Keating said they inquired 'whether the Commonwealth Bank of Australia would be prepared to buy the State Bank of Victoria'. He told them 'that the State Bank should be offered widely to other interested parties including the private banks'. Answering questions from the press, Keating conceded that the Commonwealth Bank had been told 'maybe a day or two' ahead of its competitors that the State Bank Victoria was to be sold 'because it wasn't very long after I saw them that Mr Ward-Ambler started opening up discussions with the other banks'. He also said that on 19 June he had made it clear to the Victorian government that if the Commonwealth Bank bought the State Bank Victoria it would mean a partial privatisation of the Commonwealth Bank.

It is hard to confirm whether it was Keating who put forward the Commonwealth Bank option or whether it was the Victorian government. Did Keating see the State Bank sale as part of his privatisation strategy as early as mid-June? And was it Tom Roper and David White who persuaded Keating to go open on the deal rather than the other way round? The questions are raised, but the answers are not conclusive.

What is clear is that the Commonwealth Bank was informed of a possible sale of the State Bank Victoria at least six weeks before the other bidders. Kevin Scott, Federal Secretary of the Commonwealth Bank Officers' Association said in a telephone interview from Sydney in mid-September 1990, that on 21 June 1990 Treasurer Paul Keating briefed him and two other senior officials of the CBOA in broad terms about the possible privatisation of the Commonwealth Bank. CBOA had been one of the staunchest opponents of privatisation. 'We had other preferred options,' said Scott. The union put forward the possibility of a direct government injection of funds, a dividend relief, or raising the level of debt. Keating ruled out the first suggestion. Dividend relief would not have been sufficient. And State Bank Victoria already had a high level of debt, so that additional debt of $1.6 billion would not be acceptable under the capital adequacy rules. So an issue of stock seemed to be the only alternative solution. CBOA were convinced this was the only possible way of protecting the savings of millions of Victorians. The assurance that the money raised would be used to build up the bank was palatable. Furthermore, CBOA's interests were protected by the assurance there would be no forced retrenchments and the promise of an employee share scheme. And, as Kevin Scott pointed out, at the back of everyone's mind was the probability of privatisation of the Commonwealth Bank if the federal Coalition came to power. The only difference would be that the proceeds may not have gone to the bank under a Coalition scheme.

So by the third week of June, Keating had won over a major opponent of privatisation. However, the first formal approach made on behalf of the State Bank Victoria to the four major banks, Citibank Ltd, and Chase AMP was on 2 and 3 August 1990. It was in the nature of eliciting an expression of interest if the State Bank Victoria were to be sold. That the bank was in trouble wasn't exactly news, as Haydn Park, senior manager, corporate public relations, with the National Australia Bank, said in Melbourne in September 1990. 'We all knew State Bank Victoria was going down the shute. Everyone was aware of the level of bad debts. That was market talk.' It was on 6 August that the decision was made to have a memorandum of information prepared. On 13 August, Ward-Ambler and Rizzo met with David White, Tom Roper, and the new Premier, Joan Kirner (who took office on 9 August) and it was agreed that the process should go ahead. Merrill Lynch, the international merchant bank which was dealing with the bidding process delivered the documents to the six banks on 15 August. The bid closed on 25 August.

Premier Joan Kirner said clearly at her press conference that the bid of $1.6 billion from the Commonwealth Bank was politically more acceptable than the Westpac bid which was $55 million more. However, taking into account the total package which included the reimbursement of taxation revenue by the federal government, the state government came out ahead on a net basis by $25 million. This let the state government off the hook. 'The dilemma, I think, would have been if one of the other banks [had] bid more,' Bill Gurry said in his Melbourne office in September 1990. After leaving as head of the National Mutual Royal Bank around mid-June 1990, Gurry was appointed a special adviser to the state government on the sale of the State Bank to the Commonwealth Bank. He was also advising the state government on the Pyramid Building Society and non-bank regulation.

According to Gurry, if Westpac had offered a better net price, the state government would have faced three alternatives. 'First, the state government could have withdrawn it from sale,' he said. 'Secondly, it could have sold it to the Commonwealth at a lower price. And thirdly, it could have sold it to Westpac . . . at the higher price.'

The state government accepted that the Tricontinental losses were so great as to leave it no choice but to sell State Bank Victoria. According to Gurry the government had considered the possibility of a sale as early as October 1989. 'It was one that they didn't welcome,' he said, 'but in the end the financial problem was so great, they didn't have a choice.' Once the government had accepted the necessity of a sale, difficulties arose concerning the price. Gurry proposed that the government go to the four major trading banks and have each of them put in a quarter of a billion dollars. Fix it up and in four years time sell to the highest bidder amongst the four major trading banks.

The government expressed interest in the proposal, 'but then I think it all happened too quickly ... Suddenly the reality of the losses was there. They had a Budget to present. They had to do a deal. So they did the deal.'

What is interesting is the manner in which the deal was presented to different parties as events unfolded. Even after the banks had been contacted to find out whether they were interested if the State Bank were to be sold, Premier Joan Kirner, on 9 August, ruled out selling the State Bank, the Gas and Fuel Corporation of Victoria and the State Electricity Commission of Victoria, saying they would remain in public control (*The Age*, 10 August 1990, p. 1). She said much the same thing to the State Bank branch of the Australian Bank Employees' Union, in a more careful way, in a letter dated 14 August 1990. Answering the branch's letter of 6 August 1990 concerning the possible sale of the State Bank, the Office of the Premier replied that it was the government's intention that 'major assets remain in public ownership and under public control'.

The State Bank Victoria union got the same line from its own management. Paul Rizzo who had been in on many of the meetings with the Victorian state government, sent a circular to the staff on 16 August 1990, a day after the formal bidding process had started, saying that:

> Both the new Premier, Mrs Kirner, and the State Treasurer, Mr Roper, have made it clear in public statements that SBV is not to be sold ... I am confident that we will be able to quickly put the Trico-related problems behind us, and return the bank to strong levels of profitablility as Victoria's leading bank.

In a letter to all staff on 22 August 1990, which began 'Dear Colleagues', Rizzo wrote, 'I can assure you that management is not aware of any decision by our shareholder (the state government) to sell the bank.' He continued 'I would also like to strongly refute comments in today's press that SBV is insolvent.' It is interesting to note that this was three days before the bids for the State Bank were due, though the decision to sell the bank to the Commonwealth Bank at a particular price was announced on 26 August.

Steve McKenna, secretary of the State Bank branch of the ABEU, said in September 1990 in his Melbourne office, 'I would be surprised if [Paul Rizzo] knew too much about what was going on.' Whichever way Rizzo's circular and letter are interpreted, they are an interesting reflection on communication within the bank. If, as McKenna believes, Rizzo did not know all the facts, then senior management and directors

(Rizzo is on the board) were unaware of events relating to their own bank. If Rizzo was in the know as the sequence of events may suggest, then a skilful play on words effectively kept the staff misinformed.

There is also a stark contrast in the way the respective shareholders treated the bank unions in the Commonwealth Bank and the State Bank Victoria. The CBOA was involved in the discussions to purchase the State Bank Victoria from 21 June. In early August it consulted widely with its branch secretaries and also had talks with the Australian Council of Trade Unions. The Australian Bank Employees' Union which represents approximately 10 500 of the 12 000 State Bank Victoria employees, was informed only an hour before the sale was announced on 26 August.

The privatisation of the Commonwealth Bank

The Commonwealth Bank has been too entrenched a part of Labor ideology for there not to be some hand-wringing about its partial privatisation. Putting it in historical context in a talk to the Trades Hall Council in Melbourne on 13 September 1990, John Wiseman, secretary, Victorian Council of Social Service, drew attention to the Prime Minister's earlier comments on privatisation. Delivering the Chifley lecture on 21 September 1987, Bob Hawke said:

> What in the name of reason is the justification for breaking up and selling off the great and efficient national assets, like the Commonwealth Bank, Telecom, TAA [Australian Airlines] and Qantas?... As the people of Australia come to realise the extent of the economic and social vandalism proposed by our opponents, it will be necessary for us, Ben Chifley's great heirs and successors, to keep fresh and green the memory, the example, and the experience of this great Australian.

In 1990, as the Labor conference of 24 September 1990 showed, the dominant ideology of the Labor Party had moved away from the value of public enterprise to the advantages of competition and privatisation. However, many people in Australia think the Labor Party is selling off the farm.

The Commonwealth Bank's top management and union have agreed that partial privatisation is the only way the purchase of the State Bank Victoria can be funded. Don Sanders, managing director of the Commonwealth Bank, said in a media release on 26 August 1990 that the merger of the Commonwealth Bank and the State Bank Victoria would 'not be possible without the undertaking by the Australian government to give the Commonwealth Bank the ability to issue equity capital'. He continued, 'Although debt capital has an important role to play, it is not possible to base expansion solely on debt'. He also made the point that the issue of shares will 'raise additional capital for the bank, not funds for the government.'

The proposed privatisation of the Commonwealth Bank comes with the proviso that the bank will remain dominantly owned by the government. Though it is too early to speak of the float and the way it will be conducted, it is expected that shares will be offered to superannuation funds, especially union super funds. Overseas investors and private banks will be excluded. The questions that emerge are: Will it remain a 'people's bank? Will it remain a profitable bank? Sanders sought to defuse the issue of ownership by saying in his press release:

> The issue of equity capital will allow Australians to identify even more closely with the Commonwealth Bank by investing either directly or through their pension and life funds.

An important question for bank customers is whether the Commonwealth Bank will continue its community service obligations. This is important as the bank has more low-income customers than any other Australian bank. A joint submission by seven consumer associations, in September 1990, asked that these obligations be more clearly defined and monitored.

Commercially, there is little doubt that the purchase of State Bank Victoria is a good deal for the Commonwealth Bank. It is important to note that the merger will not include Tricontinental Holdings Ltd and its subsidiaries. The Commonwealth Bank had marked the State Bank as a strategic buy in its own plans before the bank came on the market. As Tim Besley, chairman of the Commonwealth Bank of Australia said at the 26 August press conference in Melbourne, 'the cultures of our two organisations are very comparable'.

With the purchase of the State Bank, the Commonwealth Bank will be the third largest bank in Australia with the largest share of the domestic market. It will have assets of $73.5 billion, more than one-fifth (22.5 per cent) of all assets recorded on banks' Australian books, one-third of all housing loans (33.1 per cent) and more than a quarter of all deposits (26.1 per cent). (These are figures for June 1990.) It will become one of the biggest publicly owned banks in the world. More important to the changing savings pattern, it will become the largest player in the superannuation field.

But problems of productivity will loom large in the merged institution, for the Commonwealth Bank and the State Bank Victoria rank lower on the productivity scale than the three major private banks. The unions have sought and received reassurances that the jobs of the people working in the two banks are safe and there will be no forced retrenchments. However, experience with early bank mergers suggests that some degree of rationalisation is inevitable. Some of this will happen in the normal process, as there is a 25 per cent turnover in the banking industry. But as Steve McKenna of the State Bank branch of the ABEU says, the problems will be greater at the senior levels. So the union's thrust is to negotiate favourable voluntary redundancy packages for staff who want them.

The larger Commonwealth Bank will confirm its status as the bank with the largest number of customers in Australia. However, it is still a long way from extracting the full profit potential from its customer base. Neither the Commonwealth Bank nor the State Bank Victoria have complete customer information files. So, for the present, a large retail customer base may well add to the transaction costs, without increasing the profitability of customer relationships.

Not everybody is rejoicing at the Commonwealth Bank's good fortune. Allowing the Commonwealth Bank and State Bank Victoria merger to go through, while refusing the ANZ and National Mutual merger, is seen by some as a prime example of Keating's ad hoc policy making. Bob Edgar, General Manager, Strategic Planning with the ANZ Banking Group, said in Melbourne in September 1990:

> The market position achieved by the Commonwealth Bank of Australia and the State Bank Victoria is certainly more significant than what was going to be achieved by ANZ and National Mutual. This in my view seems inconsistent.

However, Bill Gurry who lost his bank because of the abortive ANZ and National Mutual deal said the two deals are not comparable. Keating did not refuse the deal on the basis of market share, but on the grounds of national interest. The crucial difference between the two mergers is that of culture. While the Commonwealth Bank and State Bank Victoria share a common retail culture, 'there is a straight cultural issue of whether you can marry insurance... with banking.'

The new banking

After the sale of the State Bank Victoria, the state banks are not expected to last too long as a breed. Keating labels them 'an anachronism'; the State Bank of New South Wales is loudly expressing its preference of merging with a non-bank partner, while the State Bank of South Australia has gone on the defensive.

More than this, Tricontinental bringing down the State Bank Victoria also marks the end of the banking style of the 1980s. Gurry says, 'I think we have been through a decade of darkness... a period where societal values changed quite dramatically.' The government, media, banks, the corporate world — all of them got it wrong. Says Gurry:

> The organisation that got it more badly wrong than anybody else in Australia is Tricontinental. They lent to every crook in Australia. They had bad management. They had bad ethical standards.

It is this kind of banking that has led to anger against banks. Gurry concedes:

> I think there is good cause to be angry with banks. I think we set bad standards during the 1980s. I think it is an inability on the part of management in Australia to be self-critical which stops us with dealing with that situation. We should be admitting it and moving on from there.

For the State Bank Victoria, the day of judgement has already come. The bank that was associated with the money boxes of childhood birthdays, the bank that housed Victoria, has been sold. For 148 years, it was one of the sureties of life for Victorians. But perhaps its failure will make bankers look more closely at how banking has been done in Australia over the last ten years. It is a sombre note on which to end. But the sale of the State Bank Victoria may well mean the start of a period of more socially responsible banking. That chapter, however, remains to be written.

Bibliography

Anon. (1877) 'The multiplication of country branches' *The Australasian Insurance and Banking Record and Statistical Register* Vol. 1

Anon. (1893) 'How to run a branch bank' *Bankers' Magazine of Australasia* Vol 7 August 1893–July 1894

Anon. (1972) 'Lady Typewriter dies' *Bankers' Magazine of Australasia* October

Appleyard, R. T. and Schedvin, C. B. eds (1988) *Australian Financiers: Biographical Essays* Melbourne: Macmillan

Arndt, H. W. and Harris, C. P. (1965) *The Australian Trade Banks* 3rd edn, Melbourne: F. W. Cheshire

Australian Bankers' Association Research (1989) *Bank Profitability in Australia* Melbourne: Australian Bankers' Association

Blainey, G. and Hutton, G. (1983) *Gold and Paper 1858–1982: A History of the National Bank of Australasia Ltd* rev. edn, Melbourne: Macmillan

Butlin, S. J. (1953) *The Australian Monetary System: 1788–1851* Melbourne: Melbourne University Press

——— (1961) *Australia and New Zealand Bank: The Bank of Australasia and the Union Bank of Australia Limited 1828–1951* London: Longmans Green

——— (1986) *The Australian Monetary System: 1851–1914* Sydney: Judith F. Butlin

Butlin, S. J., Hall, A. R. and White, R. C. (1971) *Australian Banking and Monetary Statistics 1817–1945* Sydney: Reserve Bank of Australia, Occasional Paper No. 4A

Coombs, H. C. (1981) *Trial Balance* Melbourne: Macmillan

Campbell Committee (1981) *Final Report of the Committee of Inquiry into the Australian Financial System* Canberra: AGPS

Cannon, M. (1967) *The Land Boomers* Melbourne: Melbourne University Press

Carew, E. (1985) *Fast Money 2* Sydney: Allen & Unwin

Clark, M. (1987) *A Short History of Australia* 3rd rev. ed. New York and Scarborough, Ontario: NAL Penguin

Commonwealth of Australia (1911) *Parliamentary Debates Session 1911*

(Second Session of the Fourth Parliament) Vol LXII: Government Printer for the State of Victoria

Commonwealth Banking Corporation (1980) *The Commonwealth Banking Corporation: Its Background, History and Present Operations* Sydney: Commonwealth Banking Corporation

Cooch, A. (1934) *The State Savings Bank of Victoria: Its place in the history of Victoria* Melbourne: Macmillan

——— (1929) 'The romance of savings banks' *Bankers' Magazine of Australasia* 28 February

Craddock, T. and Cavanough, M. (1967) *125 Years: The Story of the State Savings Bank of Victoria, 1842–1966* Melbourne: State Savings Bank of Victoria

Cromie, A. (1990) 'What's wrong with Westpac' *Business Review Weekly* April 26

Faulkner, C. C. (1923) *The Commonwealth Bank of Australia* Sydney: Commonwealth Bank of Australia

Fraser, B. W. (1989) 'Reserve Bank independence and all that' *Reserve Bank of Australia Bulletin* December

Game, A. and Pringle, R. (1983) *Gender at Work* Sydney: Allen & Unwin

Giblin, L. F. (1951) *The Growth of a Central Bank: The Development of the Commonwealth Bank of Australia, 1924–1945* Melbourne: Melbourne University Press

Griffiths, N. (1955) 'Success in banking, a study of personal qualities,' *Bankers' Magazine of Australasia* July, October

Hill, J. (1983) *From Subservience to Strike: Industrial Relations in the Banking Industry* St. Lucia: University of Queensland Press

Holder, R. F. (1970) *Bank of New South Wales: A History* Vol. I *1817–1893* Sydney: Angus and Robertson

——— (1970) *Bank of New South Wales: A History Vol. II 1894–1970* Sydney: Angus and Robertson

Jonson, P. (1988) 'Reflections on central banking' Talk to the Economic Society of Australia, Sydney: July 27

Johnston, R. A. (1989) '"Doing it my way": Some reflections of a retiring governor' *Reserve Bank of Australia Bulletin* August

Kelly, P. (1989a) 'Inside the Keating Treasury: The Fraser philosophy' *The Weekend Australian* April 29–30

——— (1989b) 'Inside the Keating Treasury: The trinity in Paul's power orbit' *The Australian*' May 2

——— (1989c) 'Inside the Keating Treasury: The war between the hawks and the doves' *The Australian* May 3

——— (1989d) 'Hewson's plan to unleash the Reserve Bank' *The Australian* Oct. 10

KPMG Peat Marwick Hungerfords (1989) *1989 Financial Institution Performance Survey: A Survey of Size, Growth, Profitability, Efficiency and Credit Quality Measures of Australian Financial Institutions* KPMG Peat Marwick Hungerfords

KPMG Peat Marwick (1990) *1990 Financial Institutions Performance Survey* KPMG Peat Marwick

Lee, W. (1989) 'Australian banks: comment and analysis of 1989 results' (Research paper, Nov. 22) Melbourne: A. C. Goode and Co.

Macfarlane, Ian (1970) 'Credit and debt: Part II' *Reserve Bank of Australia Bulletin* May

May, A. L. (1968) *The Battle for the Banks* Sydney: Sydney University Press
Merrett, D. T. (1985) *ANZ Bank: A History of the Australia and New Zealand Banking Group Limited and its Constituents* Sydney: Allen and Unwin Australia
——— (1988) 'Two hundred years of banking' unpublished paper
——— (1989) 'The 1893 bank crashes: the aftermath' Typescript
Moffatt, Wm (1921) *A Banker's Letters to his Son* Brisbane: Watson, Ferguson and Co.
Moyal, Ann (1984) *Clear across Australia: A History of Telecommunications* Melbourne: Thomas Nelson Australia
OECD (1988) *Bank Profitability: Statistical Supplement, Financial Statements of Banks, 1982–1986* Paris: OECD
Parliament of the Commonwealth of Australia (1937) *Report of the Royal Commission Appointed to Inquire into the Monetary and Banking Systems at Present in Australia* Canberra: Government of the Commonwealth of Australia
Peat, Marwick, Mitchell and Co. (1985) *Banking in Australia* 2nd edn, Collingwood, Vic.: Peat, Marwick, Mitchell and Co.
Phillips, M. J. (1989a) 'The changing face of central banking' *Reserve Bank of Australia Bulletin* May
——— (1989b) 'A central banking triptych' *Reserve Bank of Australia Bulletin* October
——— (1989c) 'Some thoughts on regulation' *Reserve Bank of Australia Bulletin* August
Preshaw, G. O. (1888) *Banking under Difficulties or Life on the Goldfields* Melbourne: Edwards, Dunlop and Co.
Reinecke, I. (1988) *The Money Masters: Banks, Power and Economic Control* Richmond, Vic.: William Heinemann
Reserve Bank of Australia (1989) *Report and Financial Statements 30 June 1989* Sydney: Reserve Bank of Australia
——— (1989) 'Financial system — some recent institutional developments' *Reserve Bank of Australia Bulletin* September
——— (1990) 'The banking sector in Australia' *Reserve Bank of Australia Bulletin* January
Revell, J. R. S. (1980) *Costs and Margins in Banking: An International Survey*, Paris: OECD
——— (1985) *Costs and Margins in Banking: Statistical Supplement 1978–82* Paris: OECD
Salomon Brothers (1989) *European Banking Integration in 1992: The Competitive Challenges Facing US Multinational Banks* New York: Salomon Brothers Inc.
——— (1990) *A Review of Bank Performance: 1990 Edition* April 1990
Singh, S. (1989) 'Tellers count the costs of change' *Triple A* March
——— (1989a) *Banking on the Margin: Deregulated Banks and the Lower Income Consumer* Collingwood, Vic.: Australian Financial Counselling and Credit Reform Association Inc.
T. H. (1918) 'Early days W. A. goldfields' *Bankers' Magazine of Australasia* September 30
——— (1919) 'Early days W. A. goldfields (continued)' *Bankers' Magazine of Australasia* January 31
Taylor, J. (1989) *Bank Deregulation: Is the Consumer Really Winning?* Bundoora, Vic: School of Economics, La Trobe University

Walters, M. (1989) 'EFTPOS — national asset or white elephant?' Research paper Sydney: Deloitte Haskins and Sells

Williams, C. (1988) *Blue, White and Pink Collar Workers in Australia: Technicians, Bank Employees and Flight Attendants* Sydney: Allen & Unwin

Index